VICTORIAN AND EDWARDIAN DECOR

VICTORIAN AND EDWARDIAN DECOR

From the Gothic Revival to Art Nouveau

JEREMY COOPER

ABBEVILLE PRESS · PUBLISHERS · NEW YORK

Half-title page **1** The Speaker's Drawing Room in the Palace of Westminster, photographed *c.* 1905. The furnishings and decorations were completed to A.W.N. Pugin's designs in 1859.

Frontispiece **2** View from the Botticelli Room at 49 Princes Gate, London, the home of Frederick Leyland, photographed by Bedford Lemère in 1892. The Botticelli Room, hung with some of Leyland's collection of Old Master paintings, was created by Richard Norman Shaw in 1879 as part of a triple drawing room round the stair well. The three rooms were separated by screens designed by Shaw, one of which is shown here. The ceiling design recurs throughout the house, including the Peacock Room (see 320). In the distance can be seen one of Leyland's Burne-Jones paintings.

Copyright © 1987 Jeremy Cooper. All rights reserved under International and Pan-American Copyright Conventions. No part of this book may be reproduced or utilized in any form or by any means, electronic or mechanical, including photocopying, recording, or by any information storage and retrieval system, without permission in writing from the publisher. Inquiries should be addressed to Abbeville Press, 488 Madison Avenue, New York, NY 10022. Printed and bound in Hong Kong.

First American edition

Library of Congress Cataloging in Publication Data
Cooper, Jeremy.

    Victorian and Edwardian decor.

    Bibliography: p.
    Includes index.
    1. Interior decoration—Great Britain—History—19th century. 2. Interior decoration—Great Britain—History—20th century. 3. Decoration and ornament—Great Britain—Victorian style. 4. Decoration and ornament—Great Britain—Edwardian style. I. Title.
NK2043.C65   1987   747.22   87–1335
ISBN 0–89659–768–7

Contents

Preface

In gently deriding our present 'fissiparous, disconnected age ... where the volume of critical opinion greatly exceeds its content',[1] Sir Denys Lasdun could be speaking for progressive architects and designers of almost all ages in almost all countries. During the inventive period of British furniture and interior design from 1830 to 1915 critical opinion was no less combative than it is now. The *Fortnightly Review* expressed in 1868 the robust view that 'nothing can exceed the ugliness of modern furniture, unless it be the homes into which we are obliged to put it'. A typical armchair activist of 1902, H.J. Jennings, described the work of E.W. Godwin – now prized for its crisp originality – as 'that excrescence of nineteenth century art ... effeminate, invertebrate, sensuous and mawkish'.[2] Critical comment was wide-ranging. Consider, for example, the respected opinion of the German writer Hermann Muthesius, offered in his influential book of 1904, *Das Englische Haus*: 'It is difficult to find justification for the English habit of using a knob rather than a lever to open a door. Turning a knob is the most unsuitable way of exerting pressure on a spring, especially when, as is usually the case, it is small and slippery. Whereas a German maid with both hands full can still press down the door-handle with her elbow, her English counterpart has to lay whatever she is carrying on the floor before she can open the door.'[3]

Critics of all periods chew the same old bones of contention. In the nineteenth century architects were pilloried, as they are now, for revivalism, for turning both too slavishly and too quirkily to earlier sources for their dominant motifs. In the High Victorian period this pattern-book mentality was said to have led to a style of interior design more suitable to 'a fairground booth'[4] – an apposite epitaph, some might say today, for Post-Modernism. But whatever the possible similarities between the aesthetics of the 1880s and those of the 1980s, there are at least two fundamental differences. Firstly, in the 1880s furniture and interior design throughout the world were dominated by British architects; secondly, the rich and the fashionable lived in brand-new homes surrounded by brand-new art.

Not all homes, of course, were progressive and modern in their design, for as well as harbouring the talents of a remarkably diverse band of inventive architect-designers, the nineteenth century also encouraged the commercial production of furniture and furnishings of equally remarkable ugliness. The fact remains, however, that even the most idealistic of talented church builders also concerned themselves with the decorative arts: William Butterfield produced designs for embroidery and wallpapers, A.W.N. Pugin for bookcases and dinner services decades before the better-known architectural ensembles of a C.F.A. Voysey or a Charles Rennie Mackintosh. Unlike today, the designers of the best furniture between 1830 and 1915 were mostly practising architects and much of what they produced was progressively modern, so much so that even now chairs by Pugin, for instance, retain an air of elemental originality. Concerned not merely with the external appearances of their buildings but also with every stage of construction, decoration and furnishing, many architects worked extensively with commercial manufacturers to produce designs for 'multiples', to use the modern artist-craftsman term, as well as for individual commissions. Godwin expressed the architectural belief of the time in the introduction to a commercial catalogue of his designs, published in 1877: 'The commonest article of furniture cannot be an artistic work by any happy-go-lucky process whatsoever.'[5] It is furniture of this nature, made to an authoritative design, whether one-off or mass-produced, that exclusively concerns us in this book.

The introductory first chapter, 'A Matter of Style', looks into Victorian attitudes to style and taste, taking the lead from contemporary design manuals such as Henry Shaw's *Specimens of Ancient Furniture*, Owen Jones's *Grammar of Ornament* and Mrs Haweis's *Beautiful Houses*. Whether in the 'Gothic', 'Elizabethan', or 'Louis XV' style, all furniture of the early Victorian period tended to look much the same, rounded and comfortable in form, in its way almost style-*less* – see, for example, the designs of Anthony Salvin, Philip Hardwick, or Richard Bridgens. The taste for exotic Moorish interiors is also discussed in this chapter, together with the contemporary interest in antiquarianism. In discussing matters of style in this general way, the ground is prepared for the succeeding eight specialist chapters, which begin with A.W.N. Pugin, who, despite his medievalism, was 'almost an early modern'.[6] The Pugin chapter also covers the work of his eldest son, Edward, and of his principal collaborator, J.G. Crace. Long after A.W.N. Pugin's death in 1852, Puginesque furniture continued to be produced by the cabinetmakers Gillow's and Holland & Sons, both of whom reused the original designs he had made for them, and by commercial firms such as C. & R. Light of Shoreditch, production centre of what the designer C.R. Ashbee called 'slaughtered furniture'.[7]

As William Burges was the only architect to concentrate exclusively on painted furniture, he and his assistants H.W. Lonsdale, E.J. Tarver and W.G. Saunders are allotted the next chapter to themselves. This is followed by an omnium gatherum chapter entitled 'Geometric Gothic', a term coined by the collector Charles Handley-Read[8] to describe furniture of the 1860s and 1870s designed by, among others, Bruce Talbert and Charles Bevan. This chapter also includes the spikier Ruskinesque furniture of J.H. Chamberlain, the plainer designs of C.L. Eastlake, and the Old-Englishy interiors of Alfred Waterhouse. It does not include Richard Norman Shaw or W.E. Nesfield, both of whom began their careers in the Gothic tradition but whose principal field of influence is on the aesthetic movement, discussed in the next chapter, 'From "Nankin" to Bedford Park'. (Much of the blue-and-white porcelain imported from Japan was said to come from 'Nankin'; Bedford Park, 'an aesthetic Eden',[9] is a west London suburb built by Godwin, Shaw and others, largely in the 'Queen Anne' style.) A close connection between the Gothic and Japanese revivals might at first glance seem unlikely, but many designers moved easily between the two. Burges stated of the 1862 London International Exhibition that 'truly the Japanese Court is the real medieval court'[10] and Bruce Talbert's ebonized furniture clearly combines the two influences.

In dealing with the work of Morris and Company after the aesthetic movement rather than before, direct connections can more easily be made between Morris and the arts and crafts movement, the subject of chapter seven, many of whose leaders – W.R. Lethaby, Walter Crane, etc. – were earlier employed by 'The Firm', as Morris, Marshall, Faulkner & Co. was known. Anyway, William Morris was very much a turn-of-the-century hero, whereas most of the 'Francesca da Rimini, niminy, piminy'[11] aesthetes were despised by the artist-craftsmen. (When Mrs Ashbee left London for Chipping Campden in 1902 she deeply regretted having to lease her Chelsea house to Whistler, 'the little, horrid, cantankerous, curled, perfumed creature'.)[12] The title of chapter seven, 'The Arts and Crafts Movement', defines its limits, although certain Voysey interiors discussed in that chapter might also be described as 'New Art', and one of the most important commissions of the 'New Art' designer M.H. Baillie Scott, the furniture for the Grand Duke of Hesse's palace in Darmstadt, was executed by Ashbee's Guild of Handicraft. The 'New Art', however, especially in the work of Mackintosh and the Glasgow School, was characterized not simply by the fact that one

designer was responsible for the whole interior, but also by the single unifying themes of these interiors. 'New Art' – *l'Art nouveau* in France – was also distinguished by the virulence of the criticism it attracted. The sculptor George Frampton, one-time Master of the Art-Workers' Guild, commented: 'I believe it is made on the continent and used by parents to frighten naughty children.'[13]

Finally, there is a chapter on the commercial furniture of Heal's and Liberty's – Liberty's because of the breadth of their influence (Marcel Proust owned a Liberty duvet which played havoc with his asthma), Heal's because Sir Ambrose Heal, 'that rare thing: a successful pioneer who never lost touch with economic realities',[14] was not only an excellent designer but is also one of the few from this period whose work is still neglected by collectors.

Although acres of 'Victoriana' – once ignored by the art market, now overvalued – will here remain uncultivated, it is difficult to look at architect-designed furniture without also being influenced by current collecting trends. As Richard Norman Shaw was prepared publicly to admit: 'Those of us who happen to be collectors, in even a small way, fall into error and make our homes too much like little museums – an error, this, that causes a room (and its owner, too, now and then) to be just a trifle tedious.'[15] The pieces illustrated in this book were originally created as part of often outrageously adventurous contemporary interiors, but now they must be viewed in the precious light of 'museum interest' and of colour-plate auction catalogues, their values warmed by the praise of an antiques-orientated artistic establishment. This furniture has therefore become exactly what its creators abhorred, a field of collecting approved by the fashionable rich intent on surrounding themselves with fine 'antiques' instead of commissioning living architects to build and furnish new homes. If Morris were alive today he would be tearing down his own hangings and burning his friend Burges's wardrobes, which now sell for £80,000 or more. 'I have never been in any rich man's house', Morris said, 'which would not have looked better for having a bonfire made outside of nine-tenths of what it held.'[16]

The point to be emphasized is that all the best nineteenth-century furniture was the work of individualists and iconoclasts living in a period which welcomed change. The difference between us and the Victorians is illustrated by Prince Albert's commission for the Great Exhibition in Hyde Park in 1851 of a glass and iron pre-fabricated 'palace', one of the most ambitious, technically advanced and aesthetically far-sighted buildings England has ever seen. After the opening of Prince Albert's 'Crystal Palace', Queen Victoria noted in her journal: 'The sight . . . was magic and impressive. The tremendous cheering, the joy expressed in every face, the vastness of the building, with all its decorations and exhibits . . . and my beloved husband, the creator of this peace festival uniting the art and industry of all nations on earth.'[17] The vivacity of the Victorian vision, and its optimism too, are jointly reflected in the period's furniture and interiors.

CHAPTER ONE

A Matter of Style

3 The artist E. J. Poynter in his studio at The Avenue, Fulham Road, 1884. On the easel is a cartoon for mosaic decoration in the dome of St Paul's Cathedral.

The Victorians were much concerned with matters of style and taste, and the passion of their language on the subject is a fair indication of its importance to them. The Gothic fantast William Burges called the revived Queen Anne style 'negro-language',[1] and his architect colleague J.D. Sedding followed this up with a suggestion that 'the conduct of some of the designers of this class is like unto a child in a garden picking the tops of flowers ... to make a promiscuous but malodorous nosegay'.[2] Popular pundits were as concerned as the aesthetes. The voluble Mrs Haweis, in her tour of the painter Alma-Tadema's home (32–34), noted how he could afford to be 'independent of the fashion – aesthetic or vulgar ... It is not an Owen Jones or Cottier house ... not a Morrisey house, though Morris wallpapers are brought in whenever they are wanted ... not exactly a Dutch house nor exactly a classic house ... it is essentially an Alma-Tadema house.'[3] As always, there is the problem of stylistic definition in what the *Building News* of 1868 saw as 'an age of picking to pieces ... [an age in which] the critical faculty is ... developed at the expense of creativity'. Far from ignoring matters of style, as Stracheyan detractors of the period would have us believe, the Victorians thought more about the way they and their homes looked than do all but the most ultra-fashionconscious of today. Good taste and the right style were national issues in which the principal arbiters were largely the artists and architects themselves. As an introduction, therefore, to the complex matter of Victorian style, it makes sense to see how some of the creators of contemporary taste chose to live.

In the second half of the nineteenth century leading painters were rich and sociable. Courted by their even richer clients, they earned and spent their money not on the fringes of fashionable society but at its centre. Like their patrons, many artists built themselves smart new homes in the expanding suburbs of Kensington, Chelsea, or St John's Wood, and lived on a scale it is difficult to imagine today. When in 1866 Frederick, later Lord, Leighton decided to build a studio house in Holland Park Road, his architect George Aitchison and the builders Hack & Sons were able to provide him with one in which 'we find much that revives an Italian Renascence palace'[4] at a cost of £4,500 (excluding later additions such as the Arab Hall (12) and an extra picture gallery). In the mid-1860s Sir John Everett Millais's income from society portraiture is known to have exceeded £20,000 a year, and Leighton's would have been much the same; a painter's annual earnings were therefore roughly five times the cost of building an impressive town house, in the most modern style and with the best materials. The cost today of such a venture – purely for building works, forgetting the incalculable changes in urban land values – might be £300,000 or so, meaning that today's comparably successful artist would have an annual income of £1,500,000! The rewards given by a society to its artists are realistic indicators of that society's true wealth: in the period 1830 to 1915 the industrially-dominant colony-owning British were much the richest people in the world, an important fact to remember in assessing matters of style and taste in Victorian and Edwardian furniture and interiors.

Artists' homes reflected a variety of contrasting attitudes, not all affirming the progressive ideas of Edward Burne-Jones, who aspired in an age of sofas and cushions ... to be indifferent to comfort'.[5] Millais, having dramatically married John Ruskin's ex-wife, Effie, settled down to a life of plump conservatism. Millais's sense of satisfaction – with himself as with the status quo – was reflected in his work, which became opulent and dull. The same is true of the home he and his erstwhile runaway created, 'into which the aestheticism of the day does not enter; no, not by so much as a peacock fan'.[6]

The studio of Sir Edward J. Poynter, 'that grave and industrious man',[7] is hardly a riot of modernity either, but there are a few tell-tale signs of fashionable taste (3): on the mantleshelf a recently excavated Tanagra figurine; balanced against the mirror an oriental fan; on the dado rail some vivid Isnic pottery; nearby, on the top shelf of a what-not, a large Kutani bowl; and an inlaid Savonarola chair behind the easel. The most adventurous piece of furniture is actually the most practical, an adjustable artist's stool on which the painter impatiently waits for the photographer to finish. Despite marriage to a bright, bohemian lady – Burne-Jones's sister-in-law, Agnes – the shy Poynter retreated into the shell of aloofness created by his academic achievements: Director of the National Gallery for eleven years, President of the Royal Academy for twenty-two. As a young man he had been much more outgoing, tramping the Continent with the ineluctable 'Billy' Burges, for whom he painted the Wines and Beers cabinet (151), exhibited at the 1862 London International Exhibition. Together with other, more progressive, artists Poynter objected to the separation of the 'fine' from the 'applied' arts, and in 1868 happily designed tiles for the decoration of the Grill Room at the South Kensington Museum (now the Victoria and Albert); five years later he enjoyed himself painting the Earl of Wharncliffe's billiard room. Poynter's was perhaps a fairly typical attitude: support in theory for advanced ideas in interior design but preference, in practice, for the tasteful restraint of Georgian bureau-bookcases and Hepplewhite-style shieldback armchairs.

Along the newly laid-out streets of the Holland Estate in Kensington an amicable rivalry developed between artists in the appointment of their new homes. Luke Fildes, at 31 Melbury Road, believed his house 'knocked Stone's to bits',[8] though both were designed by Richard Norman Shaw and built by W.H. Lascelles. Marcus Stone's house, No. 8, was the first of the two to be occupied, in 1875; the interior (37) was said to embody 'the spirit of an Old English Home'.[9] It is not easy to ascertain precisely what was meant by the 'Old English' style (promoted by Shaw and Nesfield in the 1870s) as distinct from the 'Queen Anne' style with which it overlapped, or from the general 'Wrenaissance' of the last quarter of the century. In 1882 Mrs Haweis tried 'to explain the apparent confusion of terms ... [and] remind readers ... that the slang term 'Queen Anne' means almost anything just now, but is oftenest applied to the pseudo-classic fashions of the First Empire'.[10] If the complex gradations in Victorian style were confusing to contemporaries they might well be assumed to be beyond precise definition by ourselves; certainly, to our eyes, the one thing 'Queen Anne' seems not to have had was any of the bold classicism of Empire design. As for the 'Old English' of Marcus Stone's Melbury Road studio, it does not look markedly different from Poynter's, save for the elegant proportions of Shaw's angled chimney-piece. The dissection and labelling of the historical origins of various Victorian styles is a difficult task, best left to committed pigeon-holers.

In choosing their architect, many painters turned to Shaw (1831–1912), one of the most stylistically versatile of them all. In 1870, for example, he produced skilful plans for F.W. Goodall's Grims Dyke, a 'country' house at Harrow Weald, only ten miles from Marble Arch. The main feature of its open-beamed structure was a large studio. Goodall soon discovered the professional inconvenience of living outside central London, and sold Grims Dyke, which passed in 1890 into the hands of W.S. Gilbert, the comic opera librettist. Gilbert's London house, in Harrington Gardens, was the work of Ernest George and Harold Peto, and it was to this busy partnership that he turned for the redecoration of Grims Dyke. Amongst other 'improvements', the architects installed a gigantic alabaster chimney piece in the studio (38), an ugly addendum, although by that time Shaw himself would probably have approved. The only piece of 'Art Furniture' is a Morris & Co. adjustable armchair in the left foreground. The lace petticoat serving as a lamp shade was much to Gilbert's taste: he died in the lake beside the house, of a heart attack, 'apparently while going to the assistance of two young ladies in distress'.[11] The photograph was taken by Bedford Lemère, who had joined his father's photographic business in the Strand in 1881 and continued working at the same address almost to his death in 1944. Lemère specialized exclusively in architectural photography, producing, it now appears, well over 50,000 negatives, the majority shot in natural light, with small apertures and long exposures, resulting in these crisp images. Carefully composed, they are remarkable house-portraits, as well as invaluable record shots.

Another Lemère photograph – of 1885 – shows the Hall of Narcissus at Leighton House (39), designed by George Aitchison. Mrs Haweis wrote of this view: 'The walls are deepest sea-blue tiles ... the floor is pallid (the well-known mosaic of the Caesars' palaces) and casts up shimmering reflected lights upon the greeny-silvery ceiling ... It possesses an imperial stateliness and strength of flavour; and the silence is like a throne.'[12] The camera leads us through to Leighton's luxurious Arab Hall, with new William De Morgan tiles to match a collection of Turkish originals, and a Walter Crane frieze 'in a beautiful running pattern of fawns and vines, carried out in gold Venice mosaic'.[13] Aitchison summoned Queen Victoria's favourite sculptor, Sir Edgar Boehm, to carve the smaller capitals in the Arab Hall; the gilded birds on the larger columns at the entrance are the work of Randolph Caldecott, like Crane better known for his children's book illustrations. As well as the building, Aitchison also designed much of the furniture, in an unfortunate combination of ill-conceived historical styles, typical of which is the table on the right in Lemère's photograph. Lauded in the popular press, the house did not please more demanding architectural critics. E.W. Godwin found the building 'altogether unsatisfactory ... Mr Webb's work in Mr Val Prinsep's house next door [399–400] comes into close comparison with it, and is chiefly admirable for the very things in which its neighbour is so utterly deficient – viz. in beauty of skyline and pleasing arrangement of mass'.[14]

George Aitchison was one of a large group of commercially successful architects working in what his friend Robert Kerr called 'the comfortable style',[15] which was, by comparison with so much exciting design of the period,

4 A map table for the Trinity Square offices of the Thames Conservancy Board, designed by George Aitchison in 1865 or 1866.

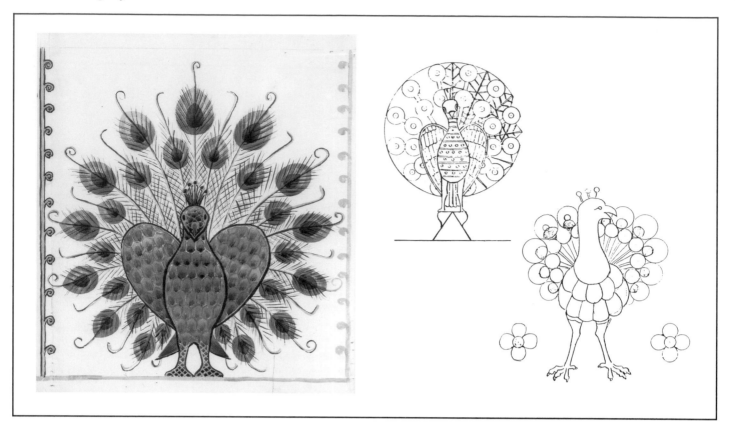

without any creative quality – the style-less style, it might be called. Aitchison, also an admired academic, turned down the offer of a knighthood on the grounds that it would add twenty percent to his bills. His father was the architect of Ivory House in St Katharine's Dock, a building noted for its early use of iron, and in 1862 the younger George had taken over as Architect and Surveyor to the St Katharine's Dock Company. In 1865 he was commissioned by the Thames Conservancy Board to redesign their offices. He produced his usual brand of mediocre furniture (4) and invited Leighton to design the frieze. The decoration of a house in Berkeley Square belonging to Frederick Lehmann M.P., however, turned out to be the extravagant apogee of Aitchison's interior design; he again turned to a painter for assistance, this time Albert Moore, who produced, in 1873, the renowned peacock frieze in the Front Drawing Room.

By then, peacocks had become the fashionable symbol of artistic taste, in life as in art. Not content with feathers in a vase, Viscountess Beaconsfield allowed her large flock of peacocks to roam free across the grounds of Hughenden Manor; the sculptor Alfred Stevens kept his peacock in the studio, pecking at his forever unfinished plaster maquettes; Alma-Tadema had his stuffed, then nailed it to the studio wall (32). 'A plump active little Dutchman',[16] Lourens Alma-Tadema became a naturalized Englishman in 1873 and was created Sir 'Lawrence' in 1899, at a celebratory dinner for which his friends sang the specially penned 'Carmen Tademare', set to music by George Henschel. 'Alma-Tad of the Royal Acad'[17] was a popular figure in society and 'all London sympathised with him when, on October 2nd 1874, his house, a very treasury of art, was

shattered by the explosion of a barge's cargo of gunpowder and benzolene'[18] on the nearby Regent's Canal. Undeterred, the painter restored Townshend House in its entirety, executing much of the decoration himself, including the Pompeian frieze in the studio. The household was famous for its private concerts, held in a music room with gold walls and ceiling, onyx windows, and one of the grandest grand pianos of the period (33). Inside the lid of the piano Alma-Tadema fixed a parchment on which famous visitors were asked to sign their names, a list that included Tchaikovsky, Paderewski, Saint-Saëns and Clara Schumann. Designed in the 'Byzantine' style by Alma-Tadema and his friend G.E.Cox, the piano was included in Christie's disposal of the deceased artist's effects on 9 June 1913. It failed to find a buyer and was picked up after the war by the furniture retailers Maples for £441 (they paid an additional £115 for the bench, the back of which was painted by Alma-Tadema himself). This piano, which Mrs Haweis had earlier declared King Solomon could not *possibly* have refused from the Queen of Sheba, remained on prestigious display at Maples's showrooms until they, and it, were destroyed by a bomb in the Second World War.[19]

A surviving suite of Alma-Tadema furniture, in a style 'which may be described as Graeco-Roman',[20] was commissioned by Henry Marquand for the music room in his New York apartment. The piano (13), piano stools, chairs (35–36) and some side tables were exhibited at the Bond Street showrooms of Johnstone, Norman & Co. in 1885 prior to shipment to America; sold in 1981 by Sotheby's in New York, one of the chairs has since returned to England and is now in the Victoria and Albert Museum.

5–7 The peacock, quintessential emblem of the aesthetic movement. *Left*, a design for an embroidered panel by Alfred Waterhouse, 1880–5; *centre*, crest for a whatnot at Dromore Castle, designed by E. W. Godwin in 1869 – a very similar peacock appears on the Dromore dining room buffet (289); *right*, a William Burges design of 1872 for a marquetry panel in the Winter Smoking Room at Cardiff Castle.

8 The popular obsession with contemporary design is demonstrated by this sheet-music cover illustrating pâte-sur-pâte vases from the Minton stand at the Paris Exposition Universelle of 1878.

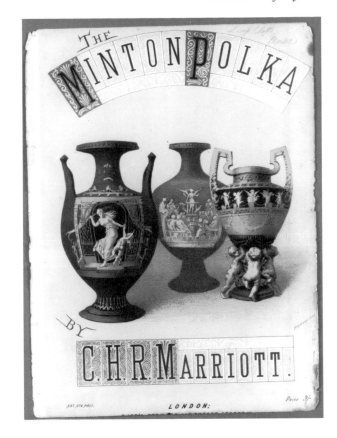

This list of artists' houses, odd and ordinary, could be extended almost indefinitely and still no stylistic consensus would emerge: exuberant and full of individuality, but hardly an ordered manual of good taste. It might even seem as if elaboration for its own sake was what the fashionable public really admired, regardless of whatever style designers might claim to adopt.

Pressurized by the revolutionary availability of manufactured fashion, styles – of dress, of interior design, of coiffure, indeed of everything – changed with increasing rapidity, and it was all written about, lectured upon and discussed with a seriousness the British have since reserved for cricket. Fashion, in all its forms, was *the* topic. Thus, in the trend-setting *Hints on Household Taste* (a collection of magazine articles first published in book form in 1868), C.L. Eastlake turned his influential attention to the question of beards, arguing that it was 'absurd that we should continue day by day, with no little pain and inconvenience, to rasp our faces for the purposes of removing an appendage which Nature has given us for use if not for ornament'. An added advantage, he pointed out, of the revival of beards, was the fact that 'the hideous and uncomfortable *Vater-mörder* – the stand-up collar ... [would be] banished from young England's wardrobe'. Herbert Minton, who died in 1858, and his successor Colin Minton Campbell were amongst the technically and stylistically most adventurous of manufacturers, not qualities which today gain popular support, and yet in the nineteenth century their ceramics became such an integral part of popular culture that the street musicians honoured them with the 'Minton Polka' (8). Just as fashion in personal appearance concerned the art critics, so the latest trends in decorative design mattered greatly to the public at large.

Perhaps it was the decorative extravagance of Minton's pâte-sur-pâte vases which gave them such a wide appeal. The architectural writer and draughtsman J.B. Waring was thinking of porcelain-mounted cabinets and lily-covered earthenware garden seats when he complained that 'exuberance of ornament, tastelessly applied ... is one of the worst points of modern furniture'.[21] The psychedelic colouring of Herbert Minton's 'Majolica' was certainly one of the wilder delights of nineteenth-century decorative art. Visitors to the London International Exhibition of 1862 were confronted by a majolica fountain forty feet in diameter and thirty-six feet high, topped by a larger-than-life-size figure of St George (68). Few dared question the artistic integrity of the sculptor, John Thomas: an exhibition guide declared: 'If there were no other object in the building but this grand work alone, it would be well worth the shilling entrance fee to see it.'[22]

Not all participants in the mid-Victorian fashion for elaboration were quite so certain of its propriety. Samuel Lloyd M.P., later Lord Overstone, hated the country house built for him in 1861–2 by W.M. Teulon, talentless brother of the architect Samuel Saunders Teulon. 'The House', Lloyd recorded, 'tho' very large and full of pretension – has neither taste nor comfort. I am utterly ashamed of it ... The principal rooms are literally uninhabitable – I shall never fit them up ... [and] I grieve to think that I shall hand such an abortion to my successors.'[23] Billiard rooms seem to have attracted some of the worst excesses. Thomas Vaughan spent a rumoured £50,000 on his at Gunnersgate, incorpor-

9 The draped entrance to Mrs Ralli's dining room at 'Iona', her house in Croxteth Park, Liverpool, 1891. This is an extravagant example of a fashionable, if much-criticized, feature of late-Victorian interiors.

10 The Rococo revival is one of the most persistent themes in Victorian interior design and continued well into the twentieth century. Despite a promising beginning in the Elizabethan Saloon at Belvoir Castle, designed by Matthew Cotes Wyatt in 1824, it rarely attracted the attention of distinguished designers. By the mid-century Rococo was firmly established as the preferred style of the *nouveaux riches*: the furnishings of this sumptuous drawing room, photographed by Bedford Lemère in the 1880s, were installed in Beaumanor Park, Leicestershire, a Jacobean-revival mansion built for Robert Herrick, a coal-mining magnate, by William Railton, 1845–7.

ating 'large and horrible'[24] paintings by Stacy Marks. At Witley Park, Surrey, the crooked company-promoter Whitaker Wright insisted on an underwater billiard room, with a glass ceiling through which to stare at unsuspecting fish. The decorative excesses of the ultra-rich were aped by the expanding middle class in, for example, the draped doorway (9) to Mrs Ralli's dining room at her house in Croxteth Park, Liverpool, decorated by Turner, Walker & Co. R.W. Edis, the fashionable architect and promoter of 'healthy furniture', criticized the way such curtains often 'trailed some feet on the floor ... and when not in the possession of the pet dog or cat becomes the receptacle for dust and dirt, or the hiding place of some pet's dinner'.[25] It was all symptomatic of what Charles Handley-Read happily described as the period's 'unselective hedonism of the sense of sight'.[26] The actual style in which the Victorians indulged themselves might change from Rococo to Gothic, but the purpose tended to remain the same – exuberant display, whether in their own drawing rooms or in a covered market for the poor of east London.

The man who tried hardest to put some order into this decorative chaos was Owen Jones (1809–74), who declared his intention to 'arrest that unfortunate tendency of our time to be content with copying ... without attempting to ascertain ... the peculiar circumstances which rendered an ornament beautiful'.[27] The vehicle chosen to bear the full weight of Jones's considerable ambition was a magnificent manual of decorative design published in 1856, containing one hundred and twelve chromolithographic plates and titled *The Grammar of Ornament* (17–20). Much more than a mere dictionary of historical style or textbook of flat-patterning, *The Grammar of Ornament* represented his whole philosophy of design and defined a new approach to interior decoration. The principles boldly advocated by Owen Jones began with general premises: 'Proposition 3. As Architecture, so all works of the decorative arts should possess fitness, proportion, harmony, the result of all which is repose.' He went on to dogmatic statement, 'Proposition 8. All ornament should be based on geometrical construction', continued with scientific instruction, 'Proposition 17. The primary colours should be used in the upper portions of objects, the second and tertiary in the lower', and ended with broad truths, 'Proposition 36. The principles discoverable in the works of the past belong to us; not the results. It is taking the end for the means.'[28] Described by a contemporary as 'our first and principal deliverer ... from the dominion of sprawling patterns',[29] Owen Jones's importance cannot be overestimated in the practice of flat pattern design, which in whatever style and whatever medium remains one of the century's most powerful and successful forms of expression.

As a practical designer Owen Jones became known to a wider public for his overall decorative scheme at the Great Exhibition, where this 'apostle of colour'[30] gave blue the dominant role. When the Crystal Palace – so named by *Punch* – was transplanted to Sydenham, re-opening in 1854,

11 Owen Jones, portrayed by H. W. Phillips, 1856. Jones is standing against a wall in the Alhambra, the subject of one of his most influential books.

he designed the Egyptian and Alhambra Courts (42–43), remembered by Mrs Haweis for 'the heart-elevation and the awe' imparted to her childhood visits. Designs for book-covers, wallpapers, carpets, silks, biscuit-tin labels (for Huntley & Palmer), silver, and even bank notes all originated at his busy commercial drawing board, earning him rightful praise for 'doing little things of this kind with grace and fitness'.[31] On contracts for furnishing and decorating Owen Jones was closely associated with the firm of Jackson & Graham, whose Oxford Street premises he redesigned in 1869 (55) and where over 600 people were employed in the 1870s (before the firm went bankrupt in 1883 and was taken over by Collinson & Lock). Jackson & Graham made Owen Jones's most elaborate furniture, including the ivory-inlaid ebony pieces for Alfred Morrison at Fonthill (57). The furniture for Fonthill was regularly exhibited by Jackson & Graham at international fairs, and a cabinet at the Vienna Exhibition of 1873 was described by Fred Smith, manager of the Union Land & Building Society, as 'a masterpiece ... the most rigid scrutiny on my part failed to expose a single flaw'.[32] In their obituary of Owen Jones in 1874 the editors of the *Builder*, however, regretted finding it 'their duty to say ... [that] this is not a type of furniture which we would wish to be imitated'. For once,

Mrs Haweis also refused to be impressed by mere luxury: while noting 'the solid perfection of miles of conscientious inlaying' at Morrison's London home (16 Carlton House Terrace), she could not refrain from criticizing 'an enormous cabinet, filled with a pretentious service of Minton's ware . . . in which the wide distinction between technical perfection and real artistic worth points a very wholesome and instructive moral'.[33] A simpler verdict from the *Builder*: 'It is . . . in the designing of purely ornamental work for flat surfaces . . . that the peculiar excellence of Owen Jones' design was best displayed.'[34]

Prior to *The Grammar of Ornament* Owen Jones published *Plans, Elevations, Sections and Details of the Alhambra* (1836–45; reprinted by Quaritch in 1877), which led the way in the colourful High Victorian revival of the Moorish style in architecture and decoration. One of the first public buildings to adopt whole-heartedly this novel style was the Royal Panopticon in Leicester Square, 'An Institution for Scientific Exhibitions, and for Promoting Discoveries in Arts and Manufactures'[35] founded in 1850 (45). At first the architect, T. Hayter Lewis, resisted the Board's preference for 'the Saracenic or Moorish style', but he eventually agreed, realizing that it would give him 'tolerably free scope in working out the design . . . [as] the Saracens had not been in the habit of building Panopticon institutions'.[36] Despite such attractions as a hydraulic lift in the shape of a birdcage, the venture flopped and the building was sold in 1857 to the eccentric showman E.T. Smith for £9,000 – £71,000 less than it had cost to build. Smith changed its name to the Alhambra Palace, first operating it as a circus and then as a music hall.

In domestic architecture Owen Jones himself had added, in 1843, some mild Moresque detail to the classical shell of 8 Kensington Palace Gardens. True oriental extravagance appeared in Palace Gardens in 1864, when Sir Matthew Digby Wyatt built a glittering Moorish billiard room for Alexander Collie, a Manchester cotton merchant who disappeared forever in 1875 with the £200,000 he had fraudulently obtained from various City institutions. In 1888 W.H. Romaine-Walker incorporated an architecturally accurate Moorish smoking room (44) in his design for a 'Tudorbethan' mansion in the middle of the New Forest. (The house also boasted a tower with a peal of bells clearly audible in the Isle of Wight.) By the 1890s, following the fashionable example of Liberty's, numerous decorators found themselves obliged to fill ordinary domestic interiors with dubious eastern promise (50). Much of the furniture came from Cairo, where it was manufactured in quantity by such men as G. Parvis, whose productions, the *Art Journal* avowed, 'have conferred great honour on the country of his adoption . . . Many visitors to a people deeply interesting to England have supplied themselves with examples of his skill.'[37] The basic form of all this 'oriental' furniture remained staunchly European wherever it was actually made, from Tokyo to Tottenham Court Road; similarly, in the British India Conference Room (47) at the Imperial

Institute, T.E. Collcutt made no attempt to adapt his architectural space to suit the Indian-style decoration.

Another important theme, the Renaissance revival, is most famously demonstrated by St George's Hall, Liverpool (52), a building begun by H.L. Elmes in 1841 and completed by C.R. Cockerell in 1856. The coffered ceiling, supported by vast red granite columns – a form inspired by the Baths of Caracalla – and strongly coloured, successfully competes with the energetic patterning of the Minton tiles on the floor. The most skilled High Victorian exponent of Italianate design, the sculptor Alfred Stevens, was commissioned in 1847 by the architect L.W. Collmann to decorate both the dining room and drawing room at Deysbrook Hall, Liverpool (51). Leonard Collmann, who was himself also a decorator and furniture designer, at first regretted the decision to employ his friend Stevens as for months nothing was heard of him; however, at the last moment Stevens 'arrived with a carpet-bag, a small portfolio of sketches and a colour box, and executed [the designs] in something less than one day each'.[38] Accustomed to contemporary neglect of his talents, Stevens might yet have been a little surprised at the writer Augustus Hare's comment on Dorchester House, a commission which had drawn from the sculptor the best Renaissance revival interiors of the period (53): 'The great charm of the house is in the immensely broad galleries which are so effective when filled with beautiful women, relieved like Greek pictures against a gold background.'[39]

Prince Albert was a keen advocate of the Renaissance style in decoration, a taste founded on the counsel of his full-time artistic adviser Ludwig Gruner and the German colour theorist Gottfried Semper, who lived in London from 1850 to 1855. Thus the interior of the Royal Dairy at Frogmore, in Windsor Park (54), designed by John Thomas, was lined with Minton majolica tiles of the most elaborately classical nature, including portrait roundels of the royal family. Decoratively indulgent and stylistically perverse though a 'Renaissance' dairy might appear to be, its design had a serious scientific *raison d'être* – hygiene and coolness – as well as the full backing of aesthetic dogma. In all this there is evidence also of the Victorian desire to impress by being different, of novelty for novelty's sake alone.

This craving for stylistic experimentation led to an interesting compromise between the Classical and the Gothic when architects turned to a style mixing Byzantine and Romanesque elements, in, for instance, Alfred Waterhouse's Natural History Museum (1873–81), Charles Harrison Townsend's Bishopsgate Institute (1892–4), John Francis Bentley's Westminster Cathedral (1895–1903)

12 George Aitchison's watercolour design for the Arab Hall at Leighton House (1877–9), based on the twelfth-century Ziza Palace in Palermo. Most of the Isnik tiles were collected by Leighton on trips he made to Turkey in 1868 and 1873; the gaps were filled with copies decorated by William De Morgan. The mosaic frieze of fawns and cockatoos was designed and executed by Walter Crane.

13

14

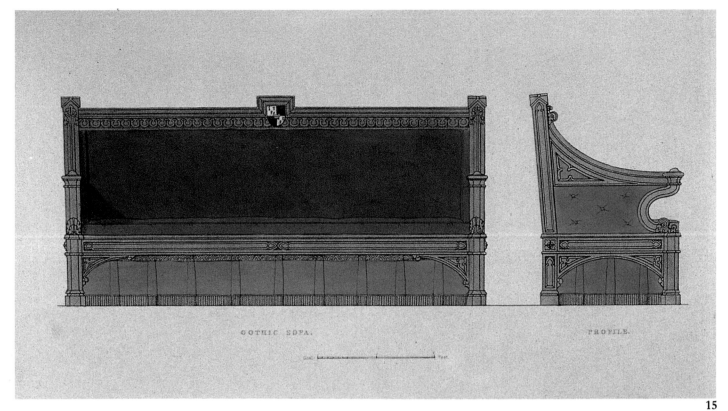

GOTHIC SOFA.   PROFILE.

15

13 This luxurious 'Graeco-Roman' piano of 1884–5 was designed by Lawrence Alma-Tadema and W. C. Codman for Henry Marquand's music room in New York (the ceiling of which was painted by Leighton). The piano was made by Johnstone, Norman & Co. of 67 New Bond Street.

14 An 'Elizabethan' wardrobe from the bedroom suite designed by Anthony Salvin in the 1830s for Sir Robert Newman of Mamhead House, Devon, as part of the preparations for a visit by Queen Adelaide.

15 A design for a 'Gothic Sofa' from Richard Bridgens's influential manual of style *Furniture with Candelabra and Interior Decoration* (1838).

16 One of the magnificent 'Renaissance' mirrors designed by Alfred Stevens for the dining room at Dorchester House, London, where work began in 1855 but was still unfinished at Stevens's death in 1875.

16

21 and **22** Lululaund (*below*), designed for Hubert Herkomer by
H. H. Richardson in 1886, is in a free style classified by the
Victorians under 'Romanesque' or 'Byzantine'. Halsey Ricardo's
house for Sir Ernest Debenham (*right*), 1906–7, combines
Byzantine mosaics with both Classical and arts and crafts
detailing.

and Halsey Ricardo's house (22) for Sir Ernest Debenham
in Addison Road, London (1906–7). The painter and
enamellist Hubert Herkomer was unusual in actually
building himself a house in what was called the Byzantine
style, Lululaund (21), to a design of 1886 by the American
architect H.H. Richardson. Herkomer's need to impress led
him to line the dining room walls at Lululaund with
lacquered aluminium.

Antiquarianism – or, as the architect Reginald Blomfield
put it, 'collector's mania', in which 'rarity and costliness
[were preferred] to beauty'[40] – was another form of stylistic
experiment. Sir Walter Scott, the best-known of these
collectors, gathered together at Abbotsford a piebald mass
of antiques, as we would call them; the much publicized hall
at Abbotsford, which became a symbol of the antiquarian

style, was dominated by two fully armoured knights
standing in pinnacled niches – one of the suits of armour
was claimed by an imaginative dealer to have been worn by
Sir John Cheney at the Battle of Bosworth. Another
dedicated collector, Thomas Lister Parker of Brownsholme
Hall, set out with the inherited kudos of two antique titles:
Bowbearer of the Forest of Bollard and Trumpeter to the
Queen. At the other end of the century the architect Harold
Peto was still surrounding himself with antiques in his
London house in Collingham Gardens (23), built in a style
Mark Girouard has so quotably described as George &
Peto's 'own overpoweringly quaint Flemish-Renaissance
manner, a kind of *pâte de foie* architecture which in small
sharp doses can be highly enjoyable'.[41] Even after ill-health
had forced an early retirement, Peto's antiquarian enthu-

Left **17–20** Four plates from Owen Jones's
The Grammar of Ornament (1856). The
effect of this influential manual on the
design of flat patterns persisted well into the
twentieth century. The styles illustrated
here are (*clockwise from top left*): 'Nineveh &
Persia', 'Turkish', 'Greek' and 'Egyptian'.

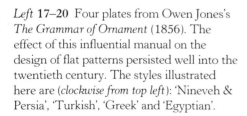

Right **23** Antiquarianism in interior design
is exemplified by the sitting room in the
architect Harold Peto's house in Collingham
Gardens, Kensington, photographed in
1891. The house itself is in a Franco-
Flemish style of *c*.1500; the interiors were
created around Peto's large and varied
collection of antiques.

24 Proposed extension to Edgeworth Manor, Gloucestershire, by Ernest George and Alfred B. Yeates, 1897. This recreation of a medieval great hall used authentic seventeenth-century furniture and fittings.

25 and **26** 'A Looking Glass from the Time of Queen Elizabeth' (*left*), from Henry Shaw's *Specimens of Ancient Furniture* (1836), and the 1860s Minton majolica mirror that it inspired.

siasm continued to have a strong influence on the work of his partner Sir Ernest George. In drawings for additions to Edgeworth Manor, Gloucestershire (24), George and his new partner Alfred B. Yeates included figures in medieval dress, and pseudo-Jacobean furniture, much of which was cobbled together for clients to the architects' specifications, using authentic seventeenth-century components.

Where decorators in the 'Egyptian', 'Celtic', 'Hindoo' or 'Chinese' styles might turn to Jones's *Grammar of Ornament*, the favoured printed sources for dressing up houses in the antiquarian manner were John Nash's *The Mansions of England in the Olden Time*, 1839–49, and Henry Shaw's *Specimens of Ancient Furniture*, first published in 1836. Many of Shaw's plates depict items from the collection of the London solicitor Sir Samuel Rush Meyrick, whose precious possessions were displayed in a brand new medieval castle in the middle of agricultural Hertfordshire. Meyrick wrote the introduction to *Specimens* and much of the text, explaining thus the instinct for elaboration in the applied arts: 'The progress of civilization has constantly a tendency to make articles of convenience become objects of luxury; and hence, the ingenuity as well as the taste of man are lavished to render splendid the common necessities of life.'[42] One of the plates illustrated Meyrick's own 'rare if not unique specimen . . . A Looking Glass of the Time of Queen Elizabeth' (25), the period elaboration of which directly inspired such monstrous conceits as majolica mirrors in the so-called 'Renaissance' style (26).

With the expanding demands of an increasingly rich professional clientele, designers and manufacturers set about producing modern suites in a wide range of named historical styles. Best qualified, in this respect, amongst early

Victorian designers was Richard Bridgens, who had worked both with the celebrated Regency furniture designer George Bullock at Abbotsford and with Henry Shaw on *Specimens* before producing, in 1838, his own popular *Furniture with Candelabra and Interior Decoration*, for which the plates were engraved by Shaw. Clearly labelled 'Gothic' (15), 'Elizabethan' (58–59), 'Grecian' and the like, all Bridgens's designs, however, look more or less the same. In their 'tepid eclecticism'[43] they are, in fact, typically early Victorian; despite attempts at definition, one comfortably rounded style is indistinguishable from another. But Bridgens was by no means a maker of taste and his various publications simply reflected the dominant architectural aesthetic of the period, best represented perhaps by Anthony Salvin (1799–1881). Salvin specialized in Elizabethan revival country houses described by E.W. Godwin as 'mostly gentle things without much character, either good or bad',[44] for many of which – notably Scotney Castle in Kent and Mamhead House in Devon – he supplied suitably inoffensive furniture. Queen Adelaide's bedroom suite at Mamhead (14), typical of the Salvin taste, has softened Baroque forms with decoration inspired by the Louis XIV furniture of Daniel Marot; the 'Elizabethan' cresting is similar in essence to Salvin's amazing pierced stone scrollwork at Harlaxton Manor, Lincolnshire, dated 1837 (an exception to his generally undramatic architecture). In the work of Charles Barry (1795–1860), architect of the Houses of Parliament, the styles were equally interchangeable: his Reform Club (28), in the 'neo-cinquecento manner',[45] is close in spirit to the romantic Gothic of Highclere Castle. Even Lewis Nockalls Cottingham (1787–1847), a noted antiquarian and author of a marvellous manual of naturalistic Gothic detail, *Working Drawings of Gothic Ornaments, etc.* (1824), was unable to escape the *Zeitgeist* (66).

The labelling of contemporary styles was a game much enjoyed in the nineteenth century. In his book *A History of the Gothic Revival in England* (1872) C.L. Eastlake (1836–1906) listed three hundred and forty three buildings of note erected in England in the Gothic style between 1820 and 1870. Each of these he placed in a particular category, ranging from the vaguely identifiable 'Tudor' of Barry's Houses of Parliament, the 'Early English' of a Richard Norman Shaw bank in Farnham and the raucously 'Venetian Gothic' of George Gilbert Scott's St Pancras Station, to the mystic distinctions between 'First Pointed' (John Prichard and J.P. Seddon's Ettington Park, Warwickshire), 'Early Pointed' (Pugin's Mount St Bernard Abbey, Leicestershire), 'Foreign Early Pointed' (G.E. Street's St James the Less, Pimlico), 'Middle Pointed' (Butterfield's All Saints', Margaret Street), 'Early Middle Pointed' (William White's St Saviour's, Highbury), 'Geometric Middle Pointed' (G.F. Bodley's St Salvador's, Dundee) and 'Late Middle Pointed' (Henry Woodyer's St Paul's, Wokingham). Alfred Waterhouse's building for Caius College, Cambridge, suffered the indignity of a Bridgens-type 'François Premier' label. Weak at spotting his own inconsistencies, Eastlake had a keen eye,

27 and 28 Sir Charles Barry moved easily between styles – Gothic, as in the Royal Gallery of the House of Lords (*above*), begun in 1840, or Renaissance Classicism, as in the Reform Club, completed in 1841 (*below*). For an example of Barry's Reform Club furniture, see 64.

29 Frederick Leyland's Botticelli Room at
49 Princes Gate exemplifies traditional
taste. The screen, which could be opened
out to create a long gallery, was designed by
Richard Norman Shaw in 1879; it is shown
in detail in 2.

30 The continuation of the Rococo revival:
the 'Louis' style as used by Frederick Sage
Ltd in their refurbishment of Harrods from
1900 to 1905. This is the Coats and Skirts
Department, photographed in 1919.

nevertheless, for the meaninglessness of fashionable jargon, and warned the uninitiated against buying anything a shop assistant described as 'handsome', that is to say 'often ponderous and almost always encumbered with superfluous ornament'; he also noted that 'elegant is applied to any object which is curved in form, no matter in what direction, or with what effect'.[46] Cottingham's supposedly Gothic *vis-à-vis* (66) and a Rococo *bureau-de-dame* (71) are both, therefore, supremely 'elegant'.

The impact of new materials on style was also a subject much debated. In the 1830s J.C. Loudon, author of the *Encyclopaedia of Cottage, Farm and Villa Architecture and Furniture*, had warned that the use of iron would transform the whole nature of architectural style and technology, but it was not until the building of Decimus Burton's Palm House at Kew Gardens, from 1844 to 1848, and Joseph Paxton's Crystal Palace, erected in less than nine months over the winter of 1850–51, that the significance of this new material was fully realized. Inevitably, the dying Pugin reacted fiercely against the threat of true modernity, snarling at the 'glass monster ... that crystal humbug'.[47] Edward Burne-Jones took the Crystal Palace less seriously: 'As I look at it in its gigantic wearisomeness ... I grow more and more convinced of the powerlessness of such a material to affect Architecture ... It is fit for fragrant shrubs, trickling fountains, muslin-de-laines, eau-de-colognes, Grecian statues, strawberry ices and brass bands.'[48] William White, a dedicated Goth, pleaded: 'Where is the massiveness so essential to architecture – the bulk – above everything else the shadow? How could there be architecture without shadow?'[49] At the University Museum in Oxford (69), begun in 1855, Thomas Deane and Benjamin Woodward 'did their best to Gothicise ironwork ... and though the attempt displayed great ingenuity it can hardly be called successful'.[50] Another contemporary commented on the

museum: 'The effect is fairy-like, we admit; and some of the perspectives are exceedingly novel ... [but] this is merely a stone vaulting system in iron.'[51] In furniture the same kind of criticism can be made, that iron was too often used simply as a marketing novelty, without any distinct difference in form from its counterpart in wood (70). In some areas of commercial furniture design – brass for bedsteads, for example – the use of new materials had considerable practical benefit, but in the majority of cases the motive was mere bravado: ladies' writing desks in *papier-mâché* (71); crystal-glass settees; chairs carved from great slabs of cannel-coal (72).

In focusing attention on the progressive architect-designers of the period, it is possible – even desirable – to forget that the mindless revivalism associated principally with the 1840s actually continued throughout the century. Take Frederick Leyland, an enlightened patron of contemporary artists, a man who employed Thomas Jeckyll and Whistler to decorate his dining room, and yet gave over most of his house at Princes Gate to antique furniture and old master pictures. The screen in a corner of his Botticelli Room (29) could be dismantled to open up the ninety-four-foot first floor into an old-fashioned gallery. Designed in one of his weaker moments by Richard Norman Shaw, the screen was made in 1879 by the off-Oxford Street firm of Charles Mellier & Company, who advertised themselves as 'specialists in the rich decorative styles of the sixteenth, seventeenth and eighteenth centuries'.[52] This kind of work indicated to a progressive designer like C.F.A. Voysey that nothing had really changed: 'Man is still very much at the monkey stage. We mock and mimic old and new, good and bad. Styles, fashions, eccentricities are immortalised – admired one season, detested the next.'[53] C.R. Ashbee, another revolutionary designer, suggested that the avant-garde had none but themselves to blame: 'We architects ...

have drifted . . . into a little backwater upon which whenever the sun shines it lights upon some momentary, some placid reflection to which we give a graceful name: Neo-Perpendicular, Queen Anne . . . or L'Art Nouveau, as the case may be . . . Each sparkles for an instant on the surface of our little architectural pool.'[54] While the Voyseys and Ashbees hand-ploughed their worthy furrows, brash members of 'the school of Accidental architecture'[55] supplied Edwardian plutocrats with the favoured Continental style of interior decoration. W.H. Romaine-Walker was one such architect, who installed, with the help of Mellier & Co., extravagant 'Louis' interiors all over Mayfair, notably at 66 Grosvenor Street for Henry Duveen, brother of the ennobled antique dealer Lord 'Jo' Duveen of Millbank. When Harrods undertook their major refurbishment of 1900 to 1905, the decorating firm of Frederick Sage Ltd turned unhesitatingly to the 'Louis' style too, and imported shiploads of Parisian shopfitters to do the work (30).

One of the pleasures of looking into Victorian and Edwardian attitudes to the decorative arts is the continuing relevance today of the major issues. Not only the ideas but also the language often continues to impress, none more so than the architect Philip Webb's sorrowful vision of bright young architectural ambitions 'carried on the crest of a wave to a frowning coast whitened with professional bones'.[56] There is a familiar ring also to an anti-style statement by W.R. Lethaby, founder and first principal of the Central School of Arts and Crafts: 'Notwithstanding all the names, there are only two modern styles of architecture: one in which the chimneys smoke, and the other in which they do not.'[57] And the *Magazine of Art* commented in February 1883: 'We regret to announce that the Treasury has reduced its grant to the British Museum . . . [demonstrating] how scant is the importance of culture in the national scheme of government.' In 1889 the *Studio* heaped praise on Lord

Carlisle's house at Kensington Palace Green (40), because the majority of its treasures were modern, 'a singularly pleasing exception to the average "palace" of today, which, if it holds masterpieces of a kind, is careful that they shall be of goodly age, hall-marked as it were with official approval of their sterling value'.

In the nineteenth century artists and critics searched ceaselessly for appropriate styles of interior design to suit new needs as they arose. The broad answer to the question of taste as supplied by William Burges in 1863 remains the same today: 'The only way to improve taste . . . is not by dissertations but by seeing beautiful objects';[58] 'a good eye was the gift of a good God', Burges averred.[59] It was considered important to take interior design seriously – but not so seriously as to lose a sense of humour. In an article of 1881 on home decorating, the designer Lewis F. Day illustrated a witty little sunflower frieze for use in the hall 'which need not be so sober as most decoration . . . [it] may even laugh without offence . . . though a perpetual grin on the face of the living-room would be intolerable'.[60]

Interior designers of the nineteenth century, in their work as in their writings, were able, it seems, to strike more easily than we today that happy balance between flippancy and solemnity.

31 A peacock tailpiece published by C. R. Ashbee in 1894.

32

35

33

Artists at home

The stylistic variety and inventiveness of Victorian furnishings is nowhere more apparent than in artists' homes. Sir Lawrence Alma-Tadema owned a sumptuous house in Regent's Park: in the studio (32) a bust of his wife (the painter Laura Epps) by E. Onslow Ford is set against 'a curtain of cloth of gold' – with a stuffed peacock nailed to the dado. An 1879 engraving of the music room (33) shows the 'Byzantine' piano designed by Alma-Tadema and G.E. Cox. The Gold Room, depicted in watercolour of 1884 by Anna Alma-Tadema, had 'Egyptian' couches designed by her father (34); he also designed in the early 1880s an elaborate suite of 'Graeco-Roman' furniture (35–36) for Henry Marquand's music room in New York.

Richard Norman Shaw was the architect of a number of studio houses, including Marcus Stones's in Melbury Road, Holland Park, decorated in 1875 'in the spirit of an Old English Home' (37); F. W. Goodall's Grims Dyke in Middlesex, built 1870–72 and photographed by Bedford Lemère in 1892 when owned by W.S. Gilbert (38); and in 1874 his own house in Ellerdale Road, Hampstead (41).

Construction of Lord Leighton's home in Holland Park Road began in 1865. The furniture in the Hall of Narcissus (39), which leads into the remarkable Arab Hall, was designed by George Aitchison. In 1867 the amateur artist George Howard commissioned Philip Webb to build a studio house on Kensington Palace Green. Burne-Jones painted the Cupid and Psyche panels in the morning room (40).

34

36

37

38

39

42

43

44

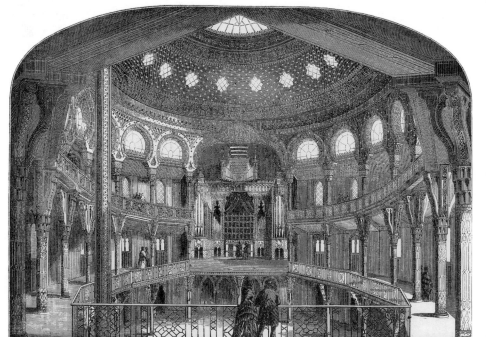

45

The taste for the exotic

When the Crystal Palace was re-erected at Sydenham (it opened in 1854) Owen Jones redesigned much of the architectural detail, including both the Egyptian Court (**42**; sculpture planned by Joseph Bonomi) and the influential Alhambra Court (**43**). Owen Jones's promotion of the Moorish style through the publication from 1836 to 1845 of *Plans, Elevations, Sections and Details of the Alhambra* led to its domestic use – for example, the smoking room of 1888–90 at Romaine-Walker & Tanner's Rhinefield Lodge in the New Forest (**44**) – as well as in public buildings, notably the Royal Panopticon of 1853–4 in Leicester Square (**45**), later the Alhambra music hall.

By the end of the century the taste for the exotic was widespread, as demonstrated by the 'Eastern Parlour' which the decorators

46

47

48

49

H. & J. Cooper installed in 1893 at 28 Ashley Place, Victoria (**46**); the 'musharabeyeh' turned-wood screens and mother-of-pearl inlaid tables were imported from Egypt and Syria – compare what the *Art Journal* in 1878 called the 'very varied as well as remarkably peculiar' cabinet (**48**) exhibited by G. Parvis of Cairo at the 1876 Philadelphia Exhibition. The Indian style is represented by the British India Conference Room in the Imperial Institute, designed by T. E. Collcutt and photographed shortly after completion in 1893 (**47**). The fashion for Far Eastern styles flourished to excess in Mrs Samuel Montagu's drawing room at 96 Lancaster Gate, decorated in 1873 largely with furniture imported from Japan, but including some London-made Anglo-Japanese pieces, such as the side-chair against the wall in the right foreground (**49**). Twenty years later, the 'Moorish' room at 2 Clarence Terrace, Westminster, is equally European in its basic appointments (**50**); the designer is unknown.

50

51

52

53

The Renaissance style

The sculptor Alfred Stevens was the foremost practitioner of the Italian Renaissance style in High Victorian interior design; this watercolour plan of 1847 is for the drawing room at Deysbrook Hall, a house in West Derby, Liverpool (**51**). Stevens designed an impressive series of sculptural cast-iron grates for the founders Hoole & Co. of Sheffield; his most important fireplace, however, was in marble, for the state dining room at Dorchester House in Park Lane (**53**) – the inlaid cushion mirrors were also designed by Stevens, but not the table or chairs.

Another sculptor, John Thomas, produced in the 1850s an impressive 'Renaissance' interior for the Royal Dairy at Windsor, covered in Minton majolica tiles and cooled by a majolica fountain (**54**). The Italianate decorative scheme of St George's Hall, Liverpool (**52**), one of the most sumptuous mid-Victorian Renaissance interiors, was designed by H. L. Elmes and completed by C. R. Cockerell (1841–56).

Most of Owen Jones's designs for furniture were made by the cabinetmakers Jackson & Graham, whose Oxford Street premises he redesigned in 1869 (**55**). His most important furniture commissions were for James Mason at Eynsham Hall, Oxfordshire, and (from 1863) for Alfred Morrison, at Carlton House Terrace and Fonthill, described by the *Builder* as being 'in the Cinquecento style' (**57**). This side-cabinet (**56**; *c*. 1865) is attributed to Owen Jones on stylistic grounds.

54

55

56

57

58   59

60   61

Early Victorian revivals

In the 1830s and 40s furniture appeared in a confusing variety of
historical styles, of which the 'Grecian', 'Gothic' and 'Elizabethan'
were represented in Richard Bridgens's *Furniture with Candelabra
and Interior Decoration* (1838): this table and chair (**58–59**) were
labelled 'Elizabethan', despite their similarity in basic character –
rounded and comfortable – to the avowedly 'Rococo' furniture
designed by Philip Hardwick in 1834 for the ladies' room at
Goldsmiths' Hall, London (**60**). Many of Bridgens's earlier designs
were made by the Liverpool cabinetmaker George Bullock,
including furniture for the restoration of Battle Abbey, Sussex,
where Bridgens worked from 1812 to 1822 (**61**). As this library
table attributed to Bullock suggests (**62**), he and Bridgens were the
leading pre-Victorian pioneers of the Gothic revival at a time when
eighteenth-century styles were more popular: the marquetry
library table (**63**) made by Robert Blake *c*. 1835 for one of Pugin's
friends, the antique dealer E. H. Baldock, is a good example of

62

63

64

65

contemporary taste. The furniture designed in the late 1830s by Charles Barry for the Reform Club (**64**), made by Taprell & Holland, has comparable stylistic origins. Barry was at ease in both the Gothic and Classical idioms; the choice of style made little difference to the structure or proportions of his buildings. The same is true of most furniture of the period.

Lewis Nockalls Cottingham, in contrast, was one of the most scholarly of early Victorian architect-designers. His influence is evident in a group of anonymous drawings of 1838 (**65**), comparable to the many pieces he supplied to Snelston Hall, Derbyshire; some of the Snelston furniture incorporated original medieval fragments, although Cottingham's drawing of *c*. 1842 for a *vis-à-vis* – or conversation settee – shows that he did not always feel the need to be archaeologically exact (**66**). His characteristic crockets around the seat backs were used to telling effect in the chapel at Magdalen College, Oxford, in the early 1830s (**67**).

66

67

68

69

New materials

Partly from genuine admiration of ultra-modernity, and partly through love of extravagant display, the mid-Victorians were bold experimenters with new materials in architecture and the decorative arts. John Thomas's vast majolica fountain at the entrance of the 1862 London International Exhibition (**68**) is a spectacular example of a genre that included ceramic garden seats, chandeliers, torchères and pedestals, all – like the fountain – manufactured by Minton's in their vast new industrial kilns. Cast-iron was also used to elaborate decorative effect, as in the painted iron vaulting of the Oxford Museum (**69**), designed on

Ruskinian principles in 1855 by Thomas Deane and Benjamin Woodward and executed by Skidmore of Coventry. In furniture the revolutionary potential of iron as a material was seldom realized, for the foundries tended to reproduce established forms, such as this imitation of Jacobean wood turning and a button upholstered cushion made by Coalbrookdale *c.* 1875 (**70**). The principal manufacturers of *papier-mâché* furniture were Jennens & Bettridge of Birmingham, who in the 1850s produced beds, chairs, settees, dressing-tables and this 'Rococo' *bonheur-du-jour* (**71**). Self-advertisment through novelty was the motive for commissioning chairs in solid cannel coal (**72**; *c.* 1850), displayed by mineowners at industrial exhibitions and offered as gifts to visiting royalty.

70

71

72

CHAPTER TWO

A.W.N. Pugin

73 The west doors of St Giles, Cheadle, by A. W. N. Pugin, 1841–6.

While working on the Pugin chapter for his book *The Gothic Revival*, first published in 1928, Kenneth Clark found it 'hard to believe that a man so little known was really so very important'.[1] It is, indeed, remarkable that from 1920 through to the mid-1950s the name of Augustus Welby Northmore Pugin (1812–52) should have been forgotten when his work at the Houses of Parliament – he designed all the external detailing and the whole of the interior – includes the decoration of the tower of Big Ben, one of the world's most familiar secular icons. So little historical value was attached to Pugin furniture that throughout this period energetic administrators discarded many of the original fittings for the New Palace of Westminster, as the Houses of Parliament were called at their rebuilding after the fire of 1834. Some of the pieces, notably Pugin's ultra-grand half-tester bed for the Speaker's House (74–75), have resurfaced in the art market and been purchased back by the Department of the Environment; others – two of the set of sixteen richly carved chairs for the Prince's Chamber (77), for example – still remain in private hands.

To his contemporaries and immediate successors Pugin's significance was self-evident. Burges described him as 'that wonderful man',[2] and George Gilbert Scott wrote: 'I did not know Pugin, but his image in my imagination was like my guardian angel, and I often dreamed that I knew him ... I was awakened from my slumbers by the thunder of Pugin's writings.'[3] Through the reformist power of publications like *The True Principles of Pointed or Christian Architecture* (1841) and the exemplary perfectionism of buildings such as St Giles, Cheadle (73), Pugin so successfully argued for a modern Gothic revival that it seemed to become 'a preternatural heaven-born impulse'.[4] Owen Jones, Christopher Dresser, William Morris, Philip Webb, Richard Norman Shaw – all the leaders of stylistic change in the half-century following Pugin's death in 1852 – publicly acknowledged his primacy. Writing in 1904 Hermann Muthesius confirmed that 'Pugin's work stands supreme ... he combined inexhaustible imaginative power with the thorough knowledge of the medieval repertoire of forms, so that it was child's play to him to find forms for every sort of commission.'[5]

Architect-designers of the arts and crafts movement, such as Ernest Gimson and C.F.A. Voysey, plainly pillaged Puginian sources in the revealed structure of certain of their furniture designs, for tables in particular, and this living example of Pugin's influence prompted Nikolaus Pevsner in the 1930s to dub him one of the 'heralds' of the modern movement. More importantly, in this context, Pevsner also sought to demonstrate how Pugin was the first architect to adapt the high ecclesiastical ideas of Perpendicular Gothic to the informal domestic setting: 'Had there not been the true Pugin principles, we would not have the robust Street, the noble Bodley, the refined Pearson',[6] and the commercial flowering of Geometric Gothic furniture in the 1860s and 1870s would never have taken place. In similar spirit Mervyn Macartney, a co-founder with Lethaby and Gimson in 1890 of the furniture makers Kenton & Co., pointed out that 'a keen and sarcastic expert was required to upset the false principles' of the first decades of the nineteenth century, 'an overthrow that was brought about by Pugin in his writings and drawings'.[7] Macartney deeply regretted the later overthrow of this Puginian revolution by modern commercial ideas.

74 and **75** The state bed in the Speaker's House, Palace of Westminster. The bed is now installed in what was the Serjeant at Arms's drawing room. Furnishing of the house, by Holland & Sons, did not begin until 1857, five years after Pugin's death, but it is firmly in the style that he established for the palace interiors. The built-in fittings are by Barry and the ceiling is gilded and stencilled in the manner of all the palace's state rooms. The bed was sold early in this century and not returned until 1986, when the hangings were restored with the aid of the anonymous design now in the Public Record Office (*left*); the newly woven brocatelle follows a design by Pugin for the Elizabethan drawing room of I. K. Brunel's house in London.

76 Late 1840s bookcase by Gillow's, to a design by A. W. N. Pugin; identical linenfold panels, metal mounts and carved Tudor roses are found on Pugin's Palace of Westminster furniture. The pottery 'Garden Seat' was manufactured by Minton in 1868, using their Pugin designs; the brass studs and tusked tenons of the armchair also follow Pugin's example.

77 A chair designed by A. W. N. Pugin in 1846 for the Prince's Chamber in the House of Lords; it is photographed against a collection of encaustic tiles of the 1840s to 60s.

78 The Consort's Throne from the House of Lords. Pugin indicated his design for this in one of the estimate drawings commissioned by Charles Barry 1836–7 (see 103).

79 Library table and candlesticks designed by E. W. Pugin for Scarisbrick Hall, Lancashire, a commission inherited from his father in 1852 and still unfinished in 1872, when the death of Anne Scarisbrick brought work there to an end. The decoration of E. W. Pugin's furniture is more elaborate and the structure less solidly architectural than his father's designs.

76

77

78

79

80 The chromolithographic frontispiece of A. W. N. Pugin's *Glossary of Ecclesiastical Ornament and Costume, Compiled and Illustrated from Ancient Authorities and Examples*, 1844. The illustrations for this influential manual of Gothic ornament were drawn by Pugin himself; the frontispiece perfectly embodies his religious and aesthetic ideas.

The portrait of Pugin by his friend J.R. Herbert (81) already hints at the self-imposed mental strains and stresses which were to lead to eight months' insanity prior to his premature death at the age of forty. Yet, though he looks tense and serious, the bright eyes and oval face tell of hope – 'En Avant' as his motto proclaims – rather than depression and death. In addition, his autobiographical notes, diaries and manuscripts, together with hundreds of surviving letters, indicate that although hysterically fanatical at times, his mind was never clinically unbalanced until the very end of his life and it seems overwork was principally to blame for his collapse. Unlike every other major architect of his day, Pugin practised without assistants, executing thousands and thousands of drawings in a characteristically worried, almost jittery, hand. 'Clerk, my dear Sir, clerk?', he is reported saying. 'I never employ one. I should kill him in a week.'[8] As Alexandra Wedgwood asserts in her impeccable catalogue of the Pugin material at the Victoria and Albert Museum, 'his fierce individualism based on his immovable religious and stylistic principles combined with his phenomenal energy'[9] made partnership impossible and breakdown almost inevitable.

The volume of commissioned work undertaken in this short working life itself defies sanity. It culminated in the invitation by Charles Barry to decorate the Palace of Westminster, where 'every inch of the great building's surface, inside and out, was designed by one man: every panel, every wallpaper, every chair sprang from Pugin's brain, and his last days were spent designing inkpots and umbrella stands'.[10] In addition to architectural and decorative commissions there were the plates and texts for his

books – nine major titles, including the magnificent *Glossary of Ecclesiastical Ornament and Costume*. As if all this were not enough, Pugin created several exquisitely executed imaginary schemes: for a Catholic college, for a precious chest of treasures, and other dreams of the ideal. Furthermore, he filled sketchbook after sketchbook with topographical studies of medieval architecture seen on his business travels in England and annual holidays on the Continent. The pace was relentless, as recorded in a letter from Liverpool to his wife at home in Ramsgate (82): 'Today I have come an immense distance, about 200 miles, continuously changing lines and carriages ... I shall have travelled a thousand miles this week and for very little good, and I must come up again on Monday.'[11] This letter was written in June 1851. Shortly before his final collapse in February 1852 Pugin wrote to the decorator J.G. Crace about a new commission, Abney Hall: '... and for £50 I will make any details and moulding full size and all ornaments, grates, fireplace, paper, and everything, curtains etc., all if you like'.[12] This time, however, his delicate health was in a critical condition and on 7 February Mrs Pugin wrote to Crace to 'beg that in future you will make some better arrangements as really ... it is *very* injurious to his health to be so driven'.[13] The seventeen drawings for Abney Hall which Pugin sent Crace were probably the last work he managed: 'I have done my best and am nearly done myself', his accompanying letter affirmed.[14]

Whereas the letters are often openly emotional, Pugin's diaries and his notes for an uncompleted autobiography are obsessive and closed. Snippets of outside information intrude only occasionally, like the observation on 12 May

81 and **82** A. W. N. Pugin by J. R. Herbert (*left*); the stencilled frame was designed in the 1850s by E. W. Pugin. The Grange, Pugin's home in Ramsgate (*above*), was begun in 1843; behind it is St Augustine's, his own church. This drawing, by his son Cuthbert, is dated 1873.

1827: 'Oxford Street begins to be Macadamised'; otherwise the only non-professional topics regularly discussed are the theatre and the sea. Even then it was only as a young man that Pugin seems to have found time to go often to the theatre, where he was fascinated by the stage mechanics – he also designed for the theatre on occasion and his sets for the ballet *Kenilworth* (1831) were in pseudo-Elizabethan style. Boating therefore remained his one life-long form of escape. Michael Trappes-Lomax quotes him as saying: 'There is nothing worth living for except Christian architecture and a boat.'[15] His diary, however, is not always revealing about his most important beliefs. He recorded the most momentous occasion of his whole life, his conversion to Catholicism, on 6 June 1835, with the entry: 'Finished alterations at Chapel received into the Holy Catholic Church.' The next day he stated simply: 'First assisted at Mass'; the day after, he returned to his habitual reportage of the weather: 'Tremendous thunderstorm at Marlborough.'[16]

Despite the cryptic quality of these pocket-diary entries there can be no doubting the passion of Pugin's convictions – indeed no other designer of the nineteenth century believed more whole-heartedly in the moral value of his work. 'England is certainly not what it was in 1440 but the thing to be done is to bring it back to that era',[17] Pugin wrote to his principal Catholic patron, the Earl of Shrewsbury. Pugin was determined by then to be associated only with buildings constructed 'in accordance with Catholic principles'.[18] 'The present condition of architecture is deplorable … Truth reduced to the position of an interesting but rare and curious relic'.[19] Furniture was also endowed by Pugin with a moral purpose, and aroused in him equal passions. The book which first communicated the full extent of Pugin's ambitions for architecture and interior design as essential weapons in the transformation of society was published in 1836, and titled *Contrasts; or, A Parallel Between the Noble Edifices of the Fourteenth and Fifteenth Centuries, and similar buildings of the Present Day; Shewing the Present Decay of Taste.* The title more or less defines the scope of the book, yet it was in fact the plates of the first edition rather than the text which attracted the most attention, for they so clearly identified Christianity with the Gothic. This witty, tempestuous book made Pugin famous, and sold out within three months of publication, largely because of his visual caricature of the Anglican Church. The clearest expression of his abstract principles of design – based, of course, on medieval precedent – appeared in 1841 in *The True Principles of Pointed or Christian Architecture*, developed from a series of lectures given at Oscott College, Warwickshire, where Pugin was Professor of Antiquities. In a pre-publication puff for *True Principles* Pugin formulated the axiom of usefulness in decorative design that Morris and others later so heavily overburdened: 'no features were introduced in the antient pointed edifices which were not essential either for convenience or propriety'.[20]

At this distance in time, grateful for the legacy of his work, it is perhaps easier for us than it would have been for

contemporaries to excuse Pugin's fanatical dual devotion to Catholicism and the Gothic. Admitting that 'Mr Pugin is a man of genius', Cardinal Newman continued: 'But he has the great fault of a man of genius, as well as the merit. He is intolerant, and, if I might use a stronger word, a bigot.'[21] True; but in Pugin's defence it is worth pointing out that he was by no means the only Victorian zealot who believed that the world had been corrupted in every way by the Reformation, 'a thing engendered in beastly lust brought forth in hypocrisy and perfidy, and cherished and fed by plunder, devastation, and by rivers of English and Irish blood'.[22]

On aesthetics Pugin was at one and the same time a bigoted reactionary and a flag-bearing revolutionary. The extent of Pugin's antiquarian expertise was extraordinary. He was a close friend of most of the leading antiquarian dealers and regularly bought medieval bits and pieces from them, for clients as well as for himself (see, for instance, a letter to Lord Shrewsbury of 1840: 'The cross you have secured at Pratts is so exquisitely Beautiful that it may be considered dirt cheap at the price').[23] At his 'Ancient Furniture Warehouse' in Wardour Street, Edward Hull not only sold old pieces to Pugin but also commissioned him to design new furniture. E.H. Baldock, another dealer, supplied quantities of Jacobean reproduction furniture to Pugin's clients, and yet another dealer, John Webb of Bond Street, also ran a high-quality cabinet workshop where the grandest Pugin pieces for the Palace of Westminster were made. Webb made copies too, including a version of the sixteenth-century Artois Jewel Cabinet at a cost to Lord Hertford of £2,500; similarly, Pugin incorporated old architectural details in new buildings. In a letter of 30 May 1844 he noted his purchase on the Continent of 'a great many casts of the most beautiful character which will be just the thing for images on the spire at Cheadle' (the same letter recorded that he had 'also established a regular correspondence in Paris for the execution of enamels for church ornaments which they do better and cheaper than we do').[24] It hardly seemed to matter to Pugin and his friends whether or not the furniture was original, providing it lived up to the stern demands of their aesthetic.

On the other hand, where most architects cribbed uncritically from Henry Shaw's *Specimens of Ancient Furniture*, E.L. Blackburne's *Sketches Graphic and Decorative for a History of the Decorative Painting Applied to English Architecture During the Middle Ages*, J. Gough's *Sepulchral Monuments*, and the many other newly available printed sources, Pugin insisted that mere revivalism meant death to design: 'Nothing can be more dangerous than looking at prints of buildings and trying to imitate them. These architectural books are as bad as the scriptures in the hands of the Protestants.'[25] Pugin attempted, instead, to abstract relevant elements from medieval examples, an ambitious aim which he fully achieved in three-dimensional work only in a few late plain pieces of furniture. As a designer of flat patterns and general ornament, however, Pugin's contribution was revolutionary for, as Eastlake pointed out at the time, his greatest 'strength as an artist lay in the design of ornamental detail'.[26] In the *Glossary* Pugin elaborated on this favourite nineteenth-century theme: 'Ornament … signifies the embellishment of that which is useful, in an appropriate manner. Yet by a perversion of the term, it is frequently applied to mere enrichment, which deserves no other name than that of unmeaning detail, dictated by no rule but that of individual fancy and caprice.'[27] It was clear to Pugin that the principal fault of early Victorian decoration was its lush, rounded naturalism, and in *Floriated Ornament* he explained how the basic structure of plants could be flattened out into geometric patterns. In this book Pugin also formulated general ideas on nature and aesthetics which remained the basis of creative design throughout the Victorian and Edwardian periods: 'Nature supplied the medieval artists with all their forms and ideas; the same inexhaustible source is open to us: and if we go to the fountainhead, we shall produce a multitude of beautiful designs, treated in the same spirit as the old, but new in form.'[28] Many examples could be given of Pugin's skill in handling flat patterns: in wallpapers, in damasks, in ceramics, in the inlay of furniture, where he neatly folded over the corners of leaves and blocked out the flat spiky forms in bold colours. Charles Handley-Read described the inlaid top of the Abney Hall octagonal table (99) as 'almost a reformer's manifesto',[29] so influential was this type of geometric design on the work of the later Goths. The table was made by Crace, to whom Pugin wrote apologizing for not having sent him more designs and explaining, however, that 'this sort of inlaid furniture takes as long as a church' to design. 'I suppose the table will be walnut', Pugin continued, referring to an almost identical piece for the Great Exhibition of 1851, now in Lincoln's Inn. 'I think it will look rich, and be something new in the old way.'[30]

The stylistic changes in Pugin's furniture designs are clear enough, if a little complicated in chronology. As a teenager Pugin worked for his father in producing engraved plates for Rudolf Ackermann's various publications (89) and his earliest work, designs for the cabinetmakers Morel & Seddon's Windsor Castle commission (90–91 and 98), was firmly rooted in the Regency 'Gothick' tradition inherited from Horace Walpole's Strawberry Hill. He began designing the Windsor furniture in March 1827, and in June was still at work, at a guinea a day, supervising the cabinetmakers at Seddon's workshop in Aldersgate. In later life Pugin turned against his father's Regency style, in which 'everything is crocketed with angular projections, sharp ornaments and turreted extremities'; he was gracious enough to admit, however, that he himself had 'perpetuated many of these enormities in the furniture designed some years ago for Windsor Castle'.[31] His chance to try out new ideas came in 1829 when he was asked by John Gough to design the furniture for Perry Hall, near Birmingham. On the strength of this commission Pugin opened his own workshop in November of that year: 'Began business for myself in the

carving and joinery line at 12 Hart Street, Covent Garden [now Floral Street].'[32] Though the break in style was complete it was not a particularly inventive change, for most of the furniture made by Pugin's ill-fated firm was directly inspired by Jacobean originals (92). The business failed in 1831 despite its successful beginning.

Throughout the 1830s Pugin's furniture remained basically backward-looking, Regency in character rather than Victorian. Though more sophisticated in design and less obviously historicist than the work of contemporaries like Richard Bridgens, it was nevertheless essentially academic, as is illustrated by his book of 1835, *Gothic Furniture in the Style of the 15th Century* (93). Handley-Read considered this period of Pugin's included 'some very fine if rather heavy designs … the exact [Gothic] equivalent of the Elizabethan designs of Anthony Salvin'.[33] Such furniture was 'unreformed' in the sense that Pugin produced nothing really structurally new; 'to this category', again quoting Handley-Read, 'belongs most of the Crace-Pugin furniture at Abney Hall … certain examples exhibited in the Mediaeval Court at the Great Exhibition of 1851 [83 and 95], and some of

83 The Minton tiled stove which A. W. N. Pugin designed for the Mediaeval Court at the Great Exhibition of 1851.

84 Pugin furniture in the Prince's Chamber of the House of Lords, photographed *c*.1905. In the background is a statue of Queen Victoria by John Gibson, 1854.

the furniture and fittings at the Palace of Westminster.'[34] Pugin was proud of his Great Exhibition bookcase, calling it 'a stirling lovely cabinet':[35] an outstanding example of High Victorian Perpendicular Gothic, it was selected by the panel of Henry Cole, Owen Jones and Richard Redgrave for the Museum of Manufactures, opened at Marlborough House in 1852, and later transferred to the South Kensington Museum, now the Victoria and Albert.

At the same time – even in the same pieces – Pugin was also developing a much simpler 'reformed' Gothic style, the earliest known example of which is the schoolmaster's desk for King Edward's Grammar School, Birmingham, one of Charles Barry's commissions of, it is thought, 1835. The Birmingham drawings are Pugin's first recorded use of tusked tenons and curved 'X' braces, which he was later to employ with such strikingly 'modern' results. The best of this furniture with progressive revealed structure was designed by Pugin for his own use at a new house in Ramsgate on the Isle of Thanet where he moved on selling his previous home in Salisbury, St Marie's Grange (sold in June 1841 for only £500 though Pugin had spent more than £2,000 on it according to his friend and biographer the architect Benjamin Ferrey). Built close to the spot where St Augustine landed on his mission to convert the barbarian British to Christianity, Pugin's house and its attendant church eventually passed into the hands of the Benedictines, at whose Oxford presbytery, East Hendred, a large group of the original furnishings was discovered in 1984. Dining tables 'can hardly be too plain', Pugin told Crace, 'so long as the framing is strong';[36] his own dining table, it now transpires, clearly demonstrates how 'the great thing is ... to keep up the beef and resist the cutting down of slices'.[37] Towards the end of his life, although still engaged in designing elaborate 'unreformed' furniture, Pugin came more and more to believe that the only way his ideas could reach the wider public that he passionately desired to influence was through this radically simple form of design. Again he wrote to Crace, in 1849: 'I am extremely anxious about this plain furniture ... rely on it, the great sale will be in articles within reach of the middling class ... you ought to frame a dozen of each to make them pay and keep them seasoned for putting together at a day's notice.' It is furniture of this kind, in which the architectural structure is given elemental emphasis, that reserves for Pugin a central position in the history of furniture design.

Not all Pugin's furniture for the Palace of Westminster was on the grand scale. 'Mr Barry wants a lot of plain useful chairs', Pugin informed Crace, 'which will not come very expensive or the board of works will be putting in modern things'[38] (in Pugin's terms 'modern things' meant over-decorated factory-made reproductions). Pugin's involvement with the Palace of Westminster dates from 1835, when he was commissioned by both Charles Barry and James Gillespie Graham to execute their competition drawings ('Is this not a regular joke? Here are two rivals competing for one prize, and I am making the designs for both.')[39] On winning the competition Barry employed Pugin throughout 1836 and 1837 on estimate drawings (103), many of which formed the basis of Pugin's massive body of Westminster work from June 1844 till his descent into insanity in February 1852. By the time Barry turned again to Pugin in 1844 the erstwhile jobbing draughtsman had become the country's leading exponent of the Gothic style, the *Builder* declaring: 'Acknowledged or not acknowledged, he is virtual pope and chief pontiff in these matters, and his bulls are received and deferred to as the canonical ordinances of the orthodox.'[40] The House of Lords Chamber was one of the first major Westminster interiors to be completed; Pugin's monumental throne (104) was in place by April 1847. Based on the coronation chair in Westminster Abbey, one of the few pieces of documented medieval furniture known to Pugin, it was carved in mahogany by John Webb, whose trade label still adheres to the underside. The original positioning of the thrones in the Lords was altered by Edward VII who, within days of his mother's death, ordered another throne to be made similar to his and only slightly smaller, so that Queen Alexandra could sit much closer to him at the Opening of Parliament than Prince Albert had done to Queen Victoria. The Consort's Throne (78) was subsequently removed from the palace; it reappeared at a provincial auction in 1985 and has been acquired by the Department of the Environment.

Although John Webb's craftsmen executed the major pieces, the bulk of the furniture in the Palace of Westminster was made by either Gillow's or Holland's; relatively little was by Crace. Gillow's in particular continued through the 1850s and 1860s to manufacture for general sale furniture identical to the plainer of Pugin's Palace of Westminster designs, notably the standard side-chair and the pedestal desk seen in a 1905 photograph of the Prime Minister's Room (106). Examples of the armchair and firescreen from the Speaker's Drawing Room (1) bearing the Gillow's trade stamp are also recorded in several private collections.

In 1837 Pugin first met the Hardmans, a Catholic family of button makers whom he persuaded to set up as church furnishers; their Birmingham workshop was soon producing metalwork of the highest quality, including most of Pugin's own. The Catholic connection had already produced for Pugin his principal client, the Earl of Shrewsbury, patron of the building Pugin himself valued above all others, St Giles, Cheadle. 'Though small and simple, it will be a perfect revival'[41] wrote Pugin, although it is 'simple' in construction only, not in design, which is subtle and complex, and 'a perfect revival' in the sense of finding new ways of expressing the old architectural forms. Lord Shrewsbury was more than merely a client of Pugin's, he was a close friend: 'Amidst the various disappointments and vexations that I am compelled to suffer from various quarters it is no small consolation to find your Lordship unchanged – and while I can carry out fine things for you I will bear the rest with resignation.'[42] In the mid-1830s Pugin made alterations to Alton Towers (107–108), Lord Shrewsbury's home near Cheadle, and in 1847 began to build the Rhineland-like Alton Castle on the hill opposite. The castle is now a convent school and Alton Towers – 'one of those tasteless monsters which tasteless wealth spawns over the land'[43] – has recently acquired new life as a pleasure park.

Seeking to reproduce his business partnership with John Hardman, Pugin tried in 1849 to set up with John Gregory Crace in furniture production. John Diblee Crace, J.G.'s son, claimed it was 'mainly at [Pugin's] instigation that he [J.G. Crace] built a factory at the back of the Wigmore Street house, and undertook the making of furniture, which hitherto he had to order from others with unsatisfactory results, and here were produced the many examples of Gothic furniture from Pugin's designs'.[44] After Pugin's death Crace continued to adapt the designs to his own use, sometimes quite successfully as in the furniture for the pious Breconshire house Treberfydd, designed by J.L. Pearson, but often outrageously as in the 1860s work at Tyntesfield for William Gibbs (who, incidentally, financed the building of Butterfield's Keble College, Oxford). Bad though Crace's designs were, Collier & Plucknett of Warwick produced for Tyntesfield some Perpendicular Gothic furniture in even worse taste. Pugin and Crace collaborated directly on a number of projects. In July 1850 Pugin visited Eastnor Castle in Herefordshire and was delighted with the Crace furniture and Hardman chandelier, all of which he had designed, whilst hating the execution of his scheme for a genealogical tree on the chimney breast: 'I assure you I never saw a fine job so completely ruined and cut to fritters.'[45] At Lismore Castle in Waterford the two of them undertook redecoration work for the Duke of Devonshire, but although the duke eventually bought for Lismore the Pugin fireplace from the Great Exhibition, it was always an unsatisfactory commission. 'The ceiling is beastly', Pugin complained, 'it is plasterer's gothic and it will never be done well.'[46]

Mention has previously been made of the correspondence between Pugin and Crace over the commission for Abney Hall – now Cheadle Town Hall but then the out-of-town home of James Watts, Mayor of Manchester. Pugin recorded producing specific designs for Abney Hall, and some of the dining room furniture is undoubtedly by him rather than by Crace, notably the chairs and the magnificent Hardman gasolier (112), though not the sideboard (111). Prince Albert stayed at Abney Hall on his trip to Manchester for the Art Treasures Exhibition in 1857, a visit which earned Watts his knighthood. Maybe it was the imminent arrival of royalty which persuaded Crace to overspice his decoration of the drawing room (115–116), which is much richer and more elaborate than Pugin would have liked.

In recent years a number of country houses with original Pugin furnishings have been sold, including, in June 1982, Adare Manor near Limerick (109). Pugin worked on the great hall and other rooms at Adare from 1846, succeeding L.N. Cottingham as favourite architect to the third Earl of Dunraven, a Catholic convert; Pugin, in his turn, was succeeded by P.C. Hardwick, who added a weighty wing in a misproportioned Pugin manner. Another disposal, at Horsted Place in Sussex, also released a body of Pugin material onto the market. The Horsted contract, dated 2 October 1850, was with Pugin's favourite builder, George

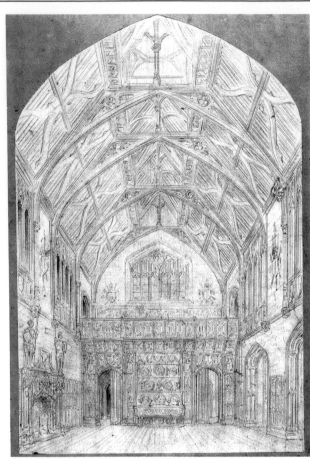

85 and **86** A. W. N. Pugin's first sketch for the Great Hall at Scarisbrick Hall (*left*) was drawn in 1836. Its antiquarian flavour was replaced in the detailed design of the following year (*right*) by a much more adventurous structure; the fireplace, however, remains close to his original concept.

87 The cardroom at Carlton Towers (1873–7) was decorated by J. F. Bentley after E. W. Pugin's death in 1875. This is a lush Venetian interpretation of Puginian Gothic by one of the most successful Roman Catholic architects of the generation following Pugin's.

88 Bentley designed furniture, chandeliers, curtains and wallpaper for Carlton Towers in a rich blend of Gothic and seventeenth-century forms. This marble-topped steel table, now in the Inner Hall, illustrates his highly personal style.

Myers, and it was he who installed there the Pugin staircase from the Great Exhibition, in a house designed not by Pugin but by Samuel Dawkes. The furniture for Horsted was all made by John Webb and much of it was designed by Myers, who demonstrates long acquaintance with Pugin's work.

On Pugin's death the architectural practice was taken over by his eldest son, Edward Welby Pugin (1834–75). One of the largest commissions in hand was for Scarisbrick Hall in Lancashire, where A.W.N Pugin had worked from 1836 to 1845. In his design for the Great Hall (85–86) A.W.N. Pugin produced a determinedly medieval interior and he incorporated in other parts of the house a 'pot-pourri of Flemish carvings'[47] – not, it is to be hoped, too many of the fake panels J.C. Loudon saw for sale by the rack at Malines in Belgium. The introduction of antique fragments would have pleased the client, Charles Scarisbrick, an odd isolated individual who left at his death a marvellous collection, auctioned by Christie's in 1860 over fourteen days, which included four oils and eleven drawings by Rembrandt. Most of the surviving furniture from Scarisbrick was designed by E.W. Pugin (79), who also undertook extensive alterations (110) for Charles's sister Anne: Crace and Hardman worked there to decorative excess until her death in 1872.

In 1873 E.W. Pugin produced a wonderfully extravagant design for huge baronial extensions to Carlton Towers, Goole, Yorkshire, which included a gigantic chapel for the private use of Lord Beaumont, a recent convert to Catholicism. Only half the Pugin plan was actually built, and the interiors at Carlton Towers were completed between 1875 and 1877 by J.F. Bentley, in the Venetian Gothic style (87).

Like his father, E.W. Pugin died early, at the age of only forty-one, ruined by his fanatical commitment to the Granville Hotel project in Ramsgate, which he both designed and financed, providing London guests with a private train which deposited them at the hotel's own railway station. The luxury of Pugin's hotel was extraordin-ary, even by Victorian standards: 'another of the most striking features . . . is made by various baths, twenty-five in number, all fitted with the latest applicances, luxuries and improvements, including Turkish, vapour, douche, shower, swimming, sitz, medicated, ozone'.[48] He designed heavy-duty Gothic furniture for use in the hotel (117) and all the metalwork was made by his brother-in-law John Hardman Powell, who had lived at Ramsgate from 1845, assisting A.W.N. Pugin with various projects. Powell had married the eldest Pugin daughter, Anne, in 1850.

Direct imitations and derivations of Pugin furniture were produced throughout the nineteenth century (120–121), and even as late as 1910 Detmar Blow and F. Billerey installed a massively Puginesque staircase in a house in Grosvenor Street (appropriately, Detmar Blow had won the Royal Institute of British Architects' Pugin Studentship in 1892). While Gillow's and Holland's liberally re-used their original Pugin designs, mass manufacturers such as C. & R. Light also cribbed from Pugin pieces at their extensive factory at 134–146 Curtain Road, Shoreditch (in 1897 Light's commissioned R. Creese Harrison to build another ten thousand square feet of factory space around the corner at 50–59 Rivington Street). In their undated catalogue of about 1880, Light's reproduced a whole page of variations on E.W. Pugin's Granville furniture (118), the kind of thing Ashbee referred to, not altogether fairly, as 'the worst machine-made Curtain Road stuff, stuff that is known as slaughtered furniture'.[49] In the early 1870s the *Furniture Gazette* opened a branch office at 79 Curtain Road, and by the end of the century Shoreditch had replaced Oxford Street as the commercial centre of the furniture trade. Ernest Gimson used to purchase his foreign woods from Sam Westlake & Sons in nearby Tabernacle Street, and the circle of contact is neatly joined by Portsmouth Museum turning, in 1985, to J.S. Crispin's of Curtain Road to supply the special veneers for the restoration of their newly acquired Pugin centre table, similar in design to the Abney Hall masterpiece (99).

From Regency to Reformed Gothic

A. W. N. Pugin's father, Augustus Charles
Pugin, earned his living primarily as an
architectural draughtsman. He worked
extensively for Rudolf Ackermann, for one
of whose publications he designed this table
of 1825 (**89**). When only fifteen years old –
in 1827 – A. W. N. Pugin received from the
cabinetmakers Morel & Seddon his first
independent commission, to design
furniture for Windsor Castle. All Pugin's
Windsor pieces are in the established
Regency Gothic style (**90** and **91**).

From 1829 to 1831 Pugin ran his own
firm of cabinetmakers in Covent Garden,
producing furniture in the Jacobean style,
some of which is stamped A.PUGIN (**92**). In
1835 he published *Gothic Furniture in the
Style of the 15th Century*, sophisticated new
designs (**93**) which are referred to as
'unreformed' Gothic; furniture made to
these designs was often in rosewood (**94**)
and still looked backwards, stylistically, to
the Regency period. A year before his death,

90

91   92

93

94

Pugin was responsible for the overall plan of the Mediaeval Court at the Great Exhibition, for which he designed several magnificent pieces, including this large bookcase (**95**).

From 1835 Pugin had also been experimenting with much plainer furniture, in what is called the Reformed Gothic style; the earliest recorded drawing of this type is his design for the schoolmaster's desk at King Edward's Grammar School, Birmingham, commissioned by Charles Barry. In this avowedly architectural furniture the structure was emphasized by the use of revealed tenons and the decoration was reduced to simple chamfering, as in the washstand (**96**) designed by Pugin for Adare Manor near Limerick, on which he worked from 1846. Pugin's reforms soon influenced commercial design: this Gillow's desk of *c.*1850 (**97**) is similar to some of the furniture Pugin supplied to Barry from 1844 onwards for the Palace of Westminster.

95

96

97

Pugin furniture

98

99

Furniture designed by Pugin in 1827 for Windsor Castle included this Regency Gothic stool (**98**), twenty-eight of which were made by Morel & Seddon. John Gregory Crace made the Pugin furniture for Abney Hall in Cheshire, notably this magnificent inlaid walnut table top for the library (**99**) and a pair of oak serving tables for the dining room (**100**). As at Abney, the decoration of Scarisbrick Hall in Lancashire remained unfinished at Pugin's death in 1852; little of the furniture was made to his design (**101**).

During his short life Pugin's output was massive: apart from executing all his own scale drawings he also engraved the plates for his many books, including *Designs for Iron and Brass Work* of 1836, from which this 'Fire-grate' is taken (**102**). Pugin's estimate drawings for the Palace of Westminster, such as the monarch's dais in the House of Lords (**103**), were produced 1836–7, the work itself commencing in 1844: the throne (**104**), modelled on the medieval coronation chair in Westminster Abbey, was made by John Webb. A photograph taken in 1905 of the Prime Minister's room (**106**) displays more Pugin-designed furniture, including the desk and its chair and the cabinet. Published Pugin designs were continuously re-used: this chair, for example, made for the Jackson family of Kelwoods Grove, Yorkshire, is dated 1864 (**105**); the manufacturer is unknown.

100

101

102

104

103

105

106

107

108

Pugin interiors

A convert to Catholicism in 1835, Pugin vowed to be associated thereafter only with buildings constructed 'in accordance with Catholic principles'. Many of his patrons were Catholics, including the greatest, the Earl of Shrewsbury, for whom Pugin started work in October 1837 on alterations to Alton Towers, Staffordshire (**107**; a detail of the Banqueting Hall ceiling); the style and quality of Pugin's work at Alton, particularly the characteristic linenfold panelling (**108**), helped secure the Palace of Westminster commission. Another Catholic convert, the Earl of Dunraven, engaged Pugin in 1846 at Adare Manor, Limerick, where the Long Gallery (**109**) was finished after Pugin's death by P. C. Hardwick. Pugin was less well served at Scarisbrick Hall, Lancashire, by his son Edward Welby Pugin, who made excessively elaborate 'improvements' for Anne Scarisbrick from 1860 to 1872 (**110**).

Pugin's last major commission, Abney Hall, Cheadle, was secured through his decorator friend J. G. Crace. The best of the furniture there, such as the dining chairs and table (**112**), were faithfully executed to Pugin's specifications; Crace designed Puginesque extravaganzas like the sideboard (**111**). John Hardman, a Catholic colleague, made the handsome chandelier designed by Pugin for the ante-room to the library (**113**); the chair, table and bookcase were made after Pugin's death, probably to his design. The alterations to Abney Hall were completed in time for Prince Albert to stay there in 1857; Crace was responsible for the furniture and decoration in the prince's bedroom (**114**) and in the drawing room (**116**), in all its overblown detail (**115**).

109

110

111

112

113

114

115

116

117

118

Pugin plagiarists

At his death in 1852, A. W. N. Pugin's practice was taken over by his eighteen-year-old son Edward Welby Pugin. E. W. Pugin's style was heavily influenced by his father's, although his furniture for the Granville Hotel in Ramsgate (1873) had its own robust individuality (**117**; the clock is by C. F. A. Voysey). Designs by both Pugins were pirated by commercial manufacturers, as a page from C. & R. Light's catalogue of *c*.1880 demonstrates (**118**): the chairs borrow features from an E. W. Pugin original (**119**). Puginesque tables are known also to have been manufactured by Howard of Berners Street, London. Holland's and Gillow's, however, simply adapted designs commissioned by them from A. W. N. Pugin – often successfully, as in the 1860s Hungarian ash bedroom suites for the Duke of Marlborough (**120**). The Crace family made less circumspect use of their hoard of Pugin drawings (**121**; this cabinet is of *c*. 1860).

119   120

121

CHAPTER THREE

William Burges

122 The Architecture Cabinet (1858) by William Burges, photographed in his
Buckingham Street offices, *c.*1876.

On superficial inspection, A.W.N. Pugin and William Burges (1827–81) might appear to have nothing in common, everything in conflict: one a religious zealot, the other an opium-smoking Bohemian; one a thrice-married family man, the other an eccentric bachelor; one a reviver of plain oak-beamed halls, the other creator of the most intoxicatingly decorative interiors of this or any period. Yet Burges remained throughout his life a steadfast apologist of Pugin's, inheriting and developing the latter's belief in medievalism as the central prerequisite of contemporary salvation. Steeped in the passionate aesthetics of Pugin's *Contrasts*, a copy of which he was given on his fourteenth birthday, Burges alone realized in architecture and interior decoration the great Victorian dream,[1] conceived by Pugin, painted by the Pre-Raphaelites, briefly lived by Morris.

Burges's father, a successful marine engineer, was a rich man – he died worth the considerable fortune of £113,000 – and his eldest son, in choosing to train as an architect, was wealthy enough never to be forced into compromise for the sake of a competitive career. To begin with, Burges was known primarily as an archaeologist and antiquarian, articled first to Edward Blore, the architect of Marlborough College, and then to Sir Matthew Digby Wyatt. In Wyatt's office Burges acquired considerable expertise in both historical and contemporary techniques by his work on the text and plates of two Wyatt publications, *Metalwork and Its Artistic Design* (1852) and *The Industrial Arts of the Nineteenth Century* (1851–3). In partnership with Henry Clutton, Burges entered designs for the Lille Cathedral competition of 1854; although Burges and Clutton won, they quarrelled and the inventive designs, which included Burges's elaborate plans for a painted and pinnacled organ-case, were never executed. His work on Clutton's *Domestic Architecture of France* (1853) and contact through the Lille competition with the leader of the Gothic revival in France, Eugène Viollet-le-Duc (1814–79), established Burges's life-long love of thirteenth-century decorative styles.

As with another equally energetic and independent contemporary, William Morris, financial freedom enabled Burges to take himself off on frequent and lengthy foreign travels. Two journeys that were especially formative experiences were his travels through France and Italy from April 1853 to November 1854, and a trip of 1857 to Greece and Turkey, where he was thrilled to find Galata 'an almost perfect copy of the middle ages ... What Oxford is to England, Nuremberg to Germany, or Assisi to Italy, Galata is to the East.'[2] Burges recorded what he saw in thousands of measured drawings, so different from the tasteful topographical sketches of many of his contemporaries. He was, as George Aitchison confirmed, a 'most rapid and brilliant draughtsman',[3] a great believer in the benefit of personal study of medieval details, and a dedicated enemy of photography. 'The sum of my advice', Burges wrote in 1861, 'would be – Measure much, sketch little, and, above all, keep

123 William Burges at the age of thirty-one, as portrayed by E. J. Poynter on an inside door of the Yatman Cabinet (1858).

your fingers out of chemicals.'[4] His friend E.W. Godwin marvelled at the man's inventiveness: 'In his little pocket-books ... the cunning fingers were ever noting down the art longings and thoughts of the yet busier brain ... [recording the] first ideas of nearly everything he carried out, and of many dreams besides.'[5] Burges transferred these private records into large-scale representations of his favourite Continental buildings for publication in *Architectural Drawings* (1870), which established itself as a key handbook for the profession.

In executed architectural and decorative work, Burges's unique contribution was the bold use of colour. There were others – Owen Jones, Gruner, Barry, etc. – who practised polychromy in the classical idiom, but nobody used colour in the medieval style as consistently as Burges. In 1864 he gave the Cantor Lectures at the invitation of the Society of Arts, the organization through which Prince Albert and Henry Cole broke ground for the Great Exhibition with displays of industrial design in 1847, 1848 and 1849. In these lectures, Burges argued strongly for the adoption of new industrial materials like Minton majolica in buildings:

124 The Summer Smoking Room in the Clock Tower, Cardiff Castle, 1871–4: chandelier by James Redfern; tiles by W. B. Simpson; the 'Eight Winds' capitals and 'Summer Love' fireplace carved by Thomas Nicholls; wall paintings by Fred Weekes and H. W. Lonsdale.

125 and **127** The drawing room at Castell Coch and a detail of its painted decoration. Burges began work here in 1875; the decoration was still incomplete at his death in 1881. The figures of the Three Fates are by Thomas Nicholls; the chairs were designed by Burges's office manager J. S. Chapple. Charles Campbell, of Campbell, Smith & Co., decorated the walls with scenes from Aesop's Fables. Here a frog doses himself with linctus for a 'frog' in the throat – a typically Burgesian joke.

126 Burges's design of 1873 for a 'Gentleman's Room' at Knightshayes, Devon. Burges was dismissed from this contract in the following year and neither room nor decoration was executed.

Overleaf **128** The dining room in the Bute Tower, Cardiff Castle, decorated 1873–4 by Charles Campbell. The chimneypiece was carved by Thomas Nicholls and the stained-glass windows were made by Lonsdale & Saunders. The table is based on a Burges design, but was not made until after his death; the chairs are of 1826 and come from elsewhere. The ceiling is one of Burges's boldest Moorish designs.

126

125

127

129 and **130** Two of Burges's own pieces of furniture: a standard Victorian chest of drawers which he had painted with joke figures (probably in the early 1860s) and a detail of the amazing Narcissus Washstand, made in 1865 (the entire piece appears in illustration 154). The washstand was discovered in a Lincoln junkshop in the 1940s by John Betjeman. He gave it to Evelyn Waugh, who described it in *The Ordeal of Gilbert Pinfold* (1957).

131 The Philosophy Cabinet, made for the guest bedroom at Burges's home, Tower House, 1878–9. The painted decoration illustrates the personal problems that undermine the lofty thoughts of philosophers. An entry in Burges's estimate book for January 1879 relates to Campbell, Smith & Co.'s decoration: 'Own wardrobe painting – 9 birds @ 5/–, 14 flies, eggs etc. @ 2/– and decoration @ £2.0.0.'

129

130

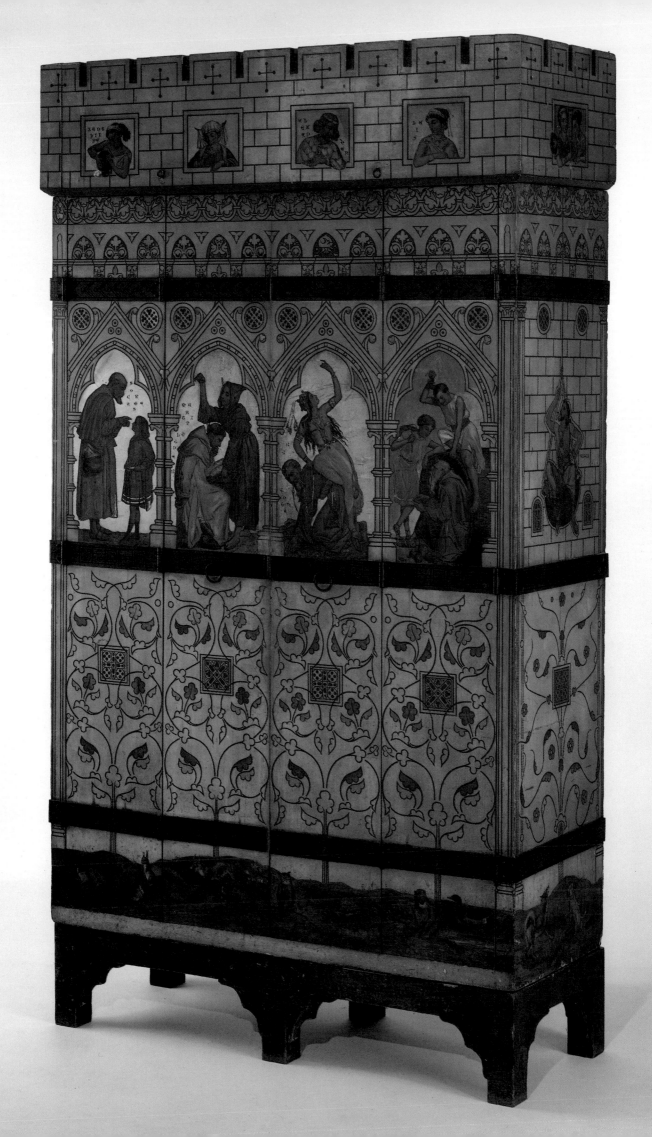

131

'With these advantages I really see no reason why we should not have buildings in smoky London glowing with imperishable colour.'[6] An avid and expert collector of medieval manuscripts, Burges – like Pugin before him – went direct to the original sources for inspiration on form and colour in interior design (133 and 136). He turned not just to manuscripts but also to medieval buildings themselves, where so much of the original painted decoration, of both stone and wood, remained to be seen. However, Burges learnt his most important lessons from the flaking remnants of once bright figurative details on the medieval armoires that lurked in the sacristies of the great cathedrals at Bayeux (133) and Noyon, sketched by him in 1853 and illustrated in 1858 by Viollet-le-Duc in his *Dictionnaire du mobilier français*. These armoires were the natural points of departure for the first pieces of painted furniture Burges produced, the Yatman Cabinet (150) and the Architecture Cabinet (122), the latter made in 1858 to house his collection of medieval manuscripts.

As well as serious historical and philosophical motives for the revival of painted interior decoration there were, as always with Burges, less sober attractions – for one thing it allowed him to indulge his whimsy. 'Excessively short-sighted ... [with] a chubby face like a cherub on a tombstone',[7] 'Billy' Burges was an eager and exuberant participant in the social world of the Strand, the centre of Bohemian London, where he lived and worked for most of his life. Were the evidence of his high spirits not ever present in his work, we could turn to one of Dante Gabriel Rossetti's 'Nonsense Verses' for information: 'There's a babyish party named Burges who from infancy hardly emerges ...'[8] The excellence of Burges's company was cherished even by the manically shy Marquis of Bute:

Above **133** The thirteenth-century armoire in the Upper Sacristy at Bayeux Cathedral, from W. E. Nesfield's *Specimens of Mediaeval Architecture* (1862).

Left **132** The Arab Room in the Herbert Tower, Cardiff Castle, *c*.1878–81: painting by Charles Campbell, stained glass by Lonsdale & Saunders. The chairs, of ebony inlaid with ivory, were intended by Burges for the Summer Smoking Room.

134 'Virgil escaping the tyranny of women', a detail of the painted decoration of the Philosophy Cabinet, 1878–9 (see 131).

'Burges is very clever, and his company is amusing, which is always such a luxury.'[9] Lady Bute said the same thing, only more appealingly: 'Dear Burges ... ugly Burges who designs lovely things. Isn't he a duck.'[10] An iconoclast himself, Burges entertained in his Buckingham Street rooms most of the avant-garde artists of the day. He was particularly friendly with E.W. Godwin and often visited him and the actress Ellen Terry at their hideaway in Wheathampstead. Ellen Terry used to trace drawings for Burges and an entry in Burges's diary for 1874 provides the only dated record of the end of the famous love affair – 'N[Nellie] left Godwin.'[11] Although in the 1870s the two friends ceased to see eye to eye on matters of style, they always remained close, and on Burges's death Godwin described their relationship as 'more intimate and sincere than any friendship of my life'.[12]

Apart from the wonderfully preserved interiors at Cardiff Castle and nearby Castell Coch (both for the Marquis of Bute) and at Tower House in Kensington (for himself), relatively little decorative work of Burges's remains. His earliest surviving painted interior, at Gayhurst in Buckinghamshire (142), is in fact more Mannerist than Gothic; the naturalistic detail was directly inspired by the Catherine de Medici 'cabinet' at the Château de Blois. Although Frederick Smallfield did not begin painting the bright gilded panels in the 'Abbess's Room' until 1861, Burges was working for Lord Carrington on the house's redevelopment from 1858. Carrington, Burges's first major patron, was a suitably eccentric character, described by a contemporary as 'a maniac, who believed that an essential part of his person was made of glass, so he was afraid to sit thereon, and used to discharge [his] legislative and judicial functions . . . standing'.[13] A by-product of this curious phobia is one of the most intriguing edifices of the Gothic revival, Burges's

Gayhurst privy, a circular building ventilated and lit by steeply arched dormer windows and surmounted by a growling Cerberus, each of his three heads inset with bloodshot glass eyes.

Burges's architectural plans for Sir John Heathcoat-Amory's home, Knightshayes, near Tiverton in Devon, are dated 1867. Building commenced in 1869 and was more or less finished by 1873 when Burges submitted to the Heathcoat-Amorys a colourful volume of interior elevations (126). The house itself, now owned by the National Trust, still retains most of Burges's external features but, pleading poverty, his clients rejected the bulk of his plans for the interior decoration and in 1874 turned to John Diblee Crace for a more modest scheme. In place of Burges's imaginative plans for the library, which included a massive castellated fireplace (145), Crace installed unpainted Puginesque bookcases with carved linenfold panels – the corbels, sculpted by Thomas Nicholls, are all that was erected of Burges's original scheme. In subsequent bouts of anti-Victorianism many Burges features already in place before his dismissal were either removed or disguised. In the hall (149) Crace first vandalized the fireplace, then in 1914 the Heathcoat-Amorys removed the arcaded wooden screen; in the drawing room the painted and gilded Burges ceiling, with his favoured jelly-mould domelets, was in the 1880s concealed beneath plasterboard and has recently been restored by the National Trust.

The Fellows of Worcester College, Oxford, and the Governors of Harrow School also failed through mistaken parsimony fully to avail themselves of Burges's talents. The estimate for redecoration of the Hall at Worcester (144) came to £3,035: 'Italian work', Burges reminded his clients, 'will not do with *little* decoration. It must either be properly done or left alone.'[14] After much to-ing and fro-ing, and under threat again from another Crace pastiche, Burges agreed in 1876 to a muted compromise, not a whisker of which is preserved in the Hall today (his flamboyant redecoration of the college chapel has been allowed to remain). At Harrow at least the Burges structure survives virtually unaltered. It is a Grecian amphitheatre in the Gothic style, but at the opening of 'Speecher' in 1877 the planned decoration had barely begun and was never seriously resumed (143). Burges fared rather better at the hands of ecclesiastical patrons and his churches and cathedral survive to vouchsafe his architectural ability in this essential form of Victorian Gothicism.

Burges's earliest recorded furniture commission was for a group of pieces in Jacobean style for Ruthin Castle in Denbighshire. They were made by W. Caldecott between 1851 and 1856 and are now missing. He received his first significant commissions in 1858 from the Yatman brothers, Henry George Yatman of Haslemere and the Rev. John Augustus Yatman of Winscombe, near Glastonbury. Two years earlier Burges had designed a jewel casket (138) for H.G. Yatman, modelled on Memling's fifteenth-century shrine in Bruges. It was inset with leather panels illuminated by Burges's young friend E.J. Poynter and the *Building News* avowed that 'Benvenuto Cellini would here have found his touch and taste'.[15] For the 1858 commission, Burges changed the scale but retained the same principles of design

135 Burges's church at Skelton, Yorkshire (1870–6), where he used many of the craftsmen who realized his secular interiors.

136 Thirteenth-century capital from Auxerre Cathedral, a building much admired by Burges, here illustrated by Nesfield in his *Specimens of Mediaeval Architecture* (1862).

137 The titlepage of Henry Shaw's *Specimens of Ancient Furniture* (1836), which had considerable influence on furniture design of the mid-century. Burges employed Shaw to copy medieval manuscripts in the British Museum.

to produce the first successfully inventive piece of painted furniture since the Middle Ages. Now known as the Yatman Cabinet, though actually a secretaire, it was exhibited with five other pieces of Burges painted furniture at the 1859 Architectural Exhibition in the Conduit Street Galleries, and again in the Mediaeval Court at the 1862 International Exhibition (150). Painted by Poynter to Burges designs illustrating the Cadmus legend and constructed in pine and mahogany by Harland & Fisher, Yatman's brilliantly colourful desk cost the substantial sum of £80; it was joined at both exhibitions by another Burges and Poynter piece, the Wines and Beers Sideboard (151), purchased in 1862 by the South Kensington Museum for £40. Although Burges thus appears to have been the first to produce this kind of furniture, others were working along the same lines and the Mediaeval Court also displayed pieces designed by J.P. Seddon and Philip Webb and decorated by various Pre-Raphaelite painters from the Morris entourage. In noting that 'the two armoires at Bayeux and Noyon had been at the bottom of it all'[16] Godwin pointed to the source of inspiration not just for the decoration of the Yatman Cabinet but also for the form of its finials. Burges's 'Woodwork' scrapbook[17] illustrates another original reference, a desk from St Lawrence's church in Nuremberg, which has similar hinged dormer-type cubby holes; in the same volume are Burges's measured sections and perspectives of the sideboard in the Hôtel de Cluny – a Pugin favourite – and Emperor Charles V's cradle from the Brussels Museum. Both the form and the decoration of this Burges furniture are equally inventive, complementing each

138 H. G. Yatman's jewel casket, 1856, painted by E.J. Poynter.

other with an architectural sophistication beyond the reach of Morris and his Pre-Raphaelite partners.

Burges lived by his beliefs, first at his office-cum-flat in Buckingham Street and then at Tower House, Melbury Road (159), the dream home in which he spent his first night on 5 March 1878 and where he died on 20 April 1881. 'Massive, learned, glittering, amazing ... and barbarously splendid',[18] Tower House was proof enough for W.R. Lethaby that 'architecture to Burges was play-acting, yet he was earnest enough and thorough, a real make-believer'.[19] For once all the pundits, popular and academic, were in agreement. Mrs Haweis ably spoke for the former: 'As a specimen of what genius can do now, as ever, treated with true poetic feeling as well as fun ... Mr Burges's home is a treat to the eye and a lesson to the mind.'[20] At Tower House Burges expressed to the full his private fantasies and feelings. He established the romanticized domesticity of his theme at the earliest opportunity, in the mosaic portrait of his pet dog Pinkie in the front porch, guarding a massive bronze door relief-cast with figures symbolizing the ages of man (163). Time passes, Burges seems to have been saying: Pinkie was dead, and in a few years time he too would die, but Tower House would long stand in memory of them all, a smallish town house built and decorated in the spirit of a medieval castle.

The decoration of each room at Tower House was designed around a different theme. The library (161) is dominated by a chimneypiece allegorizing 'The Dispersion of the Parts of Speech at the Time of the Tower of Babel'. Crammed with complicated figurative allusions, the chimneypiece also contains a typical Burgesian joke: the letter 'H' of the enveloping alphabet has fallen below the cornice – the sculptor has dropped an 'H'. Into the library Burges moved his grandest piece of furniture, the 1859 bookcase (149) on which fourteen different artists had painted illustrations of 'Pagan and Christian Art'. For his drawing room (162) Burges was able to revive the 'Love' theme rejected by the Heathcoat-Amorys in the unexecuted designs for the

SPECIMENS

of Ancient

Furniture

Drawn from

Existing authorities.

by

HENRY SHAW

F.S.A.

drawing room at Knightshayes; in the dining room (164) the chosen text was Chaucer's 'House of Fame'. In an explanatory preface to his Knightshayes designs Burges had written: 'Messrs Harland and Fisher of Southampton Street have a copy of a carpet from a picture of Van Eyck suitable for some rooms. In no case should carpets cover the rooms completely'[21] and at home he practised what he preached. Burges furnished the dining room with another of his Buckingham Street pieces, the escritoire (141) painted by C. Rossiter to illustrate the history of writing from Assyrian cuneiform inscriptions dated 'A.M. 3267' to the invention of electric telegraphy in 'A.D. 1868'. Here too was Burges's stunning display of metalwork and *objets d'art*, ranging from rare antiquities, through medieval and middle eastern oddities, to his own bizarre creations, most of which, however precious, were pressed into dinner-table service from time to time – 'what is the use of having pretty things unless one makes use of them?',[22] Burges used to say.

Upstairs the subject for decoration of the guest bedroom (165) was 'The Earth and its Productions'; Burges's own bedroom had the theme 'The Sea and its Inhabitants'. Mrs Haweis was much impressed by the guests' washstand (153): 'A fine bronze which most of us would place on some table for ornament, here makes itself useful – a bull from whose throat ajar the water pours into a Brescia basin, inlaid with silver fishes. How do you get the water in? See you that other bronze, a tortoise, which seems to creep beyond the bull's fell reach – it is a plug; twist him round and the bull fills the basin. Such is the use which Aladdin makes of bronzes.'[23] Latter-day visitors to Burges's own bedroom inspect the furniture with a more critical eye. Do the poppies on the wardrobe have a particular significance? Did the little drawer contain an opium pipe, perhaps? There can be no doubt that Burges smoked opium, for a diary entry of 1865 records that over-indulgence with the drug prevented his attending the architect C.F. Hayward's wedding. Does the portrait on his dressing table of his young aunt-by-marriage, Emma Crocker, document a disappointment in love? His friend Henry Holiday claimed that Burges 'had been "sweet" on his "auntlet", but ... marrying would not agree with his favourite tastes, such as drinking sherry at lunch out of a silver chalice of exquisite form and workmanship'.[24] The record of Burges's output – scores of learned articles and lectures, dozens of rejected architectural schemes, hundreds of full-scale executed designs in all media, and an extant legacy of furniture and buildings of prime importance – proves that there could never have been time for him to become dependent on any drug, whether women, drink or opium: he was far too busy.

It might all have been different, however, had Burges not met and impressed one of the richest men in the world, John Patrick Crichton-Stuart, the 3rd Marquis of Bute (1847–1900). The meeting took place in 1865, and by 1868, when the Marquis came of age and inherited an income of £300,000 per annum, Burges was already engaged on Cardiff Castle, a monumental project of reconstruction on

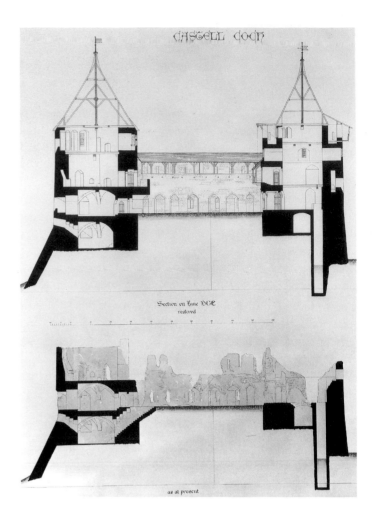

which he was to work for the rest of his life. Although Bute was a painfully shy man – '"Oh", was an exuberance with him. Twice repeated and he felt he had been talkative'[25] – he and Burges shared similar intellectual enthusiasms, and were joint creators of the patterns of conceit with which Cardiff Castle is decorated. Begun when the Marquis was still a bachelor, the Clock Tower – seven stories high, twenty-five feet square, the walls five feet thick, Winter Smoking Room at the bottom, Summer Smoking Room at the top (124) – was a 'truly fearful and wonderful' creation. In September 1873 Lord Bute, his young wife and Burges had luncheon there together for the first time and the master architect-decorator seemed 'quite content with his own work'.[26] It was just a beginning, for work continued at Cardiff Castle until the 1940s.

At Castell Coch, described by Burges as a 'country residence ... for occasional occupation during the summer',[27] the architectural form was conditioned more by the setting than by the crumbling ruin from which this 'enchanted castle' emerged (139). Castell Coch is an architectural gem, but the interior decoration (125 and 127) had barely been begun when Burges died in 1881; it was executed instead under the supervision of William Frame, an irascible ex-assistant with his own practice. Most of the furniture was designed by John Starling Chapple, who had worked in the office at Buckingham Street since 1859 and to whom Burges was 'almost all in the world';[28] Lady Bute's

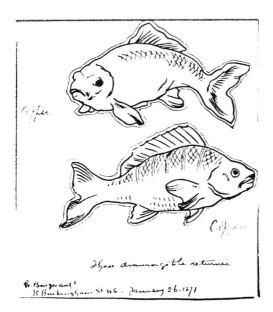

139 Presentation drawing of 1872 showing the extant ruins of Castell Coch and Burges's initial proposal for rebuilding.

140 Design by Burges for copper fishes in the Marquis of Bute's bath in the Clock Tower, Cardiff Castle (1871).

141 The 'Conditions of Life' Escritoire (1867–8) and a Moorish-inspired chair, from an engraving in the *Building News*, 17 April 1874. Now lost, the escritoire was painted by Charles Rossiter.

bed and the toy-fort washstand perfectly mimicked the master's style.

Only two of Burges's assistants built independent careers of any significance, Horatio Walter Lonsdale (1844–1919) and Edward John Tarver (1841–91), co-authors of *Illustrations of Medieval Costume* (1874), replete with chromolithographic plates of a markedly Burgesian character. Both men designed furniture, and Lonsdale remained generally loyal to the Burges idiom (168), though some of his later decorative work for the Butes rises to a quality of its own. One-time president of the Architectural Association, E.J. Tarver became a great committee man, the talkative attendant at endless meetings, to judge by the column inches of quotation in the specialist press. He was a facile practitioner in all the fashionable styles: in the *Furniture Gazette* of 12 August 1874 he went Egyptian with thong-tied ebony chairs; in the *Architect* of 23 September 1882 he went Jacobean with the new wing at Wadhurst Park (169), home of the Spanish banker José de Murietta, a boon companion to the Prince of Wales. José's father, Don Cristobal de Murietta, had commissioned Alfred Stevens to paint an important series of panels illustrating *The Faerie Queene* for their London house in Palace Gardens; when Tarver undertook some redecoration there in 1873 he gave Walter Crane his first commission for a painted frieze. Another follower, Gualbert Saunders, whose company Saunders & Co. made much of Burges's best stained glass, is

a shadowy figure. Two known pieces of painted Gothic furniture bear his inscription (170), but he apparently retired in 1880 leaving Saunders & Co. in the capable hands of his assistant William Worrall. Another assistant of Saunders's, George Smith, set up with Charlie Campbell in 1877 the decorating business on which Burges relied so heavily at Tower House, and which still specializes in painted decoration.

Despite his involvement with many mainstream progressive interests of the period – Japonisme, for example – Burges became stylistically isolated in his work, too personal, too private to have a wider influence. Socially and intellectually, however, he remained at the very centre of London artistic life, justification in itself for the special attention his extraordinary furniture commands from collectors today. Brilliantly inventive, albeit within its own formal limitations, Burges's furniture illuminates brightly this High Gothic corner of Victorian aesthetics. In an illustrated mock-advertisement the pioneering collector Charles Handley-Read wrote: '"Knockout" or "Thunderbolt" High Victorian Gothic urgently required! . . . inlaid, painted, carved or any finish. The mostest the better'[29] – and thus in 1965 acquired for only £45 the dressing table which Burges designed for himself in 1867 (157). As more and more pieces of missing furniture by Burges and his contemporaries are discovered, the jigsaw puzzle of mid-nineteenth-century design takes clearer shape.

Burges interiors

William Burges's earliest painted interior (**142**), the 'Abbess's Room' at Gayhurst, Bucks. (1858–65), is decorated with miniature floral panels against blue, green, red and gold grounds, a Mannerist feature which he later incorporated into Gothic interiors: for example, his unexecuted schemes for the decoration of the Speech Room at Harrow School (**143**) and the Hall at Worcester College, Oxford (**144**). At Knightshayes Court in Devon, Burges's plans were also frustrated: his design of 1873 for the library, with settees fitted into architectural red-stained bookcases and with a castellated chimneypiece (**145**), was rejected in favour of a tame Pugin pastiche by John Diblee Crace (**146**).

Burges's creative energy was finally released in monumental reconstructions at Cardiff Castle (**147**), on which he worked from 1868 till his death in 1881, and at nearby Castell Coch, from 1875, both for the Marquis of Bute. The Herbert Bookcase (**148**; 'Herbert' was a Bute family name) in the library at Cardiff Castle was made by Gillow's in 1878 (the electrotype 'Euripides' panel was supplied by Barkentin & Krall, the Californian marble by W. B. Simpson); although some of the detail was designed by his assistant H. W. Lonsdale, the basic form is firmly Burgesian, with wombats perched on top of the capitals. The Burges interiors at Knightshayes have been restored by the National Trust: now on display in the hall is the Great Bookcase of 1859, made for Burges's own use and painted by Poynter, Rossetti, Burne-Jones, Solomon and others (**149**).

142

144

145

146

147

150

151

153

152

Burges furniture

Burges sent five pieces of painted furniture to the 1862 London International Exhibition, two of which, the Yatman Cabinet (made in 1858 for H. G. Yatman of Haslemere) and the Harland & Fisher sideboard (now lost), can be seen in an original stereoscopic slide (**150**; the sideboard is on the left). Another sideboard shown at the 1862 Exhibition – commissioned in 1858 by James Nicholson (**151**) – was decorated by E. J. Poynter to Burges's design with 'The Battle Between the Wines and the Spirits': inside the doors four neoclassical cameos mischievously represent Ginger Beer, Lemonade, Seltzer Water and Soda Water. Burges's Wheel of Fortune table top (**155**) of 1858, for C. L. S. Cocks of Treverbyn Vean, Cornwall, was made by Crace and placed on a Pugin base. A final commission of this busy year was for the bridal bedroom in the Rev. J. A. Yatman's house in Somerset: Burges insisted on an elaborate figurative scheme for the walls, leaving the furniture itself relatively plain (**152**).

Burges's most inventive pieces were reserved for his own use, in particular two remarkable washstands, the Vita Nuova, of 1879–80 (**153**), and the earlier Narcissus, of 1865–7 (**154**), in both of which the 'Jennings patent' tip-up basins were inlaid with gold and silver fishes; the taps are Chinese bronzes. Furniture made for Burges's home-cum-office in Buckingham Street includes the Zodiac Settle of 1869–71 (**156**), painted by Henry Stacy Marks and originally hung with Turkish embroidery, and Burges's dressing table (**157**), painted red and inset with portraits of his aunts-by-marriage, the Crocker sisters. For Tower House, where he lived from March 1878, Burges made three intarsia-topped tables (**158**) to display his collection of metalwork.

154

155

156

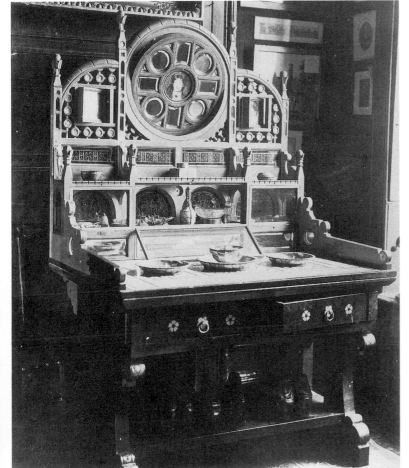

157

158

159

Burges at home

Detailed plans for Burges's home, Tower House in Melbury Road, Holland Park (**159**), were drawn up in 1875. The bronze front door (**163**), designed by Burges, was cast by Thomas Nicholls in 1876, two years before the house was ready to live in. The mosaic maze on the hall floor (**160**) symbolized 'Time', within which Burges trapped Theseus and the Minotaur, and Bacchus and Ariadne. In the library (**161**) the great chimneypiece represents the Tower of Babel, flanked by the Alphabet Bookcases, decorated with caricatures of Burges and his friends. Today, although lacking much of the original painted decoration, the *Roman de la Rose* fireplace in the drawing room still impresses (**162**).

160

161

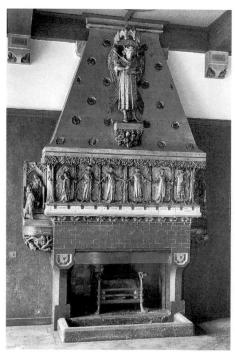

162

163

164

In photographs published in 1885 by his sister's husband, Richard Pullan, the personality of Burges himself dominates: for the dining room (**164**) he commissioned J. Walden of Covent Garden to make a hardstone inset serving buffet; to avoid the lingering smell of food, he lined the walls with Devonshire marble below a tile frieze illustrating fairy tales. After her tour of inspection in 1880 Mrs Haweis described the guest bedroom (**165**) as 'made of fire and flowers . . . like an ancient shrine or reliquary'. Burges's own bed (**167**) was decorated by Henry Holiday in 1868 with a scene from Tennyson's poem 'The Day Dream' – Burges died in this bed on 20 April 1881, of spinal myelitis. In his bedroom he installed a giltwood stand made in 1873 to display favourite caskets from his extensive collection (**166**).

165

166

167

168

169

Burges's assistants

Burges's principal architectural assistants were H. W. Lonsdale and E. J. Tarver. Lonsdale, who joined the office prior to 1868, designed a considerable body of stained glass and mural decoration for Burges buildings, notably St Fin Barre Cathedral, Cork, and Cardiff Castle. His sideboard of 1871 had Burges-like spandrels, pediment and stubby columnar supports, but lacked the master's structural strength (**168**). Tarver worked happily in whatever style his clients requested: 'Jacobean' in the 1882 design for the dining room inglenook at Wadhurst Park, Sussex, for instance (**169**). W. Gualbert Saunders, a stained glass specialist, began work on his own writing cabinet soon after arriving at the Burges office in 1865: there is a boldness in both form and decoration which suggests Burges's close participation (**170**). Henry Stacy Marks worked as a muralist and decorator for Burges, Godwin, Waterhouse and many other leading architects: tropical birds, his favourite subject, appear on an ill-composed cabinet dated 1868 (**171**).

170

171

Geometric Gothic

172 Painted sedilia in G. E. Street's St James the Less, Pimlico (1859–61).

The Victorian architectural critic J. Beavington Atkinson could 'scarcely imagine a task more agreeable for a gentleman of means, taste and leisure than to set himself to the consistent decoration and furnishing of a Gothic Villa'.[1] In the August 1862 issue of *London Society*, the pseudonymous Jack Easel similarly confirmed a victory for Gothic in the battle of the styles: 'This moyen age mania ... is pointing our windows, and inlaying our cabinets, and gothicising the plates we eat from, the chairs on which we sit, the papers on our walls.'

Evidence of the popularity from the 1860s to the 1880s of the Gothic style in new furniture and architecture surrounds us still. There is, however, no clear consensus as to what this visually complex revival should best be called. Although Ruskin forcefully recommended the use of 'geometrical coloured mosaic'[2] and Owen Jones insisted that 'all ornament should be based on geometrical construction',[3] the chapter title 'Geometric Gothic' is not a term which the Victorians themselves would have recognized. The phrase was coined in the 1960s by the collector Charles Handley-Read to describe, principally, the boldly inlaid commercial furniture of Bruce Talbert and Charles Bevan which followed on so successfully from the polychromatic decoration of buildings by, amongst others, William Butterfield. More important, however, than what the style should or should not be called is the way it looked. The essence of Geometric Gothic is marvellously exemplified in G.E. Street's sedilia of 1859–60 in St James the Less, Pimlico (172), an organized riot of flat patterning contained within a complex architectural framework. Old decorative devices are re-used in a new way on new structures: proto-Post-Modernism, it could be called.

The Gothic revival in furniture design is an architectural style, in the sense that not only was much of the furniture constructed like mini-buildings, but also many of its earliest stylistic discoveries were made in the decoration of churches and other large institutional commissions. A knowledge of Victorian architecture is a necessary precondition for the understanding of all good nineteenth-century furniture, but nowhere more so than with Geometric Gothic. In this chapter a wide-angled view of the architectural scene swings from, at one extreme, the spiky S.S. Teulon of Shadwell Park, Norfolk, through, at the centre, the decorative J.H. Chamberlain, to the eclectic commercialism of Bruce Talbert. It takes in the fussy G.G. Scott, the fustian C.L. Eastlake and the fashionable Alfred Waterhouse. Not all the furniture is inlaid, not all of it is even strictly geometric, but whether 'French', 'Venetian', 'English', 'Florentine', or whatever, it is all here grouped under the general title 'Geometric Gothic'.

Even though William Butterfield (1814–1900) designed relatively few secular buildings and virtually no domestic furniture – the one exception seems to have been at Milton Ernest Hall, Bedfordshire, his sister's house – he has always been considered an adventurous, influential figure in the development of the decorative arts of the nineteenth century. Eastlake called Butterfield 'a designer of genius and originality',[4] and suggested that 'the guiding principle of his taste is rooted in a determination to be singular ... His work gives one the idea of a man who has designed it not so much to please his clients but to please himself.'[5] Butterfield's first great statement was made at All Saints', Margaret Street, London (1850–9), the model church of the Ecclesiological Society, one of the chief propagandists of the Gothic revival. 'A bold and magnificent endeavour to shake off the trammels of antiquarian precedent', Eastlake proclaimed – whilst noting that Butterfield's determination to experiment displeased most critics who 'sneer at every specimen of modern art that departs in any marked degree from a conventional standard'.[6] Very little has changed at All Saints' since it was built (173), either in the fabric – except that the exterior is now darkened by city grime – or in the form of service: wearing Butterfield vestments the clergy process from end to end of the squat nave between acolytes swinging Butterfield censers, and preach from a Butterfield pulpit gloriously decorated with tawny Sienna, grey Derbyshire, green Irish and red Languedoc marbles, supported on solid pink granite columns. Butterfield considered All Saints' (like the chapel of Keble College, Oxford, 174) 'as a *Te Deum*, strictly ordered but magnificently triumphant'.[7] It became a favourite calling place for the poet Gerard Manley

Hopkins for whom 'the touching and passionate curves of the lilyings in the ironwork ... marked [Butterfield's] genius'.[8]

Butterfield studied under the architect and antiquarian E.L. Blackburne, author of a book on decorative painting in the Middle Ages (1847), which had beautifully detailed plates that provided many useful tips for both Burges and Morris. A devout Christian, Butterfield worked on church fittings early in his career and was encouraged by Blackburne to publish the designs, over a hundred of which appeared between 1844 and 1856, under the title *Instrumentia Ecclesiastica*. He made a specialized study of pew design, and searched for a standard form which would be at once simple, comfortable and convenient. Opinions differed as to his success – the architect H. Roumieu Gough described the pews as 'instruments of torture'[9] – but Butterfield's leaflet on the subject was popular enough to have been reprinted. He designed a large quantity of church plate, much of which was made by John Keith, and an equal body of brasswork (217), made from the early 1870s by Hart, Son, Peard & Company. For Keble College (1867–83) and Rugby School (1858–84) he produced robust undecorated furniture which has stood up well to the test of time (212). At Milton Ernest the furniture in the children's rooms, probably designed in 1858, was 'white with stripes

and cinquefoliate stars picked out in red'.[10] The main bedroom furniture, inlaid rather than painted, is more delicate and traditional in design than might be expected from Butterfield's church furnishings – like the furniture in the main reception rooms, so dutifully Georgian in inspiration it hardly seems possible that he was the designer. Butterfield also designed embroideries and wallpapers: those in a Victorian photograph of the drawing room at Milton Ernest (211) are possibly by him.

Furniture designed by Samuel Saunders Teulon (1812–73) is as rare as Butterfield's; only a few pieces – from Tortworth Court, Gloucestershire – have yet re-surfaced. However, the architectural invention of his interiors at Shadwell Park, Norfolk (1856–60), Elvetham Hall, Hampshire (1859–62), and Bestwood Lodge, Nottinghamshire (1862–64), are well-known Gothic delights. Mark Girouard finds Teulon's additions to Shadwell 'a dazzling display of Victorian fireworks' and considers the music hall to be 'one of the most impressive of surviving Victorian domestic interiors, impressive in its scale, in the inspired eccentricity of its woodwork and in the abundance and quality of its stone carving'.[11] The stonework is probably by Thomas Earp, and the metalworkers Skidmore's were involved in the organ screen (175) in the cathedral-like music hall. Although, as far as we know, Teulon's furniture was all in

173 The interior of All Saints', Margaret Street (1850–9), by William Butterfield: the *locus classicus* of Geometric Gothic.

174 Keble College, Oxford (1867–83), Butterfield's secular polychromatic masterpiece.

175 S. S. Teulon's design for the organ in his church-like music room at Shadwell Park, Norfolk (1856–60), illustrated in the *Builder* of 14 July 1860.

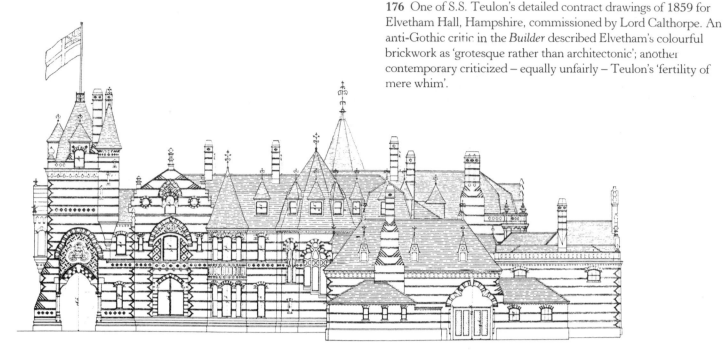

176 One of S.S. Teulon's detailed contract drawings of 1859 for Elvetham Hall, Hampshire, commissioned by Lord Calthorpe. An anti-Gothic critic in the *Builder* described Elvetham's colourful brickwork as 'grotesque rather than architectonic'; another contemporary criticized – equally unfairly – Teulon's 'fertility of mere whim'.

solid oak, elaborately carved with Perpendicular Gothic detail, the exteriors of many of his buildings are unequivocally Geometric in their decoration. 'The belligerent chaos'[12] of his 1859 elevation for alterations at Elvetham (176) is a perfect paradigm of what Eastlake referred to as 'the Streaky-Bacon style'.[13]

George Edmund Street (1824–81) received no country house commissions and in 1874, at the age of fifty, designed his only purely domestic building, Holmdale in Surrey (177), which he built for himself on a small scale but to an attractive rambling plan. Into this new home he moved 'the magnificent bookcase'[14] which Holland & Sons had made in 1865 at a cost of £59 10s (214); other equally austere furniture which Street designed for himself was destroyed in the 'Baedeker' air-raid on Bath in 1942. In his book about Scudamore organs, published in 1862, the Reverend John Baron illustrated designs by Street with tusked tenons and wide chamfering in the severest Puginian mould (192); plainer still was Street's furniture (213) for the student bedrooms at Cuddesdon College, Oxford, which he started

designing soon after his appointment in 1850 as diocesan architect to the Bishop of Oxford and finished before leaving to set up architectural practice in London in 1856. Street numbered himself with Burges amongst 'the thirteenth century men'[15] and, like Burges, travelled extensively on the Continent, producing hundreds of prettily executed topographical watercolours. Eastlake thus had reason to find St James the Less, Pimlico (172), 'eminently un-English', a fact which explains his lustreless praise of Street: 'The rich fertility of this architect's inventive power is equalled by the sagacious tact which guides its application.'[16] Street's grandest commission, for the Law Courts in the Strand, London (216), initially designed in 1866 and still unfinished at his death in 1881, was also his most controversial. Although art historians today consider Street 'achieved a classic balance between refinement and strength unequalled by other practitioners of the [Reformed Gothic] style',[17] one contemporary critic, J.C. Fergusson, wrote that he could have excused the Law Courts only 'if the Strand were the bed of a pellucid mountain stream, and this building were

177 G. E. Street's home, Holmdale in Surrey, designed by himself in 1874. This drawing of 1882 is by Maurice B. Adams.

178 The Town Hall, Bradford, designed by Henry Lockwood (1811–78) and built by Lockwood & Mawson between 1869 and 1873. The building's French and Italian Gothic splendours, here illustrated in a perspective by Axel Haig, were thought by many contemporary critics to imitate too closely Burges's unexecuted scheme for the Law Courts.

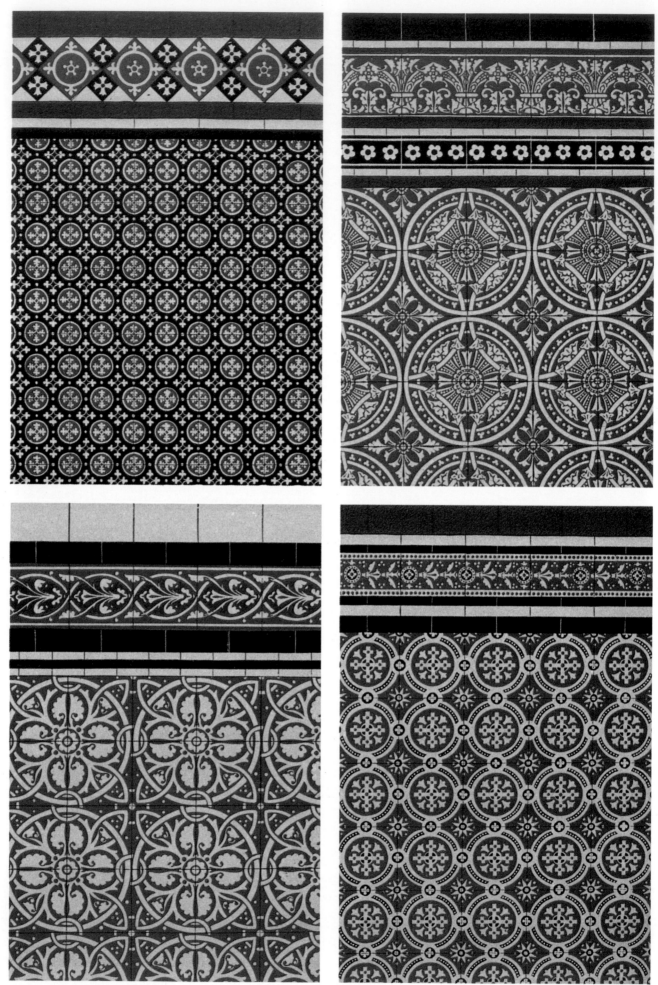

179–182

183

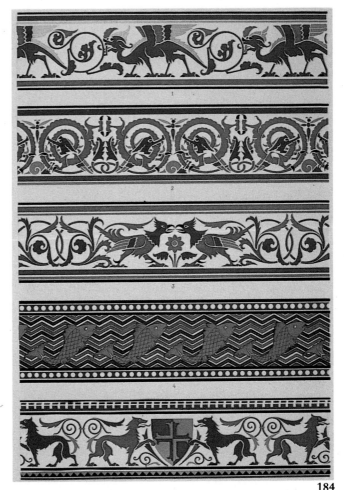

184

179–182 Designs for encaustic floor tiles by J. P. Seddon, illustrated in an elaborate chromolithographic catalogue of *c.* 1872 produced by the Shropshire firm Maw & Co., *Geometrical and Roman Mosaics, Encaustic Tile Pavements and Enamelled Wall Decorations*. Seddon's designs were inspired by thirteenth-century tiles dicovered in the 1850s at Chertsey Abbey, Surrey.

183–185 Illustrations by Firmin-Didot from William and George Audsley's *Polychromatic Decoration as Applied to Buildings in the Mediaeval Styles* (1882), depicting samples of stencilled patterns taken from Continental Romanesque and Gothic buildings. 'These few examples', the Audsley brothers maintained, 'will suggest to the decorative artist an endless number of simple combinations.'

185

186

186 This rare example of Ruskinian ideals applied to furniture is a cabinet designed by the Birmingham architect J. H. Chamberlain in 1877 for a house called The Grove, in Harborne, Warwickshire. The carcass is stained oak, with walnut and purpleheart scrolling foliage inlaid on sycamore. The two pairs of green-brown vases were designed by Christopher Dresser for the Linthorpe Pottery (1879–89) Middlesbrough; the small blue vases were made in 1906 at the Pilkington Pottery, near Manchester. See also 201.

187 A bedside table of sycamore inlaid with amboyna, purpleheart, alder and stained ash. It was made by Marsh & Jones of Leeds to designs by Charles Bevan and is similar to Bevan's 'Best Bedroom Suite' supplied by Marsh & Jones to Titus Salt Jnr of Saltaire in November 1865. The large crackle-glaze vase of *c*.1900 is by Sir Edmund Elton.

188 An inlaid oak dining chair by Bruce Talbert, whose detailed sectional design was illustrated in his *Gothic Forms Applied to Furniture, Metal Work and Decoration for Domestic Purposes*, published in 1868 (see 257). It is displayed against silk and wool curtain material designed by Christopher Dresser in the 1870s.

189 Oak sideboard inset with boxwood panels, almost identical to the Pet Sideboard designed by Bruce Talbert for Gillow's to exhibit at the 1872 London International Exhibition. Apart from a large De Morgan bowl in the centre, all the ceramics were designed by Christopher Dresser; the two silver centrepieces were designed by C. R. Ashbee for the Guild of Handicraft.

190 A cabinet decorated by Clement Heaton (left) and a Gillow's sideboard designed by Bruce Talbert, overwhelmed by a collection of C. H. Brannum's Barumware of the 1880s and 90s.

189

designed to be placed on its banks in some remote sparsely inhabited Midland valley, for the accommodation of a company of barefooted friars'.[18] Despite the bitterness of public criticism, Street continued to attract gifted people to his side, and though his own domestic output was small his influence on nineteenth-century furniture design was considerable, as gratefully expressed in the work of ex-pupils such as Webb, Morris and Shaw.

Two other muscularly Gothic architects, William White (1825–1900) and James Brooks (1825–1901), who worked one after the other at Humewood Castle in County Wicklow, also produced furniture of an admirable architectural solidity (215). White 'spent much of his life balanced on the boundary between crankiness and brilliance':[19] an enthusiastic member of the Alpine Club, the inventor of a valveless closet and wasteless lavatory, a promoter of Swedish gymnastics, he wasted the better part of his later years trying to prove that Shakespeare's plays were written by Bacon. James Brooks, though a much busier architect than White, is also known today only to devotees of the nineteenth century, for, as Eastlake asked, 'what amateur or dilettante would ever think of exploring such neighbourhoods as Shoreditch, Hoxton and Plaistow in search of architectural beauty?'[20] 'Yet', as Eastlake replied to his own rhetorical question, 'those regions contain some of the largest and most remarkable churches which have been built during the revival', a magisterial series of Geometric Gothic buildings by James Brooks (219). In 1873, the year of completion of the vicarage and clergy house at St Columba's on the Kingsland Road, the *Builder* commented on Brooks's 'exaggerated sternness and contempt for all ornamental accessory', following this with a mild rebuke: 'there *is* a medium short of absolute baldness and naked stone walls'.[21] His church furniture was equally restrained in decoration, but much admired for its formal strength and inventiveness.

As the son of a cabinetmaker, the architect John Pollard Seddon (1827–1906) designed furniture from the beginning of his career. Born in the year his father, Thomas Seddon, commissioned young Pugin for the Windsor furniture, Seddon's earliest documented furniture was for Ettington Park near Stratford-upon-Avon, a house begun by his partner John Prichard and finished by Seddon between 1860 and 1862. Some early Seddon furniture (224) is still stamped 'T. Seddon, New Bond Street', but most of his furniture designs in the Victoria and Albert Museum's extensive collection are inscribed either 'C. Seddon & Co., 58 South Molton Street', or just 'Seddon & Co., South Molton Street'. Seddon first made a public name for himself with the group of furniture shown at the 1862 International Exhibition, 'in a style much akin to that of Mr

Burges, and being less recondite in treatment ... consequently more intelligible and likely to be better appreciated'.[22] Another contemporary critic made the same comparison, noting 'some remarkable furniture ... particularly Seddon's library case for prints and maps, and library chair; he 'regretted, however, that some furniture, needlessly rude and ugly [meaning Burges's], should have been exhibited as medieval, as if rudeness and ugliness were characteristic of medieval art'.[23] Seddon's roll-top desk and chair appear in a stereoscopic slide of the Mediaeval Court (221). A drawing of the chair survives (220), illustrating the structural clarity of Seddon's furniture design, a fact appreciated by the *Illustrated London News*, which thought his chair established 'the possibility of combining beauty and utility with manifest structure'.[24]

The 2 June 1865 issue of *Building News* illustrated a large sideboard of Seddon's, the editors promising that 'another of similar character will shortly be completed'. This second sideboard (191) was yet more impressive in detail, designed in a 'style founded on Early Geometrical Gothic, but treated completely in subordination to practical requirements, to which no other style lends itself so readily'.[25] It was a style which also abstracted forms from nature, a Puginesque doctrine which J.K. Colling continued in his influential drawings of 'Art Foliage', first published in the *Building News* in 1864–5. Though the sideboard is of standard form, Seddon gave it more creative attention than he paid to two whole streets of houses in Kentish Town. Architectural details abound: an arcade of mini-columns in the base opens upwards to allow storage of dinner dishes; the mirror is supported by applied pilasters and protected by a roof. The decorative detail, too, is wonderfully inventive: the hinges are enamelled green and red; the leather panels beneath the plate shelf are painted with stylized flowers. J. Coates Carter, an occasional architectural partner of Seddon's, believed that Seddon was 'always a modern rather than a medievalist ... In his work almost alone among the early medievalists was it impossible to trace the origin of the detail to any particular medieval style.'[26]

Seddon's most famous piece of furniture at the 1862 Exhibition, his own large architect's cabinet, was always known as the King René's Honeymoon Cabinet (226), after the painted panels on that theme by Burne-Jones, Rossetti and Madox Brown (who shows King René admiring a very Victorian-looking house plan). As Burges was a pupil of Seddon at the time it may have been his idea to add the jokier elements: at the side Seddon himself is depicted as a lobster settling a dispute between client and builder, represented as snakes. Seddon kept in close contact with the Pre-Raphaelites – Rossetti actually died in one of the Seddon bungalows at Birchington-on-Sea, Kent, part of a development initiated in the late 1860s by John Taylor (they were, as it happens, the first 'bungalows' in England, a name derived from the Hindi word *Bangla*).

Another gifted pupil, C.F.A. Voysey, assisted Seddon in the renovation of his major building after it was gutted by

191 Inlaid oak sideboard designed by J. P. Seddon, 1865, and made by C. Seddon & Co. in collaboration with Kendal & Co. Three Minton breadplates by A. W. N. Pugin (1849); gilt bronze candlesticks by Chertier, design attributed to Viollet-le-Duc.

192 Design for an organ by G. E. Street, published in the Reverend John Baron's book about Scudamore organs (1852).

193 The chapter house at Noyon, from W. E. Nesfield's *Specimens of Mediaeval Architecture* (1862), one of J. P. Seddon's sourcebooks.

194 J. P. Seddon, photographed in the dining room of his Castle Hotel, Aberystwyth, begun in 1864.

fire in 1885. Designed in 1864 as the Castle Hotel, Aberystwyth, and built at a phenomenal pace to the order of the railway speculator Thomas Savin – Seddon was required to keep 500 workmen permanently on site – this masterpiece was taken over by the committee of the proposed University of Wales when Savin went bankrupt in 1866. An early photograph (194) shows Seddon seated in one of his own chairs in front of the fireplace, set with great assurance at a wide-angled corner, the panelling and double-doors typical of his bold interior decoration. Although the tall chimney breast is very much Seddon's own invention, it has its origins in twelfth-century Continental architecture (compare the chapter house at Noyon, 193, illustrated in W.E. Nesfield's *Specimens of Mediaeval Architecture*, published in 1862, the figures drawn by Albert Moore). There is a Continental quality also about Seddon's tile designs: for Godwin's of Hereford, Maw & Co. of Brosley, Shropshire (179–182), and Robert Minton Taylor. Like Pugin, Seddon successfully adapted the Gothic style to commercial ceramic production; he supplied C.J.C. Bailey with numerous designs for the pottery in Fulham which Bailey bought from Mackintosh & Clements in 1864.

Judged solely on the number of executed commissions, the two most significant architects of the Gothic revival were Alfred Waterhouse and George Gilbert Scott (1811–78), in both of whose large commercial practices projects

proliferated at an alarming rate. It is told that 'once, when Scott had left town by the six o'clock train, his office, on slackly assembling, found a telegram from a Midland station asking "Why am I here?"'.[27]

In his 1962 edition of *The Gothic Revival* Kenneth Clark admitted that he had previously overvalued the work of Scott, noting how this most ambitious of Victorian architects had 'conquered the official and, so to speak, public-speaking world ... but had never convinced the minority who really care'.[28] Certainly, in the history of furniture Scott's influence was minimal: one of his few existing designs, a table for Kelham Hall, Nottinghamshire (1858–61), either was never executed or has been lost (the design is in the Drawings Collection of the Royal Institute of British Architects). In the wider context of interior decoration, however, his impact was much greater. The elaborate stencilling at Kelham, with its 'cabbage-like roses',[29] reappears in the Midland Hotel at St Pancras Station, Scott's stupendous landmark to the Venetian Gothic ideal. Despite appearances, the Midland was highly practical, 'its hydraulic lifts and electric bells ... the height of luxury'[30] and the grand staircase (196) both a structural and a decorative *tour-de-force*, cantilevered into open space on iron girders relief-cast with Gothic tracery. The interiors have mostly been altered now, but original photographs indicate that the furniture was ordered up from commercial manufacturers – though Scott may have had a hand in a few of the more architectural pieces. A monumental sideboard (195) echoes, in the spiked quatrefoils, elements of the overall decorative scheme, and certain details, such as a subtle open-carved frieze below the drawers and the fret-carved 'cart-wheels' flanking the top of the mirror, are better organized than in most commercial furniture; as the style is more 'Old English' than would be expected of Scott, the sideboard may have been designed by T.G. Jackson, an ex-assistant of Scott's who was involved with the interior design of the dining room at St Pancras.

Alfred Waterhouse (1830–1905) was famous for both his energy and his charm, the obituarist in *The Times* confirming that 'even those who didn't like his architecture loved the man'.[31] The son of a wealthy Quaker mill-owner from outside Liverpool, most of his early commissions were secured through the Quaker network, including Hutton Hall, Yorkshire (1863–74), an 'intensely luxurious house',[32] built for Sir Joseph Whitewell Pease. Although thousands of drawings survive from Waterhouse's disciplined practice, designs for furniture are known to exist for only nine commissions, most of them institutional. Much of their furnishing is dull when compared with Waterhouse's exciting architectural detail for, say, the Natural History Museum in London. The earliest surviving documented piece of domestic furniture designed by Waterhouse is a

195 Sideboard in the dining room of the Midland Hotel, St Pancras Station, designed by either Gilbert Scott or his former assistant T. G. Jackson.

196 The main staircase of the hotel, designed in Venetian Gothic style by Gilbert Scott and built 1868–77.

197 Alfred Waterhouse, described by his obituarist in *The Times* as 'the most genial and attractive of men'.

marble-topped centre table from Hutton Hall, made in December 1867 by Hardcastle & Hall of 28a East Parade, Harrogate (233). It is commendably architectural in structure, a working through of ideas for the Romanesque style

that was forced, so successfully, onto Waterhouse for the Natural History Museum. Stylistically, Waterhouse's furniture is often difficult to define, and it perches here somewhat awkwardly in the middle of 'Geometric Gothic'. Were it not for the fact that Waterhouse was so clearly an architect of the Gothic revival, who made such wonderful use of polychrome brick in, for example, the twenty-four Prudential Insurance offices he designed, his later 'Old English' interiors (198) could easily be discussed beside Richard Norman Shaw's (and his 1872 interior design for Girton College, Cambridge, is positively Japanese).

By far the largest group of Waterhouse domestic furniture now in public and private collections originates from Blackmoor House in Hampshire, initially furnished between 1869 and 1873 by the cabinetmakers James Capel, together with a later order supplied to Waterhouse designs by Liberty's between 1882 and 1886. The *Building News* criticized this later furniture for its 'wiriness of outline, a redundancy of repeated ornament and a want of go and abandon'.[33] An earlier spindle-back chair (229) from Blackmoor is, however, 'one of his most striking pieces of furniture'[34] in its sophisticated manipulation of forms derived, Simon Jervis has suggested, jointly from a thirteenth-century chair in Hereford Cathedral and from Islamic latticework. The Blackmoor House bookcase, which Handley-Read failed to persuade the owners to part with (it was acquired at the house-auction of 1974 by the Cecil Higgins Art Gallery, Bedford), is more clearly Gothic in inspiration and closer to the architectural style of Yattendon Court, Berkshire – 'Tudor-Gothic (with Old English elements)'[35] – which Waterhouse built for himself in 1878. Above the bedroom doors Waterhouse inscribed 'Humility', 'Peace', 'Rest', 'Mercy', 'Joy', 'Valour', and 'Honour'. (The house was totally demolished in the 1960s.)

198 The library at Blackmoor House, Hampshire, designed for the Earl of Selborne by Waterhouse and built between 1869 and 1873. The furniture was supplied by James Capel to Waterhouse's designs; some pieces, like the spindle-back chair in the left foreground (an example is shown in 231) are similar in style to Bruce Talbert's later designs. The 'Old English' or 'Tudor' fitted furniture similarly shows Waterhouse moving away from High Gothic forms.

199 Waterhouse was at work on the rebuilding of Eaton Hall, Cheshire, for the Duke of Westminster between 1870 and 1882. The large drawing room, shown here in a photograph of *c*.1887, was sumptuously decorated to Waterhouse's designs by Heaton, Butler & Bayne.

Office documents now at the Royal Institute of British Architects indicate that Waterhouse habitually made only minor alterations to furniture designs from commission to commission in his extensive commercial practice. At Manchester, for instance, the furniture in the Assize Courts (230; built 1859 to 1870), the University (1869 to 1905) and the Town Hall (1869 to 1876) was closely related. Drawings exist which precisely match furniture still in the Town Hall, made by a number of different Manchester cabinetmakers, including Goodall's, Lamb's, and Doveston, Bird & Hull. Waterhouse is known to have admired the kick-back legs on Pugin seat furniture and he used them himself on a chair that appears in various forms in original photographs of the Conference Room, the Mayor's Dining Room, and the main Reception Room (232). Although no furniture was required in the rebuilding of Eaton Hall, Cheshire, for the Duke of Westminster, Waterhouse nevertheless succeeded in spending £600,000 on the job, so sumptuous were the Duke's decorative requirements. The decoration was carried out by Heaton, Butler & Bayne, for whom the influential designer Lewis F. Day was working at the time (234 and 235). An extravagant sum was expended on Waterhouse's hundred-and-eighty-three-foot clock tower, built to house a carillon of twenty-eight bells that chimed 'Home Sweet Home' to welcome the Duke's return. Eaton Hall had first been Gothicized by William Porden from 1804 to 1812, and Waterhouse's attempt at further improvement was privately disapproved of by Ralph Sneyd, the contemporary commentator, who suggested that 'any effective reform would entail demolition',[36] advice which went unheeded for eighty years, until in 1961 Eaton Hall was razed to the ground; today, only the chapel, clock tower and stables remain.

In his 1892 preface to the Kelmscott edition of *The Nature of Gothic* – reprinting a chapter from Ruskin's *Stones of Venice* of 1851–3 – William Morris stated his belief that 'in future years [it] will be considered one of the very few necessary and inevitable utterances of the century'. C.R. Ashbee also expressed a debt to Ruskin, and located the seeds of his own creed in Ruskin's 'prophetic enthusiasm'.[37] Ruskin's influence, however, extended far beyond the narrow world of the arts and crafts elite: it affected suburban villadom in every city in England. 'One of my principal notions', Ruskin confessed, 'for leaving my present house is that it is surrounded everywhere by the accursed Frankenstein monsters of, *indirectly*, my own making.'[38] In town halls too, the Venetian Gothic style that Ruskin had popularized long maintained its popular appeal (178). Ruskin's influence on furniture was, however, limited, the one magnificent exception being the redecoration by J.H. Chamberlain in 1877 of a house called The Grove, in Harborne, outside Birmingham (200). John Henry Chamberlain (1831–83) was an important figure in Birmingham artistic circles. Amongst much else, he was chairman of the School of Art Committee and, near the end of his life, architect of its fine new building, also an admirable synthesis of Ruskinian ideals. The furniture at The Grove was made by a stone and wood carver called Barfield, who had earlier worked on Chamberlain's own house, Highbury;

it is of the highest quality (186). The ante-room from The Grove was re-erected in the Victoria and Albert Museum when the house was demolished in 1963. The hanging cabinet from the hall, identified in an original photograph (201), reappeared on the London art market in 1985; both the stencilled decoration on the wall and the remarkable naturalistic inlay of the cabinet itself led Handley-Read to consider that Chamberlain had 'formalised nature very successfully, avoiding the harsh and spiky eccentricities associated with Christopher Dresser'[39] (for Dresser, see below, page 130). The *Architect* went rather further, and claimed that Chamberlain could be likened to 'the great Medieval artists . . . who stamped alike upon mass and detail the unity derivable only from individual character and original genius'.[40]

Reference has already frequently been made to Charles Locke Eastlake, the most influential writer on the Gothic revival, author of *Hints on Household Taste* – first published as a series of articles in the *Queen* in 1865 – and of *A History of the Gothic Revival*, published in 1872. Another arbiter of contemporary taste, Mrs Haweis, wrote of *Hints*: 'It is so extremely good, practical and interesting, that I cannot do better than recommend it to my readers.'[41] In an article in the *Cornhill Magazine* entitled 'Cimabue and Coal-Scuttles' a certain 'G.A.' (George Augustus Sala?) looked out from the aesthetic heights of 1880 across the previous two decades: 'Pure medievalism, well or ill understood, was all

the rage. Sir Charles Eastlake[42] became the oracle of domestic taste . . . We sat down to dinner on a sort of carved-oak bishop's throne, and we hung up our hats on a domestic variety of pinnacled sedilia . . . It was all a little ridiculous, perhaps, but it was a step towards decorative improvement.'[43] Judging from Eastlake's furniture designs alone, it is difficult to understand how he could have had any impact at all on contemporary design: the proportions of his furniture are too often top-heavy, the carved decoration crude rather than merely simple, and the formal vocabulary sadly limited. The text of *Hints on Household Taste* could scarcely be in greater contrast: it is passionate, original, combatative and convincing. In one paragraph, for instance, he brands Louis XIV-style furniture 'bad and vicious in principle' and in the next he ridicules the mid-Victorian fashion for naturalistically designed floor-covering: 'A carpet . . . may convey the preposterous notion of a bed of roses, or a dangerous labyrinth of rococo ornament – but if it is 'fashionable' that is all-sufficient. When new, it is admired; when old, everybody will agree that it was always hideous.' Carpets like these, Eastlake concluded, 'are only fit to cover the floor of Madame Tussaud's Chamber of Horrors'.[44]

Eastlake's aesthetic tenets are based on a dislike of Great-Exhibition-type decorative excess and on demands for a return to the simple propriety of medieval joinery. The illustrations in *Hints*, engraved by Eastlake, emphasize the

200 The hall of The Grove, Harborne, near Birmingham, a Ruskinian Gothic house designed by J. H. Chamberlain in 1877. This photograph was taken in 1911; the house was demolished in 1963.

201 Hanging cabinet in the hall at The Grove, Harborne, photographed in 1911. Both the cabinet and the stencilled decoration on the wall were designed by J. H. Chamberlain. See 186.

need for craftsmanship to be revealed, not concealed beneath false veneers: the plain oak planks in his bedroom chest (240) are secured by butterfly joints, and wooden dowling pins in his 'dining-room sideboard' are made provocatively clear (241). Some of Eastlake's designs were manufactured under licence by Jackson & Graham, but the many differences between design and execution in most 'Eastlake' pieces suggest that other cabinetmakers adapted the designs at will. Eastlake also designed curtains for Jackson & Graham (and for Cowlishaw, Nicol & Co.), though the textiles singled out for special praise in *Hints* are by Clement Heaton (1824–82), founder in the early 1860s of the mosaic and stained glass specialists Heaton, Butler & Bayne. Eastlake illustrated an appliqué portière decorated by Heaton with representations of Aesop's 'The Fox and the Stork', designs which Minton later reproduced on tiles and which Heaton also adapted to the stencilled decoration of furniture.

Whilst conceding that Eastlake was 'right in many views', another iconoclastic writer on design, Christopher Dresser, could not 'help regarding him somewhat as an apostle of ugliness', determined 'to despise finish and refinement'.[45] In the preface to the 1878 edition of *Hints* Eastlake himself admitted that mistakes had been made: 'I find American tradesmen continually advertising what they are pleased to call 'Eastlake' furniture, with the production of which I have had nothing whatever to do, and for the taste of which I should be very sorry to be considered responsible.' One such example is illustrated in a book published in New York in 1876 by Walter Smith, under the plagiarizing title *Household Hints*: a cabinet organ made by Mason and Hamlin (244) was described as 'without fault ... its subdued

decoration ... conceived in the Eastlake style'. By contrast, in England Eastlake was pleased to note how the large sales of his book had encouraged more and more commercial manufacturers to take advice from professional designers; there was – and is – still a long way to go, however, as 'it will take some time before this influence will extend to that unfortunately large class of the British public who are indifferent to art of any kind'.[46]

Though Bruce Talbert (1838–81) was one of the best of this new breed of professional decorator, the editor of the *Building News* overstated his case in claiming that 'Mr Talbert made a name as a designer which has not been equalled since the days of Chippendale and Adam'.[47] Both in the quality and quantity of his furniture and textile design, Talbert must certainly be seen as a leading figure in the decorative arts of the period, but his real worth was more accurately, if modestly, assessed by the *Cabinet Maker and Art Furnisher*: 'he stands forth as a pioneer in the better phases of modern taste'.[48] By the turn of the century Hermann Muthesius, leading apologist of the arts and crafts movement, had grown antagonistic to the Goths. He found Burges's Tower House particularly 'distressing ... everything solid, hard, sharp-edged, overladen'.[49] Talbert's 'simpler designs', however, were much 'less objectionable ... Everywhere there is much more rationality and down-to-earth artistic sensibility than in the work of the contemporary Gothicist architects. No wonder, then, that from the 1860's until his death in 1881 he was regarded as the leading designer of interiors.'[50]

Even before the success of his *Gothic Forms Applied to Furniture, Metal Work and Decoration For Domestic Purposes*, published by Birbeck in 1868,[51] Talbert had already

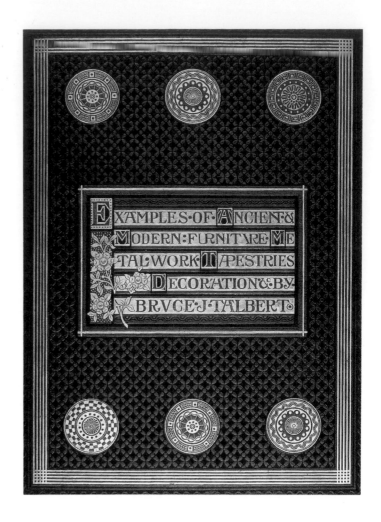

202 and **203** As a disciple of Street, Bruce Talbert (*above*) at first worked exclusively in the Gothic tradition. The linear framing, prunus blossom and abstract 'pies' on the cover of his second book of designs (*right*), published in 1876, documents his later absorption of Japanese influences.

designed furniture for Smith & Son of Dundee, Lamb's, Ogden's and Doveston, Bird & Hull, all of Manchester, Gillow's of Lancaster, Marsh & Jones of Leeds, and J.G. Crace of London; metalwork for the Coalbrookdale Iron-works in Telford, Skidmore's Coventry Art Manufactures Company and Cox & Sons; carpets for Brinton; tapestries for Cowlishaw, Nicol & Co.; and numerous textiles and wallpapers for Jeffrey & Co. Inscribed to G.E. Street, 'by his very obliged servant B.J. Talbert', *Gothic Forms* is stuffed with impressively confident designs for furniture, many with decorative detail of a quality and complexity previously seen principally in buildings (250 and 251). That Talbert was aware of the geometric basis of his style is clear: 'The recognition of this principle of economy combined with strength at once demands the adoption of a mode of framing more horizontal and vertical than at present in general use.' Furniture, he argues, should be subsidiary to other items of decoration: 'When the pictures are valuable, the quieter and more horizontal the furniture is the better, the subtle undulations of drapery, the elegances of pottery and illumination, not to mention the ever-changing curves of those for whose use the rooms are intended, will supply a sufficiency of graceful lines, rendered more valuable and pleasing by the contrast.'[52] Talbert's designs are more appealingly decorative than those of either Street or Eastlake and although his references to 'quieter' furniture may seem misleading to us, the pieces themselves often turn out to be more subdued in the flesh than the detailed drawings might suggest.

Gothic Forms was intended for use by cabinetmakers and furniture manufacturers; as well as the highly professional sectional drawings, Talbert included practical tips, like the recipe for 'dead' polish, to keep furniture clean despite city grime without the glittery effect of French polish and without destroying the natural tone of the wood ('½ gallon of Methylated Spirit; ½ lb Shellac, bleached; 1 oz of Gum of Benzoin, and ¼ oz of Gum Mastic. This is to be bruised well, and allowed to stand till it is dissolved').[53] Although he criticized excessive use of glue and veneers, Talbert was less fanatical than Eastlake, and wisely pronounced that 'there is the use as well as the abuse of things';[54] he argued that modern glues were excellent for strengthening tenons and he justified the inlay of woods too precious for use in the solid. In England, Talbert's book had much more influence than Eastlake's on popular domestic taste, and sub-Talbertian details dominated commercial furniture design for decades.

Talbert's tone in the introduction to *Examples of Ancient & Modern Furniture, Metal Work, Tapestries, Decoration & Etc*, published by Batsford in 1876, is rather more belligerent, as though he felt a need to defend himself. He took a swing at 'the revival of the so-called Queen Anne style', and laid into Chippendale, 'essentially a carver with a most redundant fancy [who] ignored every other principle of true work'; he apparently blamed Chippendale's influence for 'the monstrosities which are now-a-days so cheap and so plentiful'.[55] Many of the illustrations in this second book of Talbert designs are taken from detailed watercolours of interiors exhibited at the Royal Academy, many of which were in the possession of Sam Harris of Gillow's and Peter Graham of Jackson & Graham, two of his loyalest clients. Another watercolour, from the Academy of 1871, was then in the possession of Sir James Ramsden; the remaining designs were drawn by Talbert especially for this book, and many of the interiors have a distinctly Jacobean flavour (205). Although Talbert furniture designs were reproduced regularly in all the periodicals, including the *Workshop* (247 and 219), at his death the *Cabinet Maker and Art Furnisher* was in possession of over a hundred unpublished designs which were issued in book form in the 1880s by John O'Kane of New York as a 'unique series of elegant designs' (254), under the title *Fashionable Furniture*. Mr O'Kane greatly admired Talbert, 'the genius of whose pencil mainly lifted English Furniture into the improved position it now occupies'.[56] Even Christopher Dresser felt that *Gothic Forms* compared 'favourably with all other works on furniture'[57] – praise from Dresser is praise indeed.

Prize-winning pieces at three international fairs neatly illustrate the range of Talbert's style: the Pericles Sideboard, shown in Paris in 1867 by Holland's and purchased by the Empress of France (206); the Pet Sideboard, shown in

204 and **205** The Gothic revival modulates into the aesthetic movement: *above*, interior of The Limes, Dulwich, by Theodore Howard (1881); *below*, 'Old English' interior by Bruce Talbert, from *Examples of Ancient & Modern Furniture . . .* (1876).

206 The Pericles Sideboard, designed by Bruce Talbert and exhibited by its manufacturers, Holland & Sons, at the 1867 Paris Exhibition, where it was described by the *Art Journal* 'as certainly the most distinguished amongst competing Gothic works'.

Left **207** Talbert's Juno Cabinet, made by Jackson & Graham in their favourite medium, ebony inlaid with ivory. It won the Grand Prix at the Exposition Universelle in Paris in 1878.

Right **208** 'Medieval furniture': designs by Charles Bevan published in 1866.

London in 1872 by Gillow's and purchased by the South Kensington Museum (189); and the Juno Cabinet, shown by Jackson & Graham in Paris in 1878 and purchased for £2000 by the Viceroy of India (207). As with almost all stylistic labelling, it is a gross over-simplification to describe the Pericles simply as Gothic, the Pet as Old English and the Juno as Aesthetic, for there are as many similarities as differences, particularly in the overall structure: all three are firmly controlled in both the horizontal and vertical planes and decorated with flat naturalistic detail – Geometric, in other words. Yet each does have its own dominant characteristics. The most markedly 'Gothic' elements of the Pericles Sideboard – so named because of the sculptured decoration and the frieze quotations from Shakespeare's play – are found in the metalwork, in the capitals and in the trefoiled and crocketed pediment. The 'Old English' character of the Pet Sideboard is principally displayed in the bobbin-turned decoration, in the use of carved rather than inlaid panels, and in the fumed oak carcass – Talbert, incidentally, recommended liquid ammonia to darken furniture, in preference to stain. The Juno Cabinet is not only orientally black but also prominently displays two other key elements of 'aesthetic movement' design: the peacock (at the centre of the pediment) and the lily (in the door panels of the base).

On visiting Talbert's own house in Euston Square, the *Cabinet Maker and Art Furnisher* admired the way the sombre decoration set off the designer's collection of antique furniture, and took special note of 'various ebonised articles . . . for which Talbert set the fashion'.[58] In placing Talbert in the stylistic scheme of things it is important to remember that even when the Japanese influence is strongest the underlying structure of his design remained Gothic. Take, for example, a corner hanging cabinet (255 and 256), commercially made in ebonized mahogany in fairly large numbers: despite the gold on black stencilling of overlapping 'pies' (a decorative motif from Japanese porcelain) and the linearity of outline, the inspiration is inherently European and medieval. It is only in his excellent designs for textiles that Talbert might justifiably be deemed to fit more snugly into the next chapter; the 'Sunflower flocks' he produced for Metford Warner of Jeffrey & Co. 'became a byword in the trade'.[59]

Relatively little information has yet surfaced about another prolific designer of furniture in the Geometric Gothic style, Charles Bevan, the dates of whose birth and death are still unknown. Typical of what Handley-Read called 'the sledge-hammer blows of self-assertion and solid geometry of the 1860s and 1870s'[60] is Bevan's first published design, a davenport illustrated in the *Building News* of 1865 (260). This appealingly chunky piece of furniture, with its sophisticated geometric decoration, could not possibly be the work of an innocent outsider; given the similarities with the earlier furniture of Seddon, it has been suggested that Bevan worked at some stage for the Seddon family of cabinetmakers. The design of Bevan's 'Medieval Cabinet Organ' (263), illustrated in the *Building News* of the following year, displays yet greater self-confidence, in a manner Handley-Read described on his file copy of the engraving: 'High Victorian at saturation'. Handley-Read also noticed in this design Bevan's familiarity with avant-garde architectural styles: 'chamfers à la Seddon'; 'Shaw/Burges finials'. Luckily, a large group of totally documented Bevan furniture survives from this period: the pieces supplied by

Marsh & Jones of Leeds to the mill-owner Titus Salt Jnr in November 1865 and removed in 1872 to Milner Field, the new family home designed by Thomas Harris – 'a Wagnerian Gothic retreat in the woods above Saltaire',[61] the model industrial town built by Lockwood & Mawson to the order of Salt's philanthropic father. Comparisons with the rich variety of documented pieces for Titus Salt (265) permit other Marsh & Jones pieces to be firmly attributed to Bevan (187, 266 and 269), and an impressive corpus of work has therefore been identified.

More snippets of information about Charles Bevan can be gleaned from contemporary periodicals. In the summer of 1865 Bevan took out advertisements for his New Registered Reclining Chair (267), which he claimed 'expands the chest and gives general ease and comfort to the body ... well adapted for clubhouses, hotels, and gentleman's libraries'.[62] At the Paris Exhibition of 1867, Lamb's of Manchester exhibited a bookcase designed by Bevan, more complex but of a similar form to an undated Marsh & Jones labelled example (268). At this time the press noted that Bevan lived at 66 Margaret Street, round the corner from the Cavendish Square showrooms of Marsh & Jones, later Marsh, Jones & Cribb. By 1872 Bevan had founded his own firm, 'C. Bevan and Son, Designers, Wood Carvers and Manufacturers of Art Furniture',[63] in partnership with his son George Alfred Bevan. This same year the South Kensington Museum bought, for £30, two ebonized cabinets designed by Bevan to display Doulton pottery, and made by Gillow's (264). Like Talbert, Bevan occasionally reversed his usual practice of inlaying darker woods onto lighter oak, walnut or sycamore carcasses. Some of this ebonized furniture of Bevan's is decorative in detail, and, as the *House Furnisher* noted, there are other 'highly meritorious designs ... in which structural as well as ornamental excellence was aimed at and successfully attained'.[64]

In the pioneering *Catalogue of an Exhibition of Victorian and Edwardian Decorative Arts* (Victoria and Albert Museum, 1952), the name of Charles Bevan nowhere appears, although the evidence of furniture now known proves him to have been a designer of significance. Bevan was rediscovered in the 1960s by Charles Handley-Read, who became obsessed with his work. On the back of an invitation to Colnaghi's Dürer Exhibition of 18 June 1971, he scribbled: 'Is it true, and if so is it significant that the Bevan bros [*sic*] designed NO CHAIRS for Salt?'[65] – we know now that the answer to both questions is: 'No'.

The business of attaching designers' names to Gothic revival furniture is still problematic, and there is plenty of fine undocumented furniture of the period which it is possible only to describe as 'by someone' – by someone good that is, rather than by one of those incompetents whose names regularly appeared below 'original designs' in the *Furniture Gazette* and other periodicals: names like W.C. Brangwyn, Adolf Janquet and Owen Davis (the last two were also published in individual volumes). Although it would be tidier to know the designers of all finely composed

209 Ebonized dining chairs designed by Charles Bevan and made by Marsh & Jones of Leeds in the late 1860s.

architectural furniture, the naming of pieces can be misleading. Just because Talbert and other talented designers are known to have worked for Cox & Sons, the American writer Walter Smith was tempted to describe the indefensible mantlepiece and reading stand by Cox (278) as 'correct in principle and most artistically executed'.[66] The knowledge that a bookcase and chair (279) were produced by the reputable firm of Cooper & Holt does not change them from what they are: amazingly awful amalgams of fashionable Gothic motifs, mindlessly plundered from the published works of Talbert and Eastlake. These two must also take some of the blame for a Gothic bath (270) made of pollard oak inlaid with light oak and decorated with figures painted in blue against a gold ground, which the Birmingham firm of J. Fell & Co. sent to the Melbourne Exhibition of 1878 – 'remarkable in many respects',[67] the *Builder* commented whilst generously failing to specify in what respects this Fell bath was, indeed, so remarkable. In the same year Mr A.C. Ebbutt of Croydon sent a gigantically Gothic cabinet to the Paris Exposition Universelle; the *Art Journal* illustrated the cabinet in their review, lamely admitting that it was 'impossible to describe its more ornamental parts'.[68]

It would be incorrect to assume, however, that all well-composed Geometric Gothic furniture must necessarily have been designed by the known names. Just as Charles Bevan's was forgotten for nearly a hundred years, so the work of an architect called Theodore Howard may turn out to be more important than is presently reckoned. Inoffensive neo-Puginesque furniture made by the family firm, Howard of Berners Street, has already filtered into respectable collections; alongside the engraving published in the *Building News* in 1881 of the interior of The Limes in Dulwich, designed by Theodore Howard (204), Handley-Read inscribed the back-handed compliment: 'nothing here that could not have come out of Talbert'.[69] Some of the lesser-known cabinetmakers were also capable of producing finely designed furniture, such as the wardrobe sent by Dyer & Watts of Islington to the Paris Exhibition of 1867, the stencilled decoration 'as refreshing to the eye as if the woods imitated had been of the rarest and most costly'.[70] Like Talbert's Pericles Sideboard, it was purchased by the Empress of France.

Nor is it wise to dismiss all popular manuals as second-rate simply because they appealed to a mass middle-class audience. In their introduction to *Polychromatic Decoration as Applied to Buildings in the Mediaeval Styles*, published in 1882, William and George Audsley expressed the hope that 'their work will be of great benefit . . . to those amateurs who amuse themselves by decorating their own dwellings, furniture etc. or who lend practical help in beautifying village or country churches'. Although the Audsley designs for stencilled decoration were derived from the same original sources studied by the likes of Burges and Seddon, they are none the less admirable for the sympathy and understanding with which they are reproduced. Similarly the Gothic designs for furniture illustrated by Richard Charles in his *The Cabinet Maker – A Journal of Design*, published in 1868, need not be dismissed as merely derivative, for those bearing his own name are very superior to the illustrations by Owen Davis (for Black House, Rathbone Place) and Alfred Lormier, a French cabinetmaker working with Jackson & Graham.

In an obsequious letter to the *Furniture Gazette*, Richard Charles acknowledged his debt to E.W. Godwin as well as to Bruce Talbert: 'I entertain a very high opinion of their work, and thank them for their effort in assisting me and the trade generally in elevating the furniture trade.' Whatever else, Geometric Gothic furniture was a uniquely English style of design and, at its best, ranks amongst the most successful artefacts of the Gothic revival in Europe.

210 The barristers' reading room in an unidentified provincial court house, depicted by Joseph Wake in a watercolour dated 1865. The unpretentious furniture is clearly derived from Puginian precedents, but the architectural details reflect various High Gothic sources: G.E. Street, Gilbert Scott and – in the curiously shaped braces supporting the roof – even Viollet-le-Duc.

The 'Muscular Goths'

William Butterfield's major domestic building was commissioned in 1853 by his brother-in-law, Benjamin Storey: this photograph of the drawing room at Milton Ernest Hall was taken *c.* 1875 (**211**). No fully documented domestic furniture by Butterfield is known, though he designed quantities of ecclesiastical and institutional furnishing, including the tables and benches of the 1870s still at Keble College, Oxford (**212**; the large painting is by G. F. Watts).

Surviving furniture by George Edmund Street is also rare; it includes these puritanically plain tables (**213**) for the students' bedrooms at Cuddesdon College, Oxford (1852–4), and the architect's own bookcase made in 1865 by Holland & Sons (**214**). The furniture for the Barristers' Room in the Law Courts, London (**216**), unfinished at Street's death in 1881, was supplied by Collinson & Lock. William White, another 'Muscular Gothic' architect, designed this chair in 1850 together with other furniture for the rectory at St Columba Major, Cornwall (**215**).

Butterfield's unexecuted design of *c.* 1890 for an altar candlestick at St Augustine's, Bournemouth (**217**), is more boldly geometric than White's wrought-iron pricket stick (**218**) inset with glass and stone cabochons, designed 1860–4 for the chapel at Bishop's Court, Exeter. James Brooks took the Gothic to east London in a magnificent series of brick churches: this interior perspective of St Michael's, Mark Street, Shoreditch, was painted by Axel Haig in June 1868 (**219**).

211

212

213

214

215

216

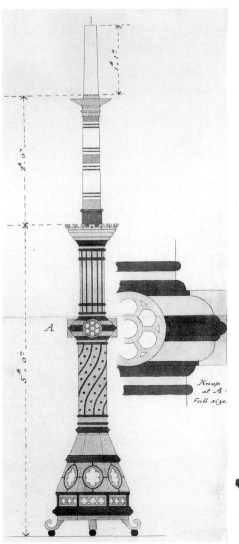

217

218

219

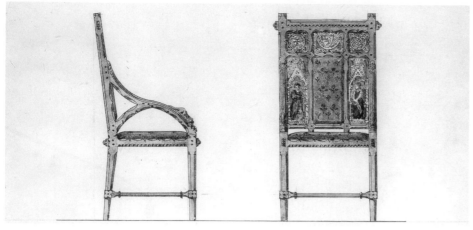

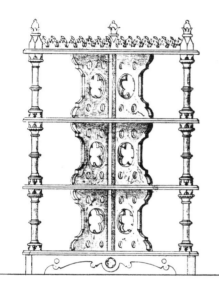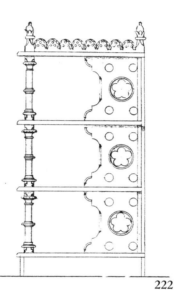

John Pollard Seddon

Seddon's best-known piece of furniture, a cabinet for his architectural drawings, was decorated by Rossetti, Burne-Jones and Madox Brown with panels on the theme of King René's Honeymoon; it was exhibited on the Morris, Marshall, Faulkner & Co. stand at the 1862 International Exhibition (226); the detail (225) shows Rossetti's 'Music' panel. A stereoscopic slide illustrates two more Seddon pieces at the same exhibition, an oak chair and an inlaid roll-top desk, the 'rawness of ornament' of which was criticized by the *Building News* (221). Seddon's drawing of the chair has survived (220); different versions known to have been made include one in solid ebony (227). Most of Seddon's furniture was manufactured by the family firm of cabinetmakers founded by his great-great-grandfather, George Seddon, and expanded

225

226

by his father, Thomas; J. P. Seddon's earlier furniture (**224**) is often stamped 'T. Seddon. New Bond Street'.

Over two thousand drawings for architecture and the decorative arts were presented to the Victoria and Albert Museum in 1896 by Seddon's daughter, including this drawing of 4 January 1865 for an architectural bookcase (**223**) and a design for a whatnot, dated 1860 (**222**). As many other designs were published in contemporary journals – this organ, for example, in the *Building News* in 1865 (**228**) – the Geometric Gothic furniture of J. P. Seddon is among the best documented of the period. It was normally in oak, with stylised foliate inlay, tongue-and-groove panelling and ebonized supporting columns; long enamelled brass hinges were also a favourite device.

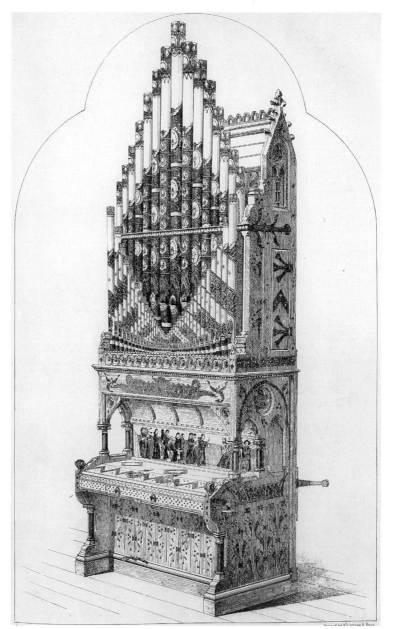

227

228

Alfred Waterhouse

Despite a large architectural practice, Waterhouse designed little domestic furniture: the earliest known piece, a centre table for Sir Joseph Pease, was made by Hardcastle & Hall of Harrogate in December 1867 (**233**; the bust is Alfred Drury's 'The Age of Innocence', 1897). He also designed all the furniture for the Earl of Selborne's Blackmoor House, Hampshire (**229**): a sturdy spindle-backed chair, supplied by James Capel in 1872 or 1873, is shown beside a Jeckyll cast-iron grate similar to those used by Waterhouse at Blackmoor (**231**).

Waterhouse's extensive institutional work in Manchester began in 1859 with the Assize Courts, for which this table was designed (**230**). Many drawings survive for the furniture at Manchester Town Hall (**232** and **237**), on which he worked from 1869 to 1876; less elaborate furniture was installed in Reading Town Hall in 1874 (**236**). From 1870 to 1883 Waterhouse rebuilt the Duke of Westminster's Eaton Hall; the Canterbury Pilgrims frieze in the morning room (**234**) and the bird panels in an ante-room (**235**) were both painted by Henry Stacy Marks.

229

230

231

232

234

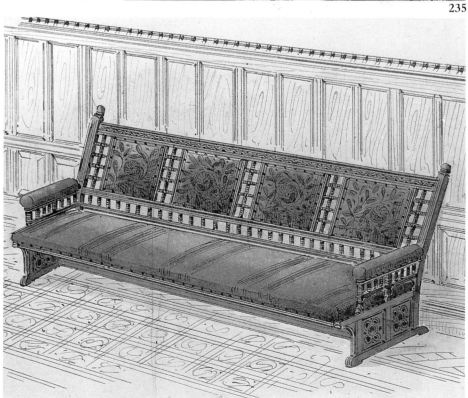

235

233

236

237

238

239

240

'Hints on Household Taste'

C. L. Eastlake's influential *Hints on Household Taste*, first published in 1868, was based on a series of articles written in 1865 for the *Queen*. Eastlake executed many of the engraved illustrations himself, repeatedly emphasizing his basic demands: furniture must be made in solid wood by traditional methods, its form and decoration decreed largely by structural necessity (**240**). Favoured decoration for chairs was simple chip-carving and turning (**238** and **239**); for larger pieces he recommended uplifting inscriptions (**241**). Although a certain amount of his furniture was made on licence by Jackson & Graham, Eastlake was not a commercial designer, but earned his living from 1878 to 1898 as Keeper of the National Gallery; the many variants on published Eastlake designs were thus produced piratically by different commercial cabinetmakers – compare the engraving of a 'drawing-room chiffonier' in *Hints* (**242**) with a cabinet is inspired (**245**). Eastlake also illustrated work by E. J. Tarver, A. W. Blomfield (**243**) and Clement Heaton (**246**). In America Eastlake was the unwilling parent of a whole 'Eastlake style': this Mason & Hamlin organ of 1876 was erroneously described as 'without fault . . . its subdued decoration . . . conceived in the Eastlake style' (**244**).

241

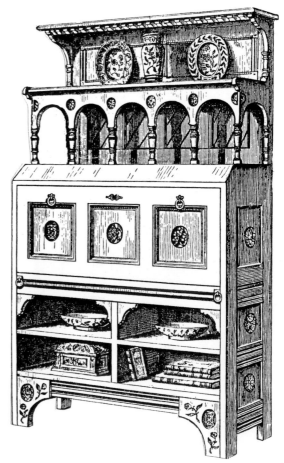

242

243

244

245

246

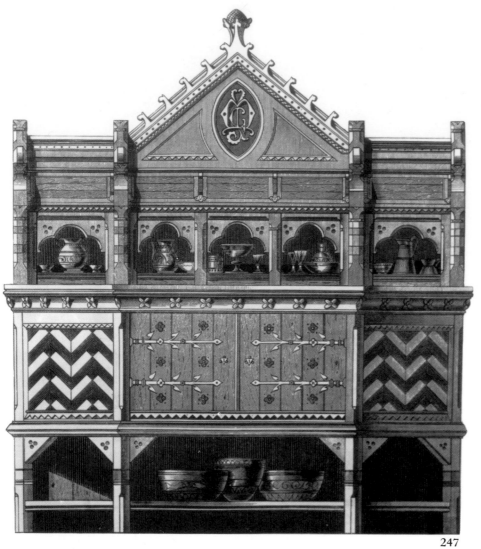

247

248

Bruce Talbert

Bruce Talbert's reputation rests today primarily on two published books of designs, *Gothic Forms Applied to Furniture, Metal Work and Decoration For Domestic Purposes* (1868), which included two typically angular tables (**250** and **251**), and *Examples of Ancient & Modern Furniture, Metalwork, Tapestries, Decoration & Etc* (1876), which documents his move from a predominantly Gothic idiom to the newly fashionable interest in the 'Old English' style (**248**). He was a fine, prolific draughtsman, publishing in all the specialist journals, including Professor Schnorr's *The Workshop* of 1871 (**247** and **249**), and in America, in *Fashionable Furniture* (**254**).

Talbert's architectural training is revealed in the skilled structural extrapolation of a dining chair, engraved in *Gothic Forms* (**257**; see also **188**). Initially he tended to favour fumed oak, embellished with relief carving and wrought-brass hinges rather than inlay (**252**; the pottery is by William De Morgan); however, firms such as Gillow's preferred him to work in more luxurious woods, such as walnut, and to use bold inlays (**253**; the jardinière on the lower shelf was designed by J. P. Seddon for the Fulham Pottery).

Over the years Talbert designed prize-winning exhibition furniture for most of the leading cabinemakers. He became an

249

250

251

innovative designer of stencilled decoration for ebonized furniture, seen to advantage in both the engraved design for a hanging corner cabinet (255) and the executed piece (256). Talbert's standard dining chair (258) was manufactured with slight variations in oak and mahogany – even ebonized – by all his regular cabinetmakers. This satinwood dining chair (259), though unmarked, was probably made by Gillow's: it is another example of what the *Cabinet Maker and Art Furnisher* referred to as 'the versatility of Talbert's genius'.

252

253

254

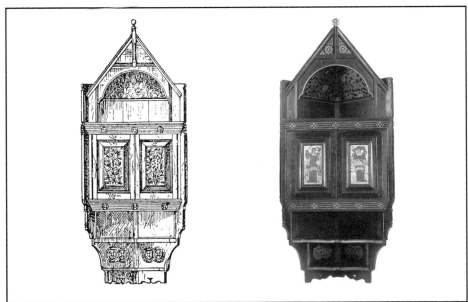

255

256

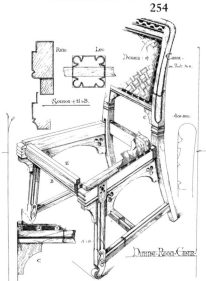

257

258

259

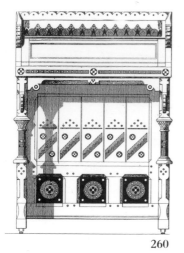

260

261

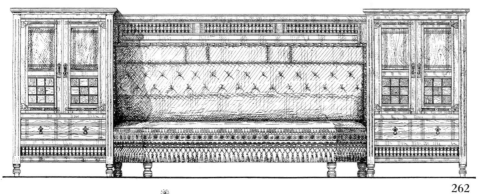

262

Charles Bevan

Bevan's first published design, a davenport in the *Building News* of 1865 (**260–261**), reveals his already well-formed understanding of the architectural qualities of Gothic revival furniture. The chamfered framing to the fielded panels of inlay on the davenport, and the architectural detailing of his 'Medieval Cabinet Organ' (**263**), published the following year, suggest that he may have been apprenticed to J. P. Seddon, though nothing has yet been discovered about his early life or training.

Bevan also turned his hand to the design of space-saving furniture for suburban homes, such as the 'drawing room commode' illustrated in the *House Furnisher* in 1871 (**262**), and to special exhibition furniture, such as the ebonized cabinet made by Gillow's to display Doulton terracotta reliefs by George Tinworth at the 1872 International Exhibition (**264**).

Fortunately, records survive for a major Bevan commission, the furniture made 1865–6 for Titus Salt Jnr and installed in

263

264

1872 in Milner Field, the Gothic mansion designed by Thomas Harris. The Salt furniture was made by the Leeds cabinetmakers Marsh & Jones (from 1872 Marsh, Jones & Cribb). Bevan's sycamore washstand (**265**) from the main bedroom at Milner Field, with its blue-grey *bardiglio* marble top, was made by Pattison; the inlay is by a Spaniard called Vert. It was invoiced on 16 November 1865 at £20 16s 0d.

Marsh & Jones marketed a quantity of Bevan furniture almost identical to the Titus Salt commission, including this music stand (**266**) and occasional table (**269**). They also made on licence the New Registered Reclining Chair (**267**) which Bevan first advertised in the trade press in 1865. The design of other imposing Geometric Gothic furniture bearing Marsh & Jones labels is confidently attributed to Bevan on stylistic grounds (**268**).

265

266

267

269

268

270

271

272

273–277

Commercial design

Wholesale manufacturers tended to bowdlerize pieces illustrated in the specialist journals. The results were predictably bad: J. Fell & Co., for example, had the temerity to send this bath (**270**) to the 1878 Melbourne Exhibition. Richard Charles attempted to capitalize on the manufacturer's need for new and varied designs with numerous short-run publishing ventures, including the *Cabinet Maker: A Journal of Design* of 1868, from which this sofa, armchair and side chairs are extracted (**271–277**). In published comment on the 1876 Philadelphia Exhibition, Walter Smith recommended this Cox & Sons furniture (**278**) for 'its substantial, massive design, correct in principle and most artistically executed'; Smith was equally mistaken in praising this Cooper & Holt bookcase as 'an education in the principles of art applied to industry' (**279**).

278
279

CHAPTER FIVE

From 'Nankin' to Bedford Park

280 Pair of cast-iron firedogs adapted by Thomas Jeckyll from his design for the railings of the Barnard, Bishop & Barnard pavilion at the 1876 Philadelphia exhibition (see 315).

At the Third General Conference of Architects in 1874, J.J. Stevenson delivered a lecture in which he argued the case for a middle way between the 'very dull prose' of the Classic style and the 'screeching, sensational poetry, or Daily Telegraphese'[1] of the Gothic revival. By the mid-1870s the middle way Stevenson recommended had already been branded 'Queen Anne', a style which found its most persuasive expression in Bedford Park, a garden suburb speculation conceived in 1875 by Jonathan Carr, initially with E.W. Godwin as architect but later – from 1877 – with Richard Norman Shaw as its key co-ordinator. Although the Queen Anne style had, as its name implies, firm roots in European domestic architecture of the early eighteenth century, the impetus towards change in the way of furnishing these comfortable new houses came not from Europe but from Japan. Indeed, it could be argued that much of the individual detailing of 'Queen Anne' buildings also derived directly from a reawakening of interest in oriental art – for example, the stylized sunflowers in the gables of Shaw's Lowther Lodge (now the Royal Geographic Society) in Kensington Gore, designed in 1872.

Trading links with Japan were reopened as a result of Commander Perry's successful expedition in 1854, and within a couple of years Whistler recorded the excitement of discovering in Paris newly imported batches of Japanese woodcuts. In England, though Burges was already collecting oriental artefacts in the 1850s, the earliest opportunity for a wider public to see any quantity of Japanese art came at the 1862 International Exhibition, where Rutherford Alcock, the British Consul in Tokyo, exhibited an instructive and varied collection. The impact on artistic circles was instant: Rossetti and Whistler became particularly keen competitors for unusual examples of blue and white 'Nankin China', as porcelain from Japan was called. Following the painters' lead, their patrons also began to collect oriental porcelain; so popular was the craze that Sir Henry Thompson, a surgeon (and founder of Golders Green Crematorium), was persuaded in 1876 to pay the dealer Murray Marks an unheard-of £250 for a pair of 'Nankin' vases. The storerooms of the principal importers became favourite haunts of the artistic elite, and Marks claimed that his business card (281) was designed jointly by Rossetti, Whistler and Morris. In 1875 Marks neatly confirmed the connection between a taste for oriental works of art and the decline in popularity of the Gothic style by commissioning Shaw to redesign his Oxford Street shop, which became, with its distinctive creamy coloured woodwork, an important landmark in the Queen Anne revival. Even such committed Goths as William Burges were ready to admit of the Japanese that 'these hitherto unknown barbarians appear not only to know all that the middle ages knew but in some respects are beyond them and us as well'.[2] Though Burges never wavered in his personal taste for elaborate figurative decoration in the High Victorian Gothic style, the younger generation all responded in their work to oriental influences,

forming part of what is now called, in its complexity of different historical echoes, the aesthetic movement.

So popular did the cult of Japan and its attendant aestheticism become that they attracted the inspired attentions of punsters and parodists. W.S. Gilbert's Japanese skit *The Mikado* and his lampoon of Oscar Wilde in *Patience* are both well known, more so than the Gerald Du Maurier poem 'Oscar' (first published in *Punch*), which describes the typical Japan-loving aesthete as 'quite too consummately utter, as well as too utterly quite'. Developing Du Maurier's joke, W.G. Eaton published his *Utterly Utter Quadrille* (283), on the cover of which Whistler and Wilde are depicted dancing with two suitably wan paisley-clad ladies, framed by the ubiquitous lily and sunflower, entwined, in order not to ignore another essential emblem, with peacock feathers. The text of the song inside offers Wildean lines like 'I'll prove to my true love untrue', followed by a series of disconnected phrases overheard at an aesthetic cocktail party: 'Too, Too'; 'How do you like London?'; 'Oh, George!'; etc. The refrain of the *Utterly Utter Quadrille* amusingly serenades a 'Half Moon Union'. Despite, or perhaps because of, critical attention in the press, the oriental style in interior design remained perennially fashionable: in 1894 Mr R. Isayama, 'a Japanese artist of long and varied experience', still found it worthwhile to advertise his 'skill and success . . . in the application of pure Japanese designs – mostly characteristic and fascinating'.[3]

Many artists, however, were much more serious about oriental art than public caricature might suggest, and although the potential for genuinely revolutionary progress was never realized in England to the same extent that it was

281 Murray Marks, dealer in 'Nankin' ware, claimed that his visiting card was designed jointly by Morris, Rossetti and Whistler.

283 The aesthetic movement and its symbols, the lily, peacock and sunflower, were parodied in popular music of the 1880s.

284 Interior of the Chelsea house designed by A. H. Mackmurdo for the painter Mortimer Menpes, 1893–5: one of the most authentically Japanese designs of the period.

282 This design for an Anglo-Japanese drawing room by E. W. Godwin was published in a catalogue of Godwin's furniture issued by the cabinetmaker William Watt in 1877. The all-over decoration marks the interior as Victorian, but the lightness of form in the furnishings shows how fashionable taste had swung against the ponderous Gothic of the previous generation.

in France or America, a number of original statements were made. In 1893, for instance, A.H. Mackmurdo designed an interesting house for the Australian painter Mortimer Menpes on the corner of Cadogan Gardens and Symons Street, the fenestration of which remains intact, though the building itself now serves as the customer collection centre for the Sloane Square department store Peter Jones. Motivated partly by his consuming admiration of Whistler, Menpes had travelled to the East in 1891 and returned with materials which he and Mackmurdo adapted for use throughout the Chelsea house (284), including several vases

which Menpes himself had decorated while in Japan. Although merely imitative rather than genuinely inventive, the use of space in Menpes's hall nevertheless points towards the creative orientalism of Frank Lloyd Wright.

Not all the cultural traffic travelled from East to West: some went in the other direction. One European architect who settled permanently in Japan, Roger Josiah Conder (1852–1920), had been a pupil of Burges and designed many Gothic-style buildings in Imperial Tokyo, including the headquarters of the Kaitakushi Export Company, a new university and the Shintomiza Theatre, in recognition of

which he was made a member of the Order of the Rising Sun – albeit only fourth class.

The earliest surviving English furniture of this period with a positively Japanese quality was designed between 1865 and 1869 by Thomas Jeckyll (1827–81) for Edward Green, at Heath Old Hall in Wakefield. The furniture was later removed to Ken Hill in Norfolk, an attractive house in eighteenth-century style built for the Green family to designs by J.J. Stevenson, who had made his name in 1871 with the Red House in Bayswater, often referred to as the beginning of a 'Re-Renaissance'[4] (by Ashbee, unkindly, as 'Queen in Anne-ity').[5] Although the structure of the Heath Old Hall sideboard (312) is basically Jacobean, the design of the relief-carved decoration clearly derives from Jeckyll's known admiration of Japanese prints. In a letter of 26 September 1866, commenting on some furniture designs submitted to Edward Green, Jeckyll wrote: 'I like the Chinese looking one';[6] he may have been referring to a circular table which does indeed look more Chinese than Japanese but remains, nevertheless, one of the most successfully inventive pieces of furniture of the whole aesthetic movement (313).

In 1870 Jeckyll designed a new wing for the Ionides's house at No.1 Holland Park. The drawing room was redecorated in the 1880s by Morris and Company, but the Jeckyll fireplace and overmantle were retained; they were specially designed to display the obligatory collection of blue and white porcelain (314). Jeckyll's new billiard room, of 1872, was described in 1897 as 'a happy example of quasi-Japanese treatment, which has in later years suffered by travesties so that its original charm no longer impresses one'.[7] The designer Lewis F. Day conjectured that 'hundreds of Japanese trays must have been slaughtered'[8] to decorate the panelled walls, and congratulated Jeckyll on producing a convincing Anglo-Japanese billiard table. Much of the furnishing for 'Aleco' Ionides was probably supplied for his marriage in September 1875. It includes Jeckyll's beautifully detailed padoukwood desk (316), the drawers of which have ebony mouldings and gilt-brass handles in the Chinese taste. From 1873 Jeckyll also helped decorate the home of Charles Augustus Howell, friend and agent of the Pre-Raphaelites – it was Howell who had organized the exhumation on 5 October 1869 of Lizzie Siddall, in order to recover a manuscript volume of poetry Rossetti regretted burying with his wife (Howell also spread the rumour that Lizzie's fabled hair had continued to grow after death, until it entirely filled her coffin). Jeckyll installed in Howell's house several of his cast-iron grates, the designs for which were first registered at the Patent Office by Barnard, Bishop & Barnard in 1873; a Norwich man himself, Jeckyll designed numerous chairs, tables and benches, as well as grates, for his local foundry (the work is of a very high quality; sometimes monogrammed with three superimposed Bs, it is mostly decorated in low relief with catherine-wheeling chrysanthemums, spread-eagled butterflies, and other orientally inspired motifs). The sunflower railings that surrounded Barnard, Bishop & Barnard's iron pavilion (315), a notable success at the 1876 Philadelphia Exhibition and again in Paris in 1878, were re-used by Jeckyll as fire-dogs (280). Executed in gilt-bronze as well as black-lacquered iron, they are the epitome of Anglo-Japanese taste.

Thomas Jeckyll was subsequently involved in the creation of one of the nineteenth century's finest surviving interiors, the dining room at 49 Princes Gate, known as the Peacock Room (320). The Liverpool shipping magnate Frederick Leyland bought the house from Lord Somers in 1876 and made three stipulations in Jeckyll's redesign of the dining room: pride of place was to be given to *La Princesse du Pays de la Porcelaine*, Whistler's 1864 portrait of Christina Spartali wearing a Japanese kimono; there were to be sufficient shelves for the Japanese porcelain collection; the walls were to be hung with the Cordova embossed leather Leyland had purchased for £1000 from Murray Marks, who claimed the hangings had been brought to England by Catherine of Aragon on her marriage. No sooner had Jeckyll finished in the dining room than Whistler turned up with his painter protégés the Greaves brothers and set about covering the whole space – expensive leather hangings, Jeckyll's sideboard, the panelled shelves, everything – with turquoise and gold peacocks (292). Leyland, who was occupied with business in Liverpool at the time, had given permission only for minor changes, along the lines of the staircase panels Whistler had painted with pale pink and white flowers on a dark green ground, imitating Japanese aventurine lacquer. He returned in February 1877 to find Whistler holding open house to admirers and distributing printed leaflets on 'The Peacock Room. Harmony in Blue and Gold'. Leyland was furious, and refused until October to pay for the work; even then the cheque was for two thousand pounds, rather than the agreed guineas, and Whistler wrote to him: 'I have enfin received your cheque ... shorn of shillings ... Well, I suppose that will do – upon the principle that anything will do – Bon Dieu what does it matter! The work just created *alone remains* the fact – and that it happened in the house of this one or that one is merely anecdote – so that in some future dull Vasari you may also go down to posterity like the man who paid Correggio in pennies!'[9] In fact, both Jeckyll's architectural design and Whistler's decoration were immediately acknowledged for their quality and Leyland's distress, in reality, concerned not money but the painter's flirtatious attention to his wife. 'Sir', Leyland wrote to Whistler, 'I am told that on Friday last you were seen walking with my wife at Lord's Cricket Ground ... if after this intimation I find you in her society again I will publicly horsewhip you.'[10]

Whistler made no attempt to patch up the quarrel with his powerful patron. Quite the contrary. In 1879 he painted *The Gold Scab*, a caricature portrait of the bearded Leyland as a piano-playing peacock, dressed in one of his habitual frilly shirts and surrounded by bags of money (319). At the Whistler bankruptcy auction, conducted by Sotheby's on 12 February 1880, the painter insisted that the portrait remain on open display in his studio, despite all Leyland's efforts to secure a court order for its removal; the picture is now owned by the California Palace of the Legion of Honor. In 1903, the year of Whistler's death, the Peacock Room was carefully removed from 49 Princes Gate – by then the Afghan Embassy – and offered for sale at Orbach's gallery in Bond Street; it was bought the following year by Charles Freer, of Washington D.C. Forgetting Jeckyll's vital contribution to the scheme, *The Studio* called the Peacock Room 'a remarkable monument to the courage of one man's convictions'[11] – Jeckyll had neglected to live long enough to claim his share of the credit; in 1877 he had gone mad and he died insane in 1881.

The most influential designer of Anglo-Japanese furniture, E.W. Godwin (1833–86), began his architectural career as the youthful confidant of William Burges and a keen admirer of the Gothic idiom. Born and brought up in Bristol, Godwin's first major commission, secured in 1861, was for the Town Hall in Northampton, a building which Eastlake correctly described as 'strongly influenced by the then prevalent taste for Italian Gothic . . . which Mr Ruskin advocated'.[12] However, in the furniture at Northampton, drawings for which are dated January 1865 (321), Godwin already revealed his desire to simplify the structure to essential elements and limit decoration to a minimum; though Gothic in form, the chairs and tables for the Council Chamber are almost childishly simple in design and must, at

the time, have been exceedingly difficult to accept. In his first substantial private commission, Dromore Castle in County Limerick, Godwin was given licence by the young Lord Limerick to take his ideas on interior design to their radical conclusion – though again within a Gothic shell.

Godwin began work on Dromore in 1866 while on a trip to Ireland with Burges, the pair of them no doubt delighted by the thought of constructing a modern-day medieval castle with fortifications of sufficient practical strength to repel a Fenian rebellion. The drawings for the Dromore furniture were executed between 1867 and 1869. Some, like 'The Eagle Chair' (322), were a direct development from the Northampton designs of 1865; this particular chair was also illustrated in the catalogue of Godwin furniture published by the cabinetmaker William Watt in 1877, and though many examples must have been manufactured none has yet been located. The Dromore pieces presently known to have survived (331) dramatically illustrate Godwin's qualities as a designer. Whatever the precise stylistic origins of his inspiration – and there is evidence of his interest in Greek, Egyptian and Jacobean design as well as Japanese – there are wide differences between his response to demands for formal simplicity and the reactions of Eastlake's disciples. When the Dromore pieces are considered alongside the ebonized 'buffet' Godwin designed for his own use in 1867 (324) and these are compared with Eastlake's published designs of the same date (241) the contrast is clear. The

285 and **286** E. W. Godwin (*above*) was called by Max Beerbohm 'the greatest aesthete of them all'; his avant-garde interiors and furniture were paralleled by radical architectural experiment such as this design of June 1878 – later revised – for the painter Frank Miles's house, 44 Tite Street, London.

differences are largely due to Godwin's determination, developed from his appreciation of oriental culture, that domestic design should 'be as light as is consistent with strength [and] in these high-pressure nervous times that the common objects of everyday life should be quiet, simple and unobtrusive in their beauty'.[13]

It is apparent from his design for the dining room buffet at Dromore (289)[14] that Godwin's demand for formal simplicity in the composition of furniture did not preclude decorative adventurousness in the interior setting. Many of the rooms were, in their way, as extravagant as Burges's. In the drawing room, the seriously oriental furniture, all made at William Watt's Art Furniture Warehouse in Bloomsbury, was in 'mahogany ebonized by penetrating stain and dry polished';[15] these black chairs, settees and central ottoman were then upholstered in 'yellow satin ... like that known in China as Imperial yellow',[16] which must have looked wonderfully exotic against walls washed in blue and green and a dark-boarded ceiling decorated with Celtic scrolls – all in a fairy castle on the banks of the Shannon.

Having established at Dromore a liberating independence of expression, Godwin went on to design a number of inventive interiors, both for himself and for various artist friends. For almost a decade Godwin lived with the actress Ellen Terry – only fifteen when they first met – and their son, Edward Gordon Craig, followed his father in becoming a professional theatre designer, the activity for which

Godwin was best known in his lifetime. The nursery in their terraced house in Taverton Street was decorated with Japanese prints; they were also among the first to buy wickerwork chairs. 'The whole effect', according to the actor Johnston Forbes-Robertson, was 'what students of my time would have called "awfully jolly"'.[17] Godwin described the colour of their drawing room frieze as 'that green sometimes seen at the stem end of a pineapple leaf when the other end has faded – indeed I may as well confess that most of the colours of the rooms have been gathered from the pineapple'.[18] Sharpness of colour was all the rage: the yellow of Whistler's breakfast room in Lindsey Row inspired in Howell the sense of walking into an egg. Whistler had barely settled into his new house in Tite Street, designed for him by Godwin, before it was handed over to the bailiffs; awarded pyrrhic damages of one farthing in his libel action against Ruskin, the legal costs of the case had bankrupted him. As with Whistler's house, the original design of No. 44 (286), for Frank Miles, was rejected by the Metropolitan Board of Works, causing Godwin to fume: 'What "judgement" have retired farmers and cheesemongers who never drew a line nor saw a drawing till yesterday?'[19] When Oscar Wilde, newly married, took a lease in the summer of 1884 on No. 16 Tite Street he too turned to Godwin for an eye-catching interior. For the loud Wilde Godwin decided on a quiet white and grey dining room, 'each chair ... a sonnet in ivory ... the table ... a masterpiece in pearl'.[20] In April of the following year Godwin fell ill and was forced to convalesce in the country, where he received from Wilde a letter of commiseration: 'I am glad you are resting – nature is a foolish place to look for inspiration in, but a charming one in which to forget one ever had any. Of course we miss you, but the white furniture reminds us of you daily, and we find that a rose petal can be laid on the ivory table without scratching it'.[21]

Godwin never recovered from this illness – acute inflammation of the bladder – and died six months later. As specifically instructed he was buried in an unmarked grave. Ellen Terry later concluded a sonnet to the father of her two eldest children: 'They tell me he had his faults – I know of one; dying too soon, he left his best undone.'[22]

The wider significance of Godwin's contribution to the history of interior design lies, however, not so much in these private commissions, as in the designs he produced for commercial manufacturers of furniture, textiles and wallpaper. After the failure of his 'Art Furniture Company of Covent Garden' - an advertisement of 1867 announced its

287 This 1880 design by Theodore Howard for a hallway in a house in St Cloud has copied the staircase and settle from Watt's 1877 catalogue of Godwin furniture.

288 Cabinet designed by Richard Norman Shaw, made by W. H. Lascelles and decorated by J. Aldam Heaton. At the Paris Exposition Universelle of 1878 Lascelles exhibited an identical cabinet, stained green.

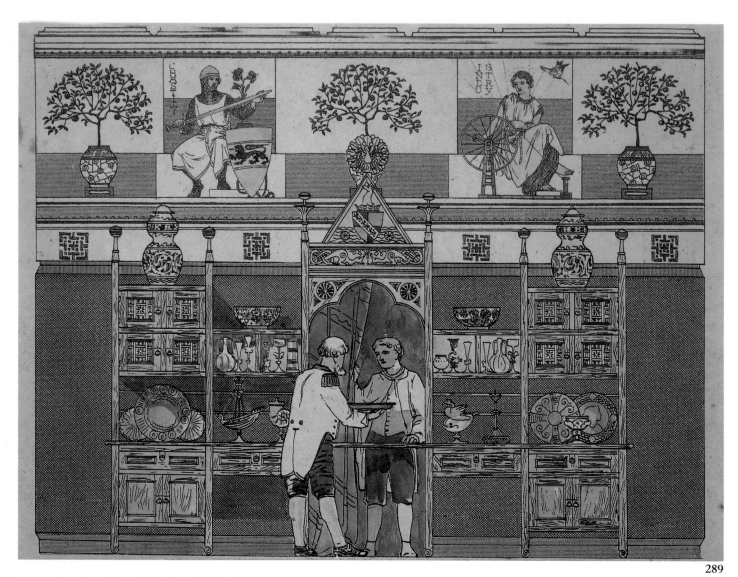

289 E. W. Godwin's design for the dining room buffet at Dromore Castle, County Limerick. This engraving, published in the *Builder* on 20 August 1870, was hand-coloured by Godwin himself. The occasional Gothic detail does not conceal the essentially Japanese inspiration of the buffet; its gable is capped by a carved peacock, one of the chief emblems of the aesthetic movement. Godwin intended the room to be painted with a frieze of allegorical figures alternating with stylised fruit-trees in blue-and-white pots, but his artist, Henry Stacy Marks, was unable to execute the scheme because of the walls' incurable dampness. This prompted Godwin to advise 'When offered a commission in Ireland, refuse it.'

290 An ebonized chair by E. W. Godwin, upholstered in its original fabric also designed by Godwin and woven by J. W. & C. Ward of Halifax. The design for the chair was registered by the cabinetmaker William Watt in 1876.

291 Anglo-Greek cabinet designed by either E. W. Godwin or Daniel Cottier. The ceramics were made by Sir Edmund Elton at his Sunflower Pottery, Clevedon, Somerset, 1895–1915.

Overleaf **292** The Peacock Room, originally at 49 Princes Gate, London. Its architectural features were designed for the shipping magnate Frederick Leyland in 1876 by Thomas Jeckyll. J. M. Whistler then spent eight months, to February 1877, covering the room with antwerp blue and gold peacocks and peacock feathers.

293 This armchair is almost identical to a design illustrated by Christopher Dresser in his *Principles of Decorative Design* (1873), described there as being 'in the Greek style'. The original colour of the upholstery has been preserved in restoration. The fireplace is lined with De Morgan tiles ('New Persian A. No. 133', 1879).

294 An 1870s Lamb of Manchester secretaire, incorporating one genuine Japanese lacquer panel and, on the lower door, a Manchester-made imitation. The pottery, also of the 1870s, is Minton Henri II, or St Porchaire, ware by Charles Toft.

295 A Gillow's ebonized mahogany bookcase designed by Bruce Talbert, with gilded panels of stylised flowers inspired by Japanese woodcuts. The hall chair was designed by Christopher Dresser and made by the Art Furnishers' Alliance (1880–3). On the wall is a Minton majolica roundel of Prince Albert, identical to one in the dairy at Windsor of 1858, and William Butterfield's design for 'St Mark' in the reredos of St Mary's, Dover (1889).

293

294

295

296 The library at Cragside, Northumberland, designed in 1870 by Richard Norman Shaw for the engineer and armaments manufacturer Lord Armstrong. The house, grafted dramatically on to a hillside, was the first in England to be lit throughout by electricity. The original decoration of the library, still largely unaltered, included the set of stylish ebonized chairs with gilded leather backs made by Gillow's probably to Shaw's design.

297 Godwin's design for a polished white deal piano, with cedar panels and ebony mouldings, published in 1874.

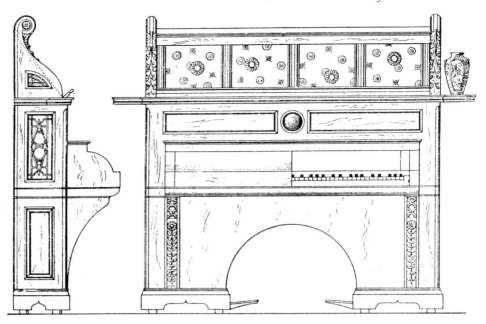

willingness 'to supply at ordinary trade prices, domestic furniture of an artistic and picturesque character, designs by C. Eastlake, A.W. Blomfield and W. Godwin and other architects'[23] – Godwin worked for a number of different manufacturers. For W.A. & S. Smee of Finsbury Pavement, for example, he supplied only designs for stock, whereas for other cabinetmakers he also accepted individual commissions, such as the £10,000 worth of Godwin furniture Waugh & Sons of Tottenham Court Road sent in 1876 to a Mr J.W. Wilson in Gothenburg. In 1872 Collinson & Lock tempted Godwin into an exclusive contract at an annual retainer of £450 (plus three guineas a design) and continued

to produce costly rosewood furniture to his designs long after he stopped working for them. It was a design for Collinson & Lock published in the *Building News* of 2 January 1874 (297), of a polished white deal piano with cedar panels and ebony mouldings, which secured Godwin some of his worst press. Correspondents inundated the editor with complaints about the piano's impracticality. 'A Furniture Manufacturer' suggested that because of 'the insecurity of its base ... it would be instant death to any child that might attempt to hang on the front of it'.[24]

Godwin's most productive business relationship was with William Watt of 26 Grafton Street (off Gower Street),

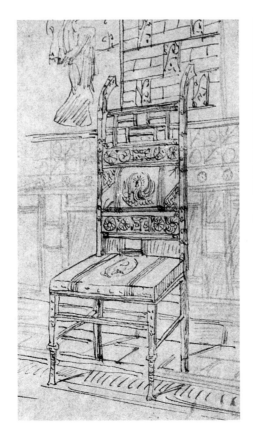
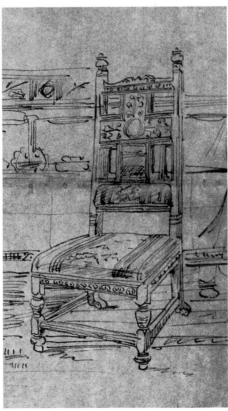

Right **298** and **299** Two Godwin designs for chairs made for the Collinson & Lock stand at the Vienna Exhibition of 1873.

London, who published a valuable record of their association in a catalogue of 1877, 'Dedicated by permission to Her Royal Highness Princess Louise'. They aimed to supply 'economic furniture', including a certain amount 'specially designed for single people living in small chambers'[25] – it was cheapness of manufacture, therefore, as well as aesthetic considerations which ordained simplicity in design (336). In a letter of 1877 to Watt, reproduced in the catalogue, Godwin complained that rival manufacturers had plagiarized their work, flooding the market with inferior versions; he mentioned in particular a small square 'Coffee Table' first made 'nine or ten years ago ... But I have seen the lines changed, the proportions altered until that which I had regarded as a beauty became an eyesore.' When Godwin asked Whistler to decorate the mahogany fireplace – since converted into a cabinet (335) – to be exhibited by Watt at the 1878 Exposition Universelle, the painter ended up covering the whole stand with wonderful yellow and gold japonaiserie. The upholstered furniture was lemon yellow and the carpets were yellow ochre, prompting one critic to label the display 'an agony in yellow'.[26] Others were more complimentary: 'Mr Watt together with Mr Godwin has a good claim to be considered the originator of the great

300 Cast-iron 'Boreas' chair manufactured by Coalbrookdale at their Shropshire foundry in the late 1870s, to a design by Christopher Dresser.

revival in the domestic arts which, with all allowances for its vagaries, is an established fact.'[27]

Although Godwin's furniture on first acquaintance might appear exclusively oriental in inspiration, the designer himself acknowledged a variety of historical debts, labelling one chair 'Anglo-Japanese' and another 'Old English or Jacobean', whilst also asserting that 'earnest study of the best Gothic work of the thirteenth century will lead us, step by step, back to Greek work' (341).[28] It must be accepted that even his most aggressively rectilinear designs may in fact have been inspired by contemporary images of Biblical Egypt rather than Japan. A drawing in Birmingham City Art Gallery which provides evidence of this is the only visual record of the sofa Rossetti exhibited in the Mediaeval Court of the 1862 International Exhibition (426). Described by Charles Dickens as 'straight and angular, and stuffed, possibly, with discarded horsehair shirts',[29] Rossetti's sofa, like some Godwin furniture, was executed in polished white deal with black geometric decoration, an idea already apparent in a biblical drawing of 1860, 'Joseph Accused Before Potiphar'. Rossetti's drawing helps confound all attempts to draw neat stylistic rings around decorative design in this remarkable period of experimental endeavour.

The art of Classical Greece and Egypt had an equally strong appeal to another devoted orientalist, the botanist-turned-designer Christopher Dresser (1834–1904). Ranked by the *Studio* as 'the greatest of commercial designers imposing his fantasy and invention upon the ordinary output of British industry',[30] Dresser was a stern theorist as well as a disciplined practitioner. 'Think not that there is a royal road to success', he wrote in a series of polemical articles published in Cassell's *Technical Educator* (1870–3), 'the road is through toil ... I am a worker, and a believer in the efficacy of work'.[31] Hence his admiration of the Egyptians for the severity of their work ethic and his belief that the dignity and appropriateness of their ornamentation was the inevitable reflection of force of character. Dresser's best furniture – such as the armchair (293) described by the *Builder* as 'of sumptuous character ... excellent in regard to outline and what might be called *expression* (for there certainly is expression in furniture)'[32] – was directly inspired by Greek and Egyptian precedent. Yet the catalyst in all this was, as for Godwin, Japan.

A graduate of Henry Cole's School of Design, Dresser was already thoroughly familiar with the South Kensington Museum's Japanese collection (bought from an exhibition held at the Old Watercolour Society in 1854) by the time he himself purchased 'a fair selection of objects'[33] from Alcock's display at the 1862 International Exhibition. Dresser concentrated on the practical application of oriental culture and he it was who received an invitation from the government to make, in 1876–7, the first official visit of a European designer to Japan. As well as advising the Japanese Ministry of the Interior on the display of European artefacts in the Imperial Museum, Dresser gave instructions for the adaptation of traditional Japanese crafts to machine

301 The opening of the Art Furnishers'
Alliance showrooms in New Bond Street in
1880, with an Egyptian chair and a Thebes
stool prominently displayed.

production, the consequences of which, even during Dresser's own lifetime, wildly exceeded all expectations. On his return Dresser bought the contents of the 'Japanese Nobleman's Room' at the Paris 1878 Exhibition and subsequently put all the objects on show at a Mr Streeter's shop in Bond Street. This was the origin of Dresser & Holme, the oriental import business he started the following year with Charles Holme, subsequently founder of the *Studio*. The Japanese connection was continued by Dresser's son Louis, who went out to Kobe to run the eastern end of affairs, married a Japanese girl and fathered a dynasty, the male line of which finally expired in 1980 with the death in Kobe of Stanley Dresser.

Except in certain pieces of Linthorpe Pottery which are virtual copies of Peruvian originals, Dresser was the least imitative of all nineteenth-century designers; although Japan was influential on his philosophy of design, not much of his furniture actually looks Japanese. Indeed, most of his furniture – an ebonized hall chair, for example (295) – is so unusual as to be beyond precise stylistic definition. Recent research[34] suggests that this black-stained furniture with deeply incised gilt decoration (350) was marketed by the Art Furnishers' Alliance, which opened showrooms at 157 New Bond Street in 1880, an event recalled twenty years later by the *Studio*: 'Attendants robed in many aesthetic costumes of the period, in demure colours, added a certain air to the place, which set it absolutely apart from a shop. So far as memory may be trusted the average work there was very good, and that the enterprise did not continue is partly owing to the fact that it was before its time.'[35] In a prospectus of 15 June 1880 the Alliance vowed that 'no object, whether an important work or mere adjunct of furnishing, will be offered for sale in the Company's

warehouse unless he [Dresser] testifies of its art qualities'. Of the furniture supplied by the Art Furnishers' Alliance to Bushloe House in Leicestershire, home of Dresser's solicitor and an Alliance backer, H.B. Ouston, some was certainly designed by Dresser himself (345), though much of the rest was merely 'approved' by him (including a settee in the Victoria and Albert Museum which was previously attributed to Dresser but is now thought to have been imported from Egypt). Dresser also designed furniture for the offices of G.H. Chubb, director of the family firm of safe-makers, and another backer, in whose workshops some Alliance pieces were manufactured (346–349). Other designs published by the *Furniture Gazette* during Dresser's brief editorship (353–355) may have been made for Sir Edward Lee with whom Dresser was 'associated in work';[36] 'art and the mart are here at one in happy combination', a contemporary noted.[37]

Given the wealth of documented Dresser material in other media – ceramics (for Watcombe, Minton, Linthorpe, Ault, Wedgwood, Old Hall, etc.), glass (for James Couper), silver (for Elkington, James Dixon, Hukin & Heath, etc.), metalwork (for Benham & Froud, Perry, Chubb, Coalbrookdale), textiles and wallpapers (for Crossley, Warner, Jeffrey, Catto & McClary, etc.) – it is frustrating that documented Dresser furniture should be so rare. The reason for this concerns the fact that, unlike most other major interior designers of the period, Dresser was not a qualified architect and therefore had no established affiliations with particular architects or builders. Instead, his connections were direct with industry, a divergence from normal contemporary practice which Dresser felt obliged to explain in the introduction to his *Modern Ornamentation*, published in 1886: 'The Author, as a designer of decoration for buildings, and of patterns for manufacturers must of necessity employ a number of assistants and pupils in his offices. The patterns now published are all original designs which are the work of the author, his assistants and his pupils collectively.' After moving from central London to Barnes in 1889 Dresser still employed ten assistants, operating much more like the head of a twentieth-century design studio than a nineteenth-century jobbing draughtsman. Owen Jones was the only near-contemporary with a work-practice comparable to Dresser's; indeed, the two were mutual admirers and Jones employed the young Dresser to produce plates at the end of *The Grammar of Ornament* to demonstrate the geometrical propensity of nature. Dresser himself went on to produce flat patterns that appear strikingly modern in their energetic forms and amazing colours. Seeing Bauhaus shapes in his teapots and a 1960s psychedelic palette in his pattern designs makes it tempting to think of Dresser as the one Englishman able to carry the lessons of Japanese structural simplicity to revolutionary conclusions. However, other designers, such as the Gothicist J.K. Colling, author of *Art Foliage for Sculpture and Decoration*(1865), made similarly harsh abstractions from nature, so it has been argued that Dresser should rightly be seen within the tradition of High Victorian Geometric Gothic, albeit heavily dosed with exotic ideas from Egypt, the Orient and South America.

Dresser's combination of the dated and dateless in design is most clearly demonstrable in the only documented furniture which appears on the market with any regularity, a series of cast-iron pieces made at the Coalbrookdale foundry at Ironbridge in Shropshire. As an isolated flat pattern, the back of one of his garden seats (352) could easily be mistaken for Jazz Age design, but when placed in the context for which it was intended the declared origins of the design in a 'water plant' brand it as distinctly nineteenth-century. Also, the concept of iron furniture itself is typically Victorian – in the 16 December 1876 issue of the *Furniture Gazette* Dresser published a design for an iron 'Gothic Hall Table' (356), intended not for hotels or public use but for ordinary homes. Furthermore, there is an essentially Victorian resonance to Dresser's booming demands for strength and power in design and his echoing derision of any display of weakness: 'Ornamentation must be *powerful* in its utterance. If power is absent from a composition weakness is the result, which cannot be pleasant. Weakness is childish, it is infantine; power is manly; power is Godlike.'[38] The way to defeat weakness was through knowledge. 'Knowledge Is Power' was painted by Dresser in bold capital letters on the outside of his study door,[39] leaving visitors with no illusions as to the kind of man they were dealing with: a man very much of his age.

Of Richard Norman Shaw the *Builder* wrote in 1873: 'Scarcely anything from his hand can be without interest.'[40] By 1900 Shaw was almost everyone's hero and a particular favourite of Hermann Muthesius, who believed that 'this

302 and **303** Two favourite Christopher Dresser devices: the hare, part of a design for a hall frieze published in 1876, and the frog, stencilled on a bedside cabinet from Bushloe House, near Leicester, in 1880.

great architect touched every nerve of his age with a beneficent hand'.[41] In his early years, however, Shaw shared the limelight with his friend and one-time partner W.E. Nesfield (305), and the two were jointly credited with the creation of the Old English style in interior design, out of which, nurtured on an oriental diet, grew the illustrious Queen Anne revival. Though a contemporary described the Queen Anne movement as basically 'a Gothic, bah! Classic, ah!' period,[42] the educational grounding of these two young architects was firmly Gothic, a subject on which each of them published a book. Nesfield's *Specimens of Mediaeval Architecture* (1862) aimed to 'stimulate the growing appreciation of the noble buildings of the Middle Ages' (to Nesfield this meant exclusively twelfth- and thirteenth-century French and Italian architecture). After working for first William Burn and then Anthony Salvin, Shaw took over from Philip Webb in 1859 as G.E. Street's chief assistant and came under the most rigorous of Gothic influences, leaving the younger Nesfield to take the initial steps down a different path. The first sign that Nesfield's interest in Japanese prints might fundamentally affect his work appeared in the fountain he exhibited at the 1862 Exhibition in London, described by one critic as 'the most artistic basin that butter ever floated in – with the wonderful peacock of inlaid marbles'.[43] Then at Cloverley Hall, Shropshire, begun in 1864, he incorporated Jeckyll lead sunflowers into the eaves, and about a year later installed an

inglenook in H. Vallance's house at Farnham Royal, Buckinghamshire, which contains most of the basic elements of a style Shaw was to make his own.

In a letter to Swinburne, the painter Simeon Solomon described Nesfield as 'a fat, jolly, hearty fellow, genuinely good natured, very fond of smoking and, I deeply regret to say, of women'.[44] Nesfield was, undoubtedly, a keen Bohemian and often pulled on the gloves for an after-dinner bout with Whistler. He also had a reputation as a furniture designer, although no documented pieces have yet been discovered, with the possible exception of a remarkable Anglo-Japanese screen (361) about which everything is known for certain except the name of the designer. The screen, which incorporates painted panels of Chinese silk, was made by the wood and stone carver James Forsyth and given by him to Richard and Agnes Norman Shaw on 16 July 1867, the day of their marriage at Hampstead Parish Church. Attribution of the design to Nesfield rather than Jeckyll – only they, and Godwin, would have been capable at the time of such sophisticated manipulation of Japanese motifs – is made on the grounds firstly that Forsyth was then working extensively for Nesfield and secondly that Nesfield had made a speciality of its overlapping 'pies', a term which he himself had invented to describe a motif used in the decoration of Japanese porcelain and which he used to such telling effect in his work at Kinmel Park, Denbigh (1866–74). In the absence of actual furniture to match

304 and **305** Richard Norman Shaw (seated) and W. E. Nesfield, photographed in 1873 in the office they shared in Argyll Street (previously occupied by Nesfield's uncle, Anthony Salvin, to whom both men were articled). Shaw and Nesfield were partners from 1866 to 1868, when Nesfield was a pioneer of the Japanese influence, as demonstrated by his inglenook at Farnham Park, Buckinghamshire (*c.* 1865), illustrated in C. L. Eastlake's *History of the Gothic Revival* (1872).

306 A painting by the Northumbrian artist H. H. Emmerson of William Armstrong in his dining room inglenook at Cragside, designed by Richard Norman Shaw. The magnificent carving was carried out by James Forsyth 1873–4; the Morris & Co. stained glass was designed by Burne-Jones.

307 Design for the library at Flete in Devon, a house rebuilt 1877–83 by Richard Norman Shaw for a banking magnate, H. B. Mildmay. Much of the interior detail is the work of Shaw's assistant W. R. Lethaby.

Nesfield's known designs, this marriage screen remains the only generally accepted piece by this important designer.

Furniture by Richard Norman Shaw is also rare. In 1952 the organizers of the trail-blazing exhibition of Victorian and Edwardian decorative arts at the Victoria and Albert Museum could locate no documented Shaw furniture, since when only two significant pieces have surfaced. The first appeared at a Sotheby auction in 1962, consigned for sale by the Anglican Sisters of Bethany. It was Shaw's own secretaire-bookcase, which had found its way to their nunnery in Clerkenwell through his eldest daughter, Bessie, or Sister Elizabeth as she became on joining the Order in 1896. Made by James Forsyth, and first placed on public display at the London Architectural Exhibition of 1861, the secretaire (360) is Gothic in style, oddly proportioned and unhappily decorated. The second Shaw piece was unveiled at the Fine Art Society's 1981 exhibition 'Architect-Designers: Pugin to Mackintosh'. It is a cabinet (288) made by W.H. Lascelles and decorated by J. Aldam Heaton, similar to one stained green which Lascelles used in furnishing the two 'Croydon Cottages' he erected at the 1878 Paris Exposition Universelle. The enterprising Lascelles, at this stage Shaw's principal domestic builder, also made all the fitted and much of the free-standing furniture for the houses Shaw designed at Cragside, Northumberland (296 and 306), and Ellerdale Road, London (41, 359 and 362). (The extent of Shaw's involvement in the design of furniture for his houses is undocumented.) After 1876, when Shaw persuaded Heaton to come down from Leeds and set up business in Bloomsbury, the three men worked even more closely together in the decoration and furnishing

of Shaw commissions, and many of the pieces in Heaton's catalogue of 1887 were of earlier designs by his architect-patron. However, Heaton soon turned to mere decorative revivalism, such as the incongruous adaptation of intarsia panels copied from the choirstalls in San Miniato, Florence, to use in some bookcases he installed in the S.S *Teutonic* and in the panelling of dining cars on the London and North-Western Railway. In his *Record of Work*, published in 1893, Heaton condemned Shaw's Early English style in furniture as 'rubbish . . . [or] at best outrageously clumsy', a judgement with which Shaw himself would by then have more or less agreed.

In comparison with his buildings, Shaw's furniture is, indeed, disappointing, and his principal contribution to the history of interior design lies not in individual pieces or even in complete decorative schemes, but in the creation of a new kind of interior domestic space, light and practical and relatively informal (367). Shaw's use of space, in both small and large buildings, in effect offered a twentieth- rather than nineteenth-century style of life, and it is no coincidence that an 1881 prospectus for one of his favourite projects, Bedford Park, proclaimed 'this aesthetic Eden'[45] to be: 'The Healthiest Place in the World (Annual Death Rate under 6 per thousand). About 500 Houses all in the picturesque Queen Anne style of Architecture . . . A Kindergarten and good Cheap Day Schools on the Estate, and a School of Art. Also Church, Club (for Ladies and Gentlemen) . . .' The Club, designed by Shaw with the help of his assistant E.J. May, was decorated with Godwin and Morris furniture, Japanese wallpaper, De Morgan tiles and the fireplace which J. Aldam Heaton exhibited at Paris in 1878; in the Tabard

Inn there are Walter Crane relief panels and, again, De Morgan tiles. According to the American painter Edwin Abbey, a stroll in Bedford Park felt 'like walking through a water-colour sketch'.[46] It was an image Shaw liked, for this scheme proved that different designers and manufacturers could work together in harmony to produce a unified ambience. Towards the end of his life he much regretted the passing of an age 'when the great architect was the bandmaster of art, the employer of many perfectly skilled players in the making of that "frozen music" to which Goethe likened the structural symmetry of consummate building'.[47] It was this kind of attitude which made Shaw's office the natural home for the next generation of arts and crafts architects, men like Sidney Barnsley and W. R. Lethaby, who were later to produce important furniture. Despite his own unimpressive record in design for the decorative arts, Shaw thus exerted a crucial influence on furnishing style in England from the early 1870s until well into the twentieth century.

Amongst the followers rather than leaders of fashion, Thomas Edward Collcutt (1840–1924) commands attention both as an architect – most memorably at the Imperial Institute, London, now largely demolished, and D'Oyly Carte's Palace Theatre, opened in November 1891 – and as a furniture designer for Gillow's, Jackson & Graham, Collinson & Lock (379–380) and Maples. His name is associated in particular with Collinson & Lock, for whom he designed a rosewood cabinet universally acclaimed by the critics on its tour of the world fairs: London in 1871, Vienna in 1873, and Philadelphia in 1876 (372). Moving on to the Paris Exhibition of 1878, Collcutt built a house in the Street

of Nations, furnished entirely with pieces designed for Collinson & Lock, mostly in rosewood and in a style to match his 'Wrenaissance' architecture. After buying up the bankrupt cabinetmakers Jackson & Graham in 1884, J.S. Lock himself began to design furniture in the Collcutt mould, commissioning Stephen Webb to decorate the pieces with intricate ivory inlay; when Collinson & Lock were themselves taken over by Gillow's in 1897, Webb continued to work for the new management (378) until he took up his post as Professor of Sculpture at the Royal College of Art.

The house-style also impinges on a cabinet illustrated by H.W. Batley, another Collinson & Lock designer, in his *Series of Studies for Furniture, Decoration etc.* of 1883 (382). In an article in the 1887 *Art Journal* Lewis F. Day described Batley as a pupil of Talbert's, although Batley's work has a much more pronounced oriental flavour, which is particularly noticeable in his satinwood and purpleheart furniture inset with boxwood panels which both Shoolbred & Co. (383–384) and Henry Ogden & Son exhibited in Paris in 1878. None of the furniture Batley designed for his own house in Upper Richmond Road, London, has yet been identified – nor have any pieces by the Guild of Decorators Syndicate Ltd, which he co-founded in 1908 with W.G. Paulson Townsend, Alfred Martin and Henry Poole.

Where Batley was a designer who also drew, J. Moyr Smith (fl. 1868–94) and Maurice B. Adams (1849–1933) were primarily draughtsmen who also designed. A close friend of Collcutt, Adams is known to have designed furniture for William Watt (385), Gillow's (a bedroom suite at the 1886 Manchester Exhibition), Holland's, Shapland &

308 Commercial Anglo-Japanese furniture of the 1870s, designed by Owen W. Davis and manufactured by James Shoolbred & Co. of Tottenham Court Road, London. Davis designed much furniture for Shoolbred's, in a wide variety of styles.

Petter and Robertson & Son of Alnwick. None of his work displays the slightest originality; as editor of the *Building News* he was, in the words of Reginald Blomfield, 'a well-known draughtsman, though not a very good one'.[48] Moyr Smith is mainly remembered for jokey pseudo-medieval illustrations readily adaptable to almost any decorative use: by Minton & Hollins and W.B. Simpson & Sons to tiles, or by Marcus Ward to Christmas cards, for example. However, Moyr Smith also worked in Christopher Dresser's studio, where he not only executed the majority of plates for *Modern Ornamentation* but is also assumed to have been independently responsible for some of the designs. Indeed, as draughtsman of the whole of the 1871 Collinson & Lock catalogue, Moyr Smith, not Collcutt, may well have designed some of the details in the catalogue also.

Documentary evidence may yet be discovered proving Moyr Smith to have been a more significant furniture designer than he is at present considered (389), the author perhaps of important pieces currently attributed to Dresser. The same is true of Daniel Cottier (1838–91), who, after working briefly in partnership with Bruce Talbert, opened offices of his own in 1873 in both New York and Sydney. The few known pieces of furniture bearing a Cottier manufacturer's stamp (390) are in ebonized mahogany, decorated with incised borders and a type of painted design normally associated with Godwin – it is conceivable that a significant body of work presently attributed to Godwin will at some time in the future be transferred to the Cottier file (391).

Knighted in 1919 as war-time commander of the Artists' Corps of Volunteers, Colonel Sir Robert William Edis

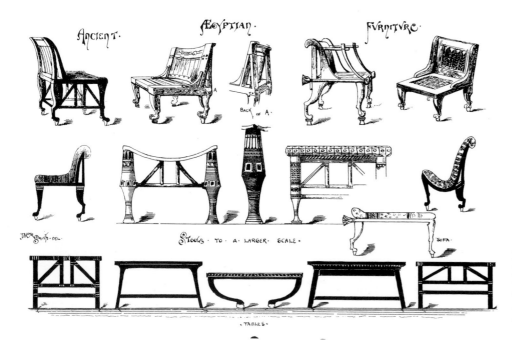

309 'Ancient Aegyptian Furniture' in the British Museum, a page of drawings by J. Moyr Smith published in the *Building News* of 17 December 1875: such illustrations were a source of inspiration for designers of 'Art Furniture'.

310 Inferior commercial furniture in the aesthetic taste, from R. W. Edis's *Decoration and Furniture of Town Houses* (1881), for which Maurice B. Adams drew the illustrations.

(1839–1927) trained as an architect but made his name as a decorator. He lived in Upper Berkeley Street, one of the earliest commercially built terraces in the Queen Anne style, and illustrated many of his own rooms (392) in his influential *Decoration and Furniture of Town Houses* (1881). The dado frieze in his dining room was painted with medieval figures symbolizing 'Welcome', and inscribed: 'The Friends thou hast and their adoption tried, grapple them to thy soul with hooks of steel. Welcome ever smiles and farewell goes out sighing.' Edis was a busy but undistinguished designer who, undeservedly, received in 1883 a commission from Queen Victoria to build and decorate the new ballroom and other additions at Sandringham House.

Two other professional purveyors of popular fashion, the cousins Rhoda and Agnes Garrett, worked in a similar vein next door to Edis at 4 Upper Berkeley Street, home of Agnes's sister Elizabeth Garrett Anderson, the first Englishwoman permitted to qualify as a doctor. The Garretts trained as clerks in the architectural office of J.M. Brydon before setting up their own interior design company, which aimed to bring fresh designs in the Queen Anne style to a wider middle-class public.

A last comment in defence of the Queen Anne school can best be left to 'G.A.' in his essay 'Cimabue and Coal-Skuttles', which has already been quoted: 'Under a thin disguise of archaism, it really recognised the needs of modern comfort. Moreover, it penetrated the serried phalanx of British Philistinism and induced it to discover its own hideousness.'[49]

311 Boldly decorated aesthetic movement bedroom furniture manufactured by Audas & Leggott, illustrated in the *Furniture Gazette* of 2 December 1876.

312

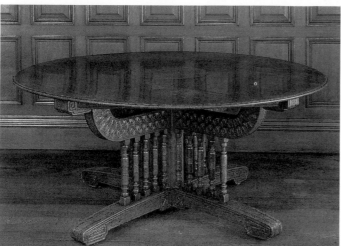

313

315

Jeckyll and Whistler

Thomas Jeckyll designed some of the earliest surviving furniture inspired – in decoration if not in form – by interest in Japan: this sideboard (312) and centre table (313) were made in the late 1860s for Edward Green of Heath Old Hall in Wakefield. From 1870 to 1875 Jeckyll worked on an extension to the Ionides house at 1 Holland Park: the mantlepiece in the dining room (314) was the first of its kind, a precedent thereafter poorly imitated throughout suburban London. Alexander Ionides's desk (316), in padoukwood with ebony mouldings, is an outstanding example of the Anglo-Japanese style. In the pavilion for his home-town founders, Barnard, Bishop & Barnard of Norwich – here photographed at the Paris Exposition Universelle, 1878 (315) – Jeckyll developed the oriental sunflower motif; a scale drawing for one of the pavilion's spandrels shows his delicate style (317)

Jeckyll was also responsible, in 1876, for structural alterations to Frederick Leyland's dining room at 49 Princes Gate to display the fashionable collection of blue and white porcelain (320): the sideboard on the right was designed by Philip Webb, but the one at the far end is Jeckyll's. A year later Whistler produced plans (318) for peacock panelling and proceeded to decorate the whole room in gold and turquoise (see 292). The resulting quarrel with Leyland inspired Whistler to caricature his client as 'The Gold Scab: Eruption in Frilthy Lucre' (319).

314

316

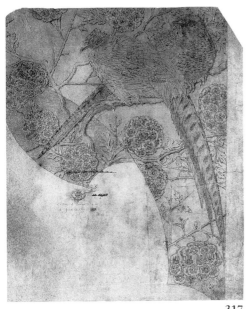

317

318

319

320

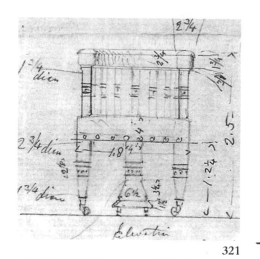

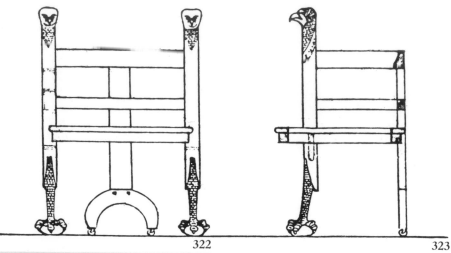

321

322

323

324

Early Godwin furniture

E. W. Godwin's first significant commission was the Town Hall at Northampton (1861), a Gothic revival building into which he introduced some remarkably stylised furniture. His drawing of the 'Councilmen Chairs' (**321**), dated 1865, was covered with instructions to Green & King for their production in honey oak, with maroon stencilled decoration and seats upholstered in dark green leather. Godwin's 1869 design for the 'Eagle Chair' at Dromore Castle, near Limerick (**322–323**), clearly derives from his Northampton experience, though other Dromore designs were more distinctly oriental (**328–329**). All the Dromore furniture was made by William Watt, and both the form and decoration were radically simple for their time (**331**).

325

326

327

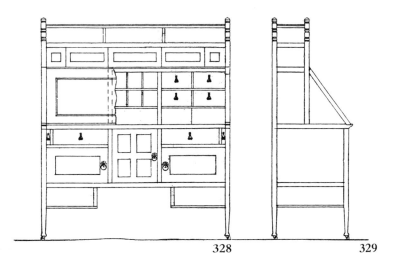

328   329

330

Before this, in 1867, Watt made for
Godwin's own use the first of a series of
ebonized sideboards inspired directly by
interiors studied in Japanese woodcuts and
subsequently manufactured for commercial
retail (**324**). The furniture Godwin designed
at this time for his mistress, Ellen Terry,
was also attractively Japanese (**325** and **326**).

In 1872 Godwin signed a design contract
at £450 per annum – plus 3 guineas a
drawing – with the London cabinetmakers
Collinson & Lock, who produced various
rosewood versions of this octagonal centre
table (**327**); an ebonized version made by
Watt had out-splayed feet, shod in brass.
Godwin's 'Lucretia Cabinet' (**330**) was made
by Collinson & Lock in 1873 and painted
by Charles Fairfax Murray; it was rather
more practical than his equally angular
couch (**332**), about which a contemporary
complained: 'With all respect to Mr
Godwin's undoubted talent, where is the
repose for back and head?'

331

332

Later Godwin furniture

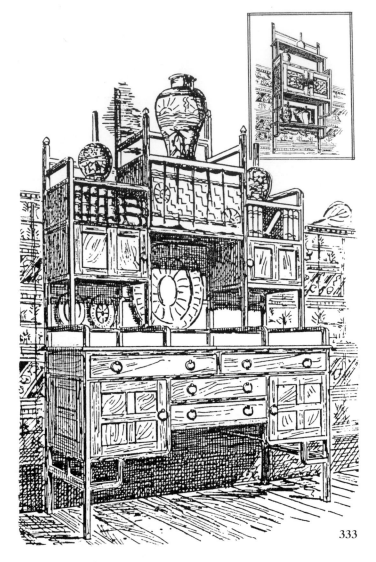

In 1877 Watt produced a catalogue of Godwin furniture made by his firm over the previous decade; it records some of the architect's personal favourites, such as his oriental 'Buffet' and 'Hanging Cabinet' (**333**), as well as illustrating some simple, inexpensive interiors (**336**). The catalogue was pirated by other manufacturers: numerous misproportioned copies are to be found of Godwin's 'Sofa-Settee' (**338**), 'Jacobean Chair' (**339**) and 'Coffee Table' (**340**).

The stylistic origins of Godwin's furniture are not always as clearly displayed as they are in a small cabinet (**342**) incorporating actual Japanese fragments – carved boxwood panels on the doors, and ivory monkeys as handles. The architectural detail of the Godwin cabinet exhibited by Watt at the 1878 Paris Universelle (**335**) is actually more 'Queen Anne' in basic style: the oriental flavour is supplied by Whistler's elaborate decoration. Other furniture designs – in the *Building News* of 1 May 1885, for example (**334**) – reveal Godwin's interest in ancient Greek and Egyptian furniture: the bulbous turned legs and incised gilt decoration on two more pieces (**337** and **343**) precisely match museum notes in his sketchbooks. Another of his 'Greek' chairs, made by Watt in plain oak (**341**), was advertised in the *Building News* in December 1884 as a 'Cheap Chair'.

333

334

335

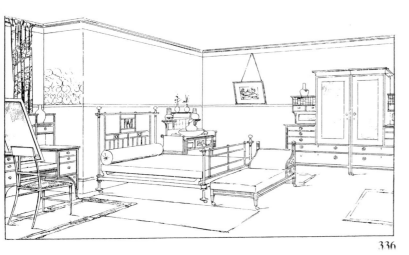

336

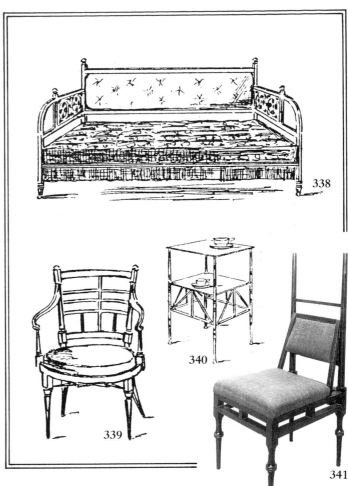

338

337

339

340

341

342

343

344

345

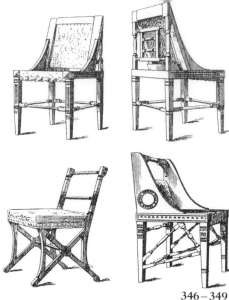

346–349

351

350

352

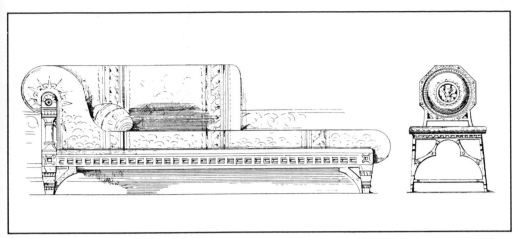

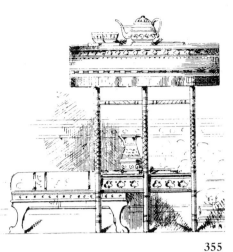

353   354   355

Christopher Dresser

In 1880 Christopher Dresser set up the Art Furnishers' Alliance, with himself as manager and G. H. Chubb (owner of the firm of safe-makers), H. B. Ouston (a lawyer) and A.L. Liberty (founder of Liberty's) as its principal backers. Documentary material is scarce, but the Chubb & Son works at 128 Queen Street, London, are known to have made certain pieces of furniture (346–349), all of which are assumed to have been designed by Dresser – he definitely designed the 'Egyptian' chair (345) supplied to Ouston in the redecoration of his home in Leicestershire, Bushloe House. Other pieces (344 and 350) are firmly attributed to Dresser on stylistic grounds; they have the deeply incised gilt lines typical of furniture marketed by the Art Furnishers' Alliance (the plates displayed in the cabinet were also designed by Dresser).

During 1880 Dresser was editor of the *Furniture Gazette*, in which many anonymous designs were drawn by R. A. Boyd and other draughtsmen employed in Dresser's own office (353–355). Records at Coalbrookdale, the Shropshire ironfounders, prove that Dresser was regularly employed by them; the design for his remarkable hall stand (351) was patented on 5 July 1876; his 'Water Plant' garden seat (352) was sold by Coalbrookdale either bronzed, at 49 shillings, or painted green or chocolate at 47 shillings – all with seats of grained pine. In 1876 the *Furniture Gazette* ran a series of articles on cast-iron furniture, illustrating Dresser's 'Gothic Hall Table' (356), an extraordinary display of technical bravado by Coalbrookdale, and this umbrella stand (357), with characteristic stylised leaf decoration and animal feet.

356   357

Richard Norman Shaw

Shaw's earliest known piece of furniture, a monumental secretaire exhibited at the 1862 International Exhibition, is unequivocally Gothic in inspiration (**360**). His main contribution, however, was interiors, notably the dining room at Cragside, decorated between 1870 and 1872 (**358**), and at his own house in Ellerdale Road, Hampstead (**359**); for the smaller fireplace in the front drawing room at Ellerdale Road (completed 1876) he introduced De Morgan tiles (**362**).

The remainder of Shaw's furniture was mostly 'Old English': this settee (**363**), for example, or the sideboard illustrated in 1870 in *The Workshop* (**364**). Most of Shaw's 1870s furniture (**365**) was made by his favourite builder, W. H. Lascelles. A drawing of *c*.1865 for a secretaire (**366**), though vaguely oriental in flavour, was actually derived from European eighteenth-century precedent. Shaw certainly produced nothing so obviously Anglo-Japanese as the screen (**361**) made for him as a wedding present in 1867 by the carver James Forsyth (the design is attributed to W. E. Nesfield).

By 1885, when Shaw built a house in Hampstead for Kate Greenaway, his interiors were handled by J. Aldam Heaton: the double drawing room (**367**) contains no furniture by Shaw himself and emphasizes propriety and comfort – almost style*less*, in fact.

360

361

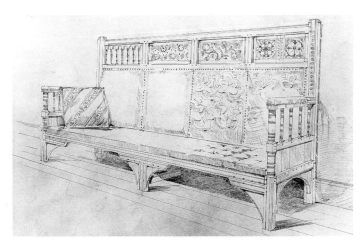

362

363

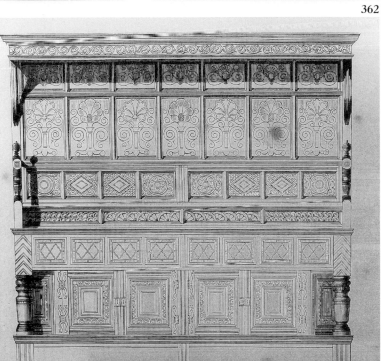

364

365

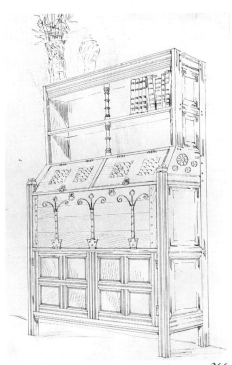

366

367

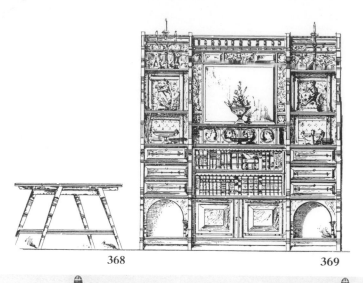

368   369   370   371

Collinson & Lock

The cabinetmakers Collinson & Lock produced in 1871 a catalogue of their latest 'Artistic Furniture': the plates (368–371 and 374–376) were engraved by J. Moyr Smith, one of Dresser's assistants, and their style is clearly influenced by both Godwin and Talbert. Collinson & Lock's principal designer, however, was T. E. Collcutt, a partner in the firm of Woodzell & Collcutt, architects of the cabinetmakers' new premises in St Bride Street, London, here illustrated in the *Architect* of 10 May 1873 (373). Collcutt was responsible for what Handley-Read considered 'one of the most original, attractive and influential pieces of furniture ever designed by a Victorian architect', a painted rosewood cabinet of 1871 (372).

373

372

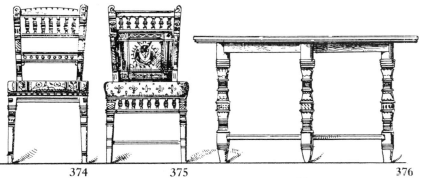

374   375   376

377

At one time Collcut occupied offices below Godwin's in Essex Street, off the Strand, and an 1880s Collinson & Lock sideboard (**377**) has stylistic affinities with both their architect-designers. It was produced to a very high standard of craftmanship in solid rosewood with ivory inlay. Other pieces (**379**) are more clearly the work of Collcutt, who presumably also designed this 'Wrenaissance' cabinet photographed in the Imperial Institute, London, of which he was architect (**380**). Having in 1884 absorbed Jackson & Graham, Collinson & Lock were themselves taken over in 1897, by Gillow's. A page in a Gillow's catalogue of *c*.1900 illustrates a group of ivory inlaid rosewood furniture (**378**) identical to pieces designed by J. S. Lock himself and decorated for Collinson & Lock by Stephen Webb from 1885 onwards.

378

379

380

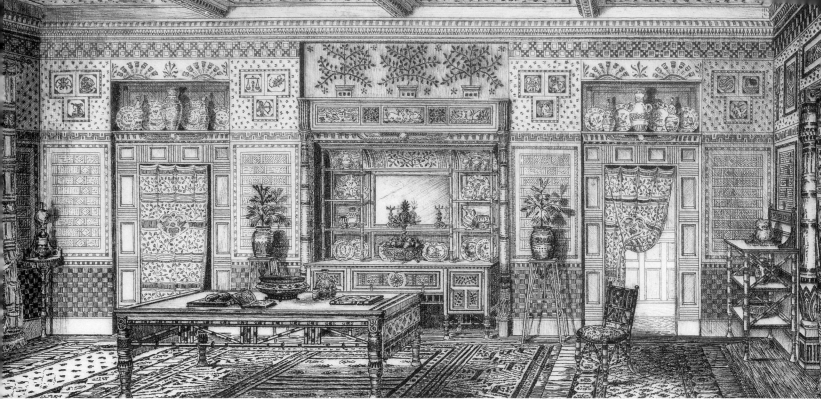

Aesthetic variety

In a drawing of 1872 H. W. Batley aimed 'to adapt Egyptian ornament and detail to the modern dining room' (**381**): it was praised by the *Magazine of Art* as 'altogether admirable; here, indeed, is a real suggestion'. Batley gathered ten years' work on interior design into his *Series of Studies for Furniture, Decoration etc.*, published in 1883. In plate 9 (**382**) the vase balanced on the dado was designed by James Hadley and exhibited by Worcester at the 1878 Paris Exposition Universelle; the extravagant 'oriental' wallpaper is Batley's own invention, adapted from a Jeffrey & Co. commission. For the Universelle Batley himself designed furniture for James Shoolbred & Co., whom the *Art Journal* described as 'eminent among the most extensive cabinetmakers and upholsterers in England'. This group was in satinwood, inset with carved boxwood panels (**383** and **384**). Dealing with able designers

382

383

384

385

like Batley only for prestigious international exhibitions, the quality of Shoolbred's commercial furniture declined. Even Watt, a friend of Godwin, with a less commercial firm than Shoolbred's, sank in 1883 to commissioning Maurice Adams for this nauseating piece of neo-Chippendale (385). Howell & James were one of the few retailers exclusively committed to the avant garde: their two similar clockcases of 1878, designed by the architect Thomas Harris, were trendily labelled 'Jacobean' (386) and 'Queen Anne' (387). Though Godwin, Dresser and Batley were the leaders of the Egyptian revival, Alma-Tadema also designed Anglo-Egyptian furniture (388), mainly for portrayal in his luscious paintings of Pharaonic interiors. The versatile J. Moyr Smith, author of *Ornamental Interiors* (1887), published in the *Building News* of 17 December 1875 a sheet of illustrations of 'Ancient Aegyptian Furniture' from the British Museum, a source of inspiration to them all (see 309); this ebonized side-chair (389) is thought to have been designed by Moyr Smith himself.

386   387

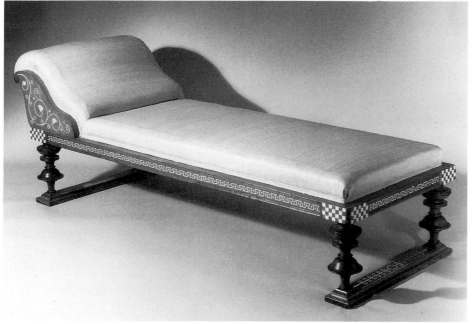

388   389

390

391

Cottier and Edis

Despite the Glasgow designer Daniel Cottier also having offices in New York and Sydney, very little documented furniture by him has been discovered. Of those pieces bearing his trade stamp, even the most Jacobean-looking cabinet (**390**) is clearly part of the aesthetic movement; similar unmarked pieces (**391**) attributed to Godwin may actually be by Cottier. This curious chair (**393**), with its complex structure and specially designed castors, could be by Dresser, Godwin or Cottier.

One of Godwin's 'Jacobean' chairs is the best piece of furniture in the decorator R. W. Edis's own drawing room at 3 Upper Berkeley Street, Mayfair (**392**): an engraving of this image appears in his *Decoration and Furniture of Town Houses* (1881).

393

392

CHAPTER SIX

Morris and Company

394 Fireplace at 1 Kensington Palace Green, 1869–70, by Philip Webb. The 'Cupid and Psyche' frieze is by Burne-Jones.

Despite the shocks and challenges of his busy public life and the emotional disappointments of his private life, William Morris retained from birth to death a beguiling optimism. In an address delivered to the Trades' Guild of Learning he declared: 'I neither, when I think of what history has been, am inclined to lament the past, to despise the present, or despair of the future ... I believe all the change and stir about us is a sign of the world's life, and that it will lead – by ways, indeed, of which we have no guess – to the bettering of all mankind.'[1] Morris did not simply accept change, he demanded it with the whole force of what Ashbee described as his 'titanic energy'.[2]

As a textile designer, visionary poet, socialist revolutionary and preservationist William Morris (1834–96) commanded the respect and admiration of a wide range of distinguished contemporaries. Ruskin likened him to 'beaten gold',[3] while Henry James, on meeting Morris in 1869, praised his earthier qualities: 'He is short, burly, corpulent, very careless and unfinished in dress ... an extraordinary example of a delicate sensitive genius and taste, saved by a perfectly healthy body and temper.'[4] Shortly after his death, the *Studio* went so far as to claim that Morris was 'not only the greatest but the only leader' of meaningful change in the decorative arts of the period.[5] His influence extended far into the twentieth century. In 1936 George Bernard Shaw noted that with the passing years Morris 'towers greater and greater above the horizon beneath which his best advertized contemporaries have disappeared'.[6] By the 1970s his importance as a designer was seen to have been over-rated by earlier eulogies, but the power of his personality was still strong enough for the Marxist historian and international anti-nuclear campaigner E.P. Thompson 'to say that Morris claimed me'.[7] This is the kind of comment Morris would have appreciated, bored as he was with the narrow life of the art world and with the barren conservatism of elitist academics. 'I do not want art for a few', he proclaimed, 'any more than education for a few, or freedom for a few. No, rather than art should lead a poor thin life among a few exceptional men, despising those beneath them for their ignorance for which they themselves are responsible – rather than this, I would rather that the world should indeed sweep away all art for a while.'[8] Whatever the inherent contradictions in his work, Morris here expressed the kind of emotional idealism which motivated his young admirers, Ashbee, Lethaby and the other leaders of the arts and crafts movement. The early designs of Morris, Marshall, Faulkner & Co. were pedestrian compared with Pugin's, and the later products of the renamed Morris & Co. were no better than Maples', yet William Morris remains a central figure in the history of Victorian and Edwardian furniture and interiors.

Born the son of a stockbroker in a country house in what is now the east London suburb of Walthamstow, Morris was sent away in 1848 to the newly founded Marlborough College where he 'learned next to nothing, for indeed nothing was taught'.[9] Moving on to Exeter College, Oxford, in 1853 Morris quickly established a close friendship with

395 and **396** Edward Burne-Jones and William Morris, photographed by Frederick Hollyer in the 1870s and caricatured in the early 1860s by Burne-Jones, who shows himself falling asleep while Morris reads from the manuscript of his long poem *The Earthly Paradise*, eventually published in four volumes 1868–70.

Edward Burne-Jones (1833–98) and his serious young socialist friends from home in Birmingham. In their company Morris learnt a great deal, not least to replace expectations of becoming a clergyman with the bluff ambitions of a practical artist, on account of which he used to recite: 'I sits with my feet in a brook – And if anyone asks me why – I hits them a crock with my crook – For it's sentiment kills me says I.' [10] On entering the architectural office of G.E. Street in 1856 Morris made another contact that was to have important consequences for the history of the decorative arts – Philip Webb (1831–1915), Street's office manager in Oxford since 1854. Later that year Street moved his practice to London, and with him went Morris, to share rooms at 17 Red Lion Square with Burne-Jones. It was here that the lack of any contemporary furnishing to suit their taste is said to have inspired them to set up business as decorators; the only furniture Morris himself ever designed or made were those first roughly hewn pieces for his bachelor digs. The one item of distinction made in these early days was a wardrobe designed by Webb and painted by Burne-Jones with scenes from Chaucer's 'Prioress's Tale' as their wedding gift to Morris and Janey Burden, who became engaged in February 1858. Webb admitted that 'it was finished in a great hurry at the end for exhibition at the Hogarth Club [1860] and we all worked getting it done' (407). [11]

For his new family home Morris automatically turned to Webb. The first known sketches of the 'Red House' are to be found on the back of Morris's copy of Murray's Guide to France which he, Charles Faulkner – best man at the wedding, later an Oxford mathematics don – and Webb used on their rowing holiday on the Seine in August 1858. Though an important event in the development of Philip Webb's ideas about design (of furniture as well as architecture), the Red House had little impact on current styles; William Butterfield's contemporary experiment in the Gothic vernacular at Milton Ernest received much wider notice. Keen on claiming a place for Webb as founder of the modern movement, W.R. Lethaby praised the undecorated brick fireplaces as the first domestic display of constructional decoration; others have commandeered the Red House as the foundation stone of the Queen Anne revival. Amidst the constant barrage of art-historical claims and counter-claims a key quality is often ignored – the sustained individuality of Webb's search for a modern, a-historical style. The painter William Bell Scott appreciated this, noting of the drawing room at the Red House 'that the adornment had a novel, not to say startling, character, but if one had been told it was the South Sea Island style of living one could have believed such to be the case, so bizarre was the execution' (415–417). [12]

Founded in April 1861, Morris, Marshall, Faulkner & Co. was financed by a loan of £100 from Morris's mother and the £1-share contributions of Webb, D.G. Rossetti, Ford Madox Brown, Burne-Jones and the three named members (Peter Paul Marshall, a friend of Brown's, was a surveyor and sanitary engineer). Soon referred to as Morris

397 Philip Webb in 1873, painted by Charles Fairfax Murray.

& Co., though the name was not officially adopted till 1875 when Morris became sole proprietor, 'The Firm' was initially a co-operative of artists who drew on additional assistance from Albert Moore and Simeon Solomon for the design of stained glass. The Pre-Raphaelite contribution was thus considerable: Rossetti, for example, is often credited with the re-design of the 'Sussex' chair, a traditional eighteenth-century form (429), as well as with the lyre-back chair that bears his name (428), both of which were first produced in 1865 and remained part of standard stock till the company eventually folded in 1940. It is, however, as unwise to put one artist's name rather than another's to these early ebonized chairs – praised by Edis for being 'comfortable for use, pleasant to look at and cheap in price' [13] – as it is to define their stylistic origins precisely as eighteenth-century English, nineteenth-century oriental, or ancient Egyptian. Variations on a particular theme are a common feature of almost all their work and another version of the Sussex chair manufactured by Morris & Co. is confusingly attributed to Ford Madox Brown. Brown's earliest furniture, however, is well documented. He made a group of designs for another Pre-Raphaelite, William Holman Hunt, soon after Hunt's return from travels in Egypt and Palestine in 1854. The anonymous author of an article in the *Artist* (May 1898) informs us that Brown went on to design for Morris & Co. eight different chairs, four tables, a piano and several bookcases and couches, mostly decorated with green stain, using oxides of chromium (421–423). Morris acquired a suite of Brown's green bedroom furniture for his own use (424); the pieces are now at Kelmscott Manor, Oxfordshire, from 1871 Morris's country retreat. Madox Brown also supplied the furniture for an ideal working man's cottage at the Manchester Jubilee Exhibition in 1887, including a chest of drawers (420) that Lethaby chose to show again at the 1890 Arts and Crafts Exhibition and which directly inspired, both by its colour and its cut-out handles, Ambrose Heal's 'Simple Bedroom Furniture' of 1899.

When Burne-Jones married and moved from Red Lion Square to a small flat overlooking the British Museum he continued to paint furniture for his own use (he finished the decoration of his deal sideboard (436) only a week before the wedding in June 1860). For 'The Firm's' first major public appearance, at the Mediaeval Court of the 1862 International Exhibition, he painted 'The Backgammon Players' on the doors of a Webb cabinet, a much more successful endeavour than another exhibition piece, the St George Cabinet painted by Morris. 'Who would' have believed it represented manufacturers of the nineteenth century – the age, par excellence, of cog-wheels and steam rams and rifled cannon?' asked one of the critics.[14] The *Building News* was even less sanguine, suggesting that the Morris exhibits would 'suit a family which might suddenly be awakened after a sleep of four centuries and which was content to pay enormous prices suitably to furnish a barn'.[15]

Figurative painting of furniture, however, was a passing phase in Morris productions and total responsibility for the design of almost all their commissioned furniture, both fitted and free-standing, soon passed to Philip Webb (397). Writing in 1925, Lethaby pronounced that 'all our better new house furniture owes something to Webb's experiments'.[16] Twenty years earlier Muthesius had praised

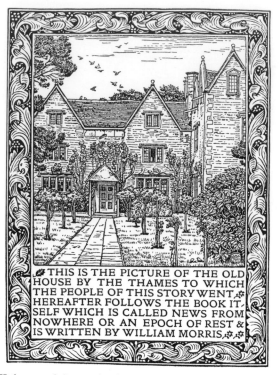

398 Kelmscott Manor: the frontispiece of Morris's *News from Nowhere* (1893), published by the Kelmscott Press.

him for 'an independence amounting almost to genius . . . he is the embodiment of maximum honesty'.[17] Webb's puritanical attention to detail was a quality also admired by Lutyens, who felt it 'the duty of the present generation to make a faithful technical record of his work . . . for there was no item in the fabric of his building too small or trivial for him to consider and design to fit its purpose'.[18] Sketchbooks reveal the origin of Webb's formal structure in his

399 and 400 In 1864 Philip Webb designed this studio house for the artist Val Prinsep at 1 (now 14) Holland Park Road, London. The high-windowed studio, shown in a photograph of 1884, has the curved cornice characteristic of many of Webb's interior designs.

401 Drawing of a hare by Webb, incorporated by Morris into his tapestry 'The Forest', designed for Alexander Ionides in 1887.

402 The Green Dining Room, South Kensington Museum, by Webb, 1866–7. Windows and small wall-panels by Burne-Jones; embroidered screen by Morris and his wife; piano decorated by Kate Faulkner, in front of Morris's St George Cabinet.

observations in nature: the shape of trees, birds in flight, cats at play, the skeletal hulls of abandoned boats. There are few major buildings in his sketchbooks, except for the occasional photograph pasted in: Battle Abbey, and Hurstmonceaux Castle, for example. Webb's designs themselves are incredibly detailed, with delicate pencil shading and minutely precise instructions to cabinetmaker or silversmith.

Webb designed the architectural detail of Morris, Marshall, Faulkner & Co.'s two reputation-making commissions of 1866, the decoration of the Green Dining Room at the South Kensington Museum (402) and of two rooms in St James's Palace (441). In the same year the artist Val Prinsep moved into the first in an important group of studio houses in Holland Park (399–400) built by Webb. Prinsep, one of the painters who had joined Rossetti and Morris in Oxford in 1857 to decorate the Union with Arthurian murals, was also an ardent collector of Japanese ceramics. His studio, however, was much more workmanlike than most of his contemporaries', with a curved cornice which reappears in many other Webb and Morris interiors, and a curious striped floor-covering which does not (400). Webb immediately moved on to another artist's commission, for George Howard, later Lord Carlisle. The house was to be built on a vacant plot at the southern end of Palace Green, 'a wooded lane opening directly off the busiest part of High Street Kensington',[19] but Webb's initial proposals fell foul of the Crown Commissioners, led by Sir James Pennethorne and seconded by Anthony Salvin and T.H. Wyatt. Philip Webb's reaction to the criticism was typical: 'That Messrs Salvin and Wyatt are "unable to discover what actual style or period of architecture" I have used, I take to be a sincere compliment'.[20] A compromise was agreed and by June 1869

the structure was ready for Morris & Co. to start on the interior decoration, a task which was not finally completed till 1887. Howard's wife never really liked the house, complaining that it was designed principally for parties, with Burne-Jones's St Cecilia organ at the top of the stairs and a show-piece morning room (40) decorated with scenes of Cupid and Psyche's doomed love affair (taken from Morris's *Earthly Paradise*) above Webb's blue-green dado painted with stylized foliage. In the end the Howards lost patience with Burne-Jones, and Morris called in Walter Crane to finish off the job.

Webb's influence on Morris at this time was crucial. At a personal level his seriousness balanced the others' waywardness, complained of by the firm's manager, Warrington Taylor, in July 1869: 'Ned [Burne-Jones], W.M. and Gabriel [Rossetti] egg one another on to every kind of useless expense. How long do they intend to play boy? They have all got grey hairs in their head.'[21] In May 1867 the admirable Taylor had forced Webb to accept a regular consultancy fee for all his extra work: 'We could not move another step without your professional assistance, and therefore if you will not be paid the firm must come to a stop – because sponging on you is degrading.'[22] Throughout the 1870s and 1880s Webb continued to share his architectural commissions with Morris & Co. At Northallerton Webb worked on Rounton Grange for the ironmaster Sir Lowthian Bell from 1872 to 1876; the decoration installed during the next three years included the *Romaunt de la Rose* frieze, designed by Burne-Jones and embroidered by Lady Bell and her daughters (445). While Rounton Grange was being decorated, Webb built Smeaton Manor, Yorkshire, for Major Godman, husband of the eldest Bell girl (403), who herself embroidered in thick bright wools Morris's Artichoke wall panels, a fine example of his luxuriant naturalism.

Although Thomas Jeckyll had already completed significant work at the Ionides house in Holland Park, Webb made important architectural contributions to the alterations carried out by Morris & Co. from 1877 to 1888, 'in the more or less Persian manner which Mr Morris very often adopts when he forgets to be Gothic',[23] at a total cost of £2,361 2s 10d. Webb created a new staircase, decorated by Kate Faulkner to designs by Morris, as well as the dining room, the upper walls of which he left Walter Crane and Osmund Weekes to decorate with scenes from Aesop's Fables (he retained the Jeckyll fireplace). Of the entrance hall (446), which doubled as a smoking room, Gleeson White, editor of the *Studio*, wrote: 'so cleverly has Mr Philip Webb employed his material that a sense of translucency, almost of transparency, is its dominant note'.[24]

In 1885 Webb was commissioned by the M.P. Wickham Flower to make substantial alterations to Great Tangley Manor (451) in Surrey. His solution was much admired by Muthesius: 'It is without pomp or decoration, and has that natural decency which is so rare in our present culture.'[25] Morris had already decorated Flower's London home, Old Swan House in Chelsea, designed by Richard Norman Shaw in 1875. Photographed by Bedford Lemère before the furniture was removed in 1890 to Great Tangley, the drawing room at Old Swan House provides an interesting period record of a wide range of the finest of the firm's work (447–448), set off by one of Morris's boldest carpets, designed in 1881, whose border of large repeating palmettes was directly inspired by Persian originals at the South Kensington Museum. In the corner by the fire is Webb's settle decorated in gilt gesso by the firm's specialist in this field, Charles Faulkner's sister Kate. Flower's is the most elaborate of these 'medieval' settles, plain versions of which were advertised in a 1910 Morris & Co. catalogue at £30 (£35 with the addition of embossed leather panels); a black stained settle, polished and inset with Webb-designed leather, appears in a photograph of Morris's house in Hammersmith.

No sooner was the decoration of Webb's magnum opus, Clouds, near Salisbury, completed in 1889 than a chambermaid's carelessness with a candle caused the whole place to be gutted by fire. Undeterred, the owner, Percy Wyndham, claimed his £27,000 from Sun Insurance and set Morris & Co. to work for a further three years on its precise restoration. The interiors were decorated with numerous Morris tapestries and fabrics hung against a white ground. White walls were not approved of by Mrs Haweis, who blamed this new fashion for 'the staring suites of furniture which positively scream at one in their obtrusiveness with the result of obliterating the company, who vainly struggle to be conspicuous by still gaudier fantasies in dress'.[26] There is a Puginian tone to Webb's letter to Wyndham thanking him for his refusal to listen to the popular critics: 'Your pleasant expression of satisfaction with

the house at Clouds was very cheering, and will continue to be a help in my work when a sense of hopelessness at times creeps upon me, that all one's efforts to make modern architecture in some way genuine seem to be futile.'[27] Webb's individuality and independence were well understood by his clients; when the building of Standen (450) was finished in 1894 Mr Beale gave Webb, who was an inveterate snuff-taker, a snuff-box inscribed: 'When clients talk irritating nonsense I take a pinch of snuff.'[28]

Webb had no direct architectural involvement in two later Morris & Co. schemes: at Wightwick Manor near Wolverhampton (409), a large 'Elizabethan' house designed by Edward Ould on which Morris & Co. worked on and off for forty years; and at Bullers Wood, Chislehurst, Kent, the country house Ernest Newton built for the Sanderson family. Decorative work began at Bullers Wood in 1889; it was probably the last commission in which Morris himself had a hand. He designed a scarlet pimpernel pattern for the ceiling of the drawing room, where he also installed his last grand carpet (404). The Sandersons ordered from Broadwood in 1893 a square-ended piano, the design of which Burne-Jones had pioneered in his Orpheus piano of 1878–9 for William Graham, and had repeated in a remarkable piano of 1883 for Ionides, decorated by Kate Faulkner with 'varying tints of coloured silver upon a groundwork of Celadon Green ... [to] very fine effect'.[29] The elaborate inlay on the Sanderson piano (453) was designed and executed by George Jack; the leaf scrolls reflected the Morris carpet on which the piano stood and the birds were inspired by Webb drawings in the office.

Philip Webb also designed some of the earliest of Morris, Marshall, Faulkner & Co.'s stained glass (454), though most of the best work in this medium must be credited to Burne-Jones. Amongst the most important early commissions for stained glass were three in Cambridge, for Jesus College Chapel, 1866 to 1878 – the culmination of a

403 Mrs Ada Phoebe Godman (*née* Bell), drawn by Frank Bramley as she was working on the embroidered panels Morris designed for her at Smeaton Manor, Yorkshire.

404 The drawing room at Bullers Wood, Chislehurst, built by Ernest Newton and furnished by Morris & Co., 1889. The ceiling and frieze were decorated with a scarlet pimpernel pattern on a white ground, designed by Morris. This drawing, by T. Raffles Davison, was made in 1890, before the installation of the piano decorated by George Jack (see 453).

restoration scheme begun by Anthony Salvin in 1846 – for All Saints, Jesus Lane, designed by G.F. Bodley in 1861 (the marvellous glass was installed 1866–7), and for G.G. Scott's rebuilding programme at Peterhouse from 1868 to 1870. The firm's first decorative commission in Cambridge had actually been for the tiled fireplace in Bodley's restored Hall at Queens' College, executed between 1862 and 1864, to which Morris added the elaborate painted roof decoration in 1875. In the past Morris has also been credited with the stencilled wall decoration at both Queens' and Peterhouse but it now appears that the architects were themselves responsible for these schemes; their work, like Morris's, was inspired by the same medieval sources first exploited in this manner by Pugin.

William Morris's unique contribution, however, was in the design of flat patterns, of which he was a master. He made subtle distinctions not just between patterns for floor or wall but also between materials, insisting that a design suitable for curtains in woven wool was likely to be disastrous in printed cotton. The Morris style in textile and wallpaper design dominated the later nineteenth century, a fact noted by Richard Norman Shaw – without much enthusiasm: 'The art teaching of today follows in the steps of William Morris, a great man who somehow delighted in glaring wallpapers.'[30] Lethaby tells an amusing story of a self-important customer in the firm's shop in Oxford Street frowning at the brightness of some material: 'This, too, is delightful', she said, 'but I wish the colours were more harmonious.' Apparently Morris replied by opening the door to the street and pointing: 'If it's mud you want', he said, 'you'll find plenty out there!'[31] Morris textiles and wallpapers have a tangible richness, in quality as well as in style, a reflection of his instinctive opposition to half measures. 'Shoddy is King', he complained. 'From the statesman to the shoemaker everything is shoddy.'[32] Despite a passionate attachment to the craft ethic, it was not

machine production in itself which he objected to, but inferior workmanship of any kind. Morris's earliest registered design for floor covering was, in fact, a trellis of African marigolds printed in two colours onto cheap 'corticine floor cloth', as linoleum was then called. Also, his first carpets were designed in the mid-1870s to be machine woven, not wall to wall but with separate borders of varying widths. Five different weaves were officially authorized: Kidderminster three-ply; Wilton pile; Brussells loop; patent Axminster; and 'hand-knotted' Axminster – although Morris designs were pirated and plagiarized in many other weaves too.

Before setting up the commercial production of tapestries at Merton Abbey in 1881, Morris had experimented at length with colours and techniques, working first at Thomas Wardle's factory in Leek and then, from 1879, on his own loom at his London home, Kelmscott House in Hammersmith. Although Morris himself provided much of the vegetable detail and Webb the animal (401), the dominant images associated with Merton tapestries are the female figures by Burne-Jones, modelled on Morris's wife, Jane (456–458). After Morris's death fine-quality tapestries continued to be produced at Merton Abbey under the management of J.H. Dearle, who also contributed numerous designs of his own, for carpets and embroideries as well as for tapestries, mostly in the master's style (460). Patterns (and the wool) for embroidery continued almost till the firm's demise to be successful sellers: a twentieth-century catalogue advertises designs for 'Curtains, Bedspreads, Billiard Covers, Table Cloths, Overmantels, Wallpanels, Fire-Screens, Bookcovers, Blotters, Photograph Frames, Work-bags or sachets, Doylies and Cosies'.[33] The majority of surviving 'Morris' textiles were probably made after his death, many of them to designs by Dearle.

At Red Lion Square, and from 1865 at 26 Queen Square, the Morris enterprise worked principally on commission; it

405 The drawing room, Windleshaw House, East Sussex, designed for himself by W. A. S. Benson. In the foreground of this 1911 photograph, a Morris & Co. table and Madox Brown chair; the table by the window and the chandelier are by Benson.

406 'Margarete', a wallpaper design by Walter Crane for Jeffrey & Co., 1876.

was not until opening a retail outlet in Oxford Street in 1877 that they began both to manufacture 'on spec' and to take in stock from selected outside sources. The potter William De Morgan (1839–1917) – called 'the mouse' because of the shape of his head – was the earliest of such Morris & Co. associates. Before installing a kiln at his home in Fitzroy Square in 1869, De Morgan had provided painted panels for several pieces of Webb furniture (462); then, on moving to Chelsea in 1872, he began lustre-tile production in earnest. Some of the early animal tiles may have been designed by De Morgan's brother-in-law Reginald Thompson, and Morris certainly designed at least one large foliate panel, first used by J.D. Sedding at Memland House in Devon but subsequently offered on order through Morris's Oxford Street premises. De Morgan went to the same Middle Eastern sources as Morris for instruction on running patterns; his 'New Persian A' (293) first appears as No. 133 in the catalogue of 1879, *Painted Tiles to be had of William De Morgan at Orange House Pottery, 36 Great Cheyne Row*. Some of the tiles in this catalogue bear a 'BBB' identification to notify their use by Barnard, Bishop & Barnard in fire-grates. In 1882 Morris persuaded his friend to erect kilns next door to the dye works at Merton Abbey, a venture which lasted only four years and was followed by De Morgan's most prolific period of production in partnership with the architect Halsey Ricardo at the Sands End Pottery from 1888 to 1897 (459 and 461). Ricardo decorated – inside and outside – the house he built for Sir Ernest Debenham in Addison Road, London (22), with an astounding display of De Morgan lustre tiles; completed in 1907, the decoration also includes fine plaster ceilings by Ernest Gimson and stained glass by E.S. Prior.

Another Morris protégé, W.A.S. Benson (1854–1924), 'made his name ... as the reformer of oil-lamps and candelabra which he redeemed from the bondage of early Victorian taste'.[34] Persuaded by Morris in 1880 to leave his apprenticeship with the architect Basil Champneys and set up business as a metalwork manufacturer, Benson made rapid progress, first building a factory in Hammersmith, and then in 1887 opening his own shop in New Bond Street. As well as a wide range of metalwork – kettles, candlesticks, firescreens, etc., in addition to electric chandeliers – produced under his own name, Benson also designed furniture for J.S. Henry & Co. and grates for the Coalbrookdale and Falkirk foundries. On Morris's death he became chairman of Morris & Co. and designed furniture for them (465) which is depressingly traditional in comparison with some of his earlier pieces that were decorated by the sgraffito specialist Heywood Sumner (411 and 466). Sumner, an eccentric Old Etonian who had shared a flat with Benson in the late 1870s and married his sister in 1883, also worked with Dearle on a group of Merton Abbey tapestries.

Walter Crane (1845–1915) received his initiation into commercial design when in 1874 Bruce Talbert introduced him to Metford Warner, for whom he went on to design over fifty wallpapers. Crane also developed a talent for relief plasterwork, and executed his first major commission, for Dr William Spottiswoode, President of the Royal Society, between 1878 and 1880. As a result of that Morris gave him the Aesop's Fables reliefs in the dining room of the Ionides's home in Holland Park. From the inception of the arts and crafts movement Crane was an influential figure, yet in 1902, when two of the three British rooms at the Turin

407

407 A collection of early Morris furnishings. The wardrobe, settle, oak table and copper candlesticks were all designed by Philip Webb in his heavy Gothic manner of the 1860s. The wardrobe, a wedding present to William Morris, was painted by Edward Burne-Jones with illustrations of Chaucer's 'Prioress's Tale' (he also designed the framed tiles on the wall). The 'Fruit' wallpaper and 'Lily' carpet were both designed by William Morris. The chairs are variants of the vernacular 'Sussex' chair of turned wood with a rush seat. That on the right is the simplest; in the background is one green-stained in the fashion made popular by the Morris firm; the elaborate version on the left may have been designed by D. G. Rossetti.

408 The 'Daffodil' chintz, one of Morris & Co.'s most successful fabrics. It was designed by J. H. Dearle in 1891.

Overleaf **409** The Great Parlour at Wightwick Manor, Staffordshire, part of the extension added by Edward Ould in 1893. This is one of Morris & Co.'s finest surviving interiors: the plaster frieze of roses above the fireplace, the painted Orpheus and Eurydice frieze below the roof (both executed by C. E. Kempe), the antique oak furniture, the George Jack electric light brackets, the William Morris 'Diagonal Trail' wall-covering and a selection of the firm's upholstery and embroidery all contribute to the comfortable effect of modern-day medievalism.

408

410

411

410 Many of the Edwardian revivalist interiors installed by Morris & Co. across the world from Brisbane to Boston were designed by B. Stafford. This example is a dining room for a house in Bournemouth, illustrated in W. Shaw Sparrow's *Hints on House Furnishing* (1909).

411 'The Charm of Orpheus' Cabinet by W. A. S. Benson, who became chairman of Morris & Co. on Morris's death in 1896. The cabinetwork is by C. Rogers; the sgraffito decoration was designed by Heywood Sumner and executed by G. H. Walton. The cabinet was exhibited at the Arts and Crafts Exhibition Society in 1889.

412 No Walter Crane furniture is known to survive. This settle, exhibited in 1889, was made for Crane by Edward Miles. It was enamelled white, with reddish-brown painted decoration.

Exhibition were given over entirely to his work, the *Studio* commented: 'though twenty years ago a pioneer, few workers have followed in his footsteps'.[35] No Crane furniture seems to have survived, though he did exhibit a settle beside Benson's 'Orpheus' music-cabinet at the New Gallery in 1889 (412): 'the whole thing is rather dwarfish and slight', the *Building News* commented, 'and does not promise to survive the wear and tear of many years'.[36]

George Jack (1855–1932) joined Webb's small office in the late 1870s principally to help with interior work. A skilful inlayer and carver (463), Jack became involved with furniture production at Morris & Co. when the workshop moved to Merton in 1881. When in 1890 the company came under the control of the brothers F. and R. Smith, an extensive new furniture factory was opened in Pimlico, managed part-time by the unimaginative Jack. By the turn of the century Morris & Co. furniture had become barely distinguishable from the work of purely commercial manufacturers (470) and their interior schemes conformed to the safe Edwardian ideal of eighteenth-century imitation (410). In 1905 the firm was purchased jointly by H.C. Marillier, a partner of W.A.S. Benson, and a rich Morris client, Mrs Wormald of Berkeley Square, whose sole stipulation on providing most of the cash was that a place on the board be found for her son-in-law, the Hon. Claud Lambton. Marillier, already the owner of Morris's Kelmscott House, 'soon found that the Smiths had been too clever for us and that the Morris business which seemed so prosperous on the figures supplied, had been let down and was actually making a loss when we took over'.[37] There seemed no alternative but to become yet more grossly commercial, and the company's stand at the Franco-British Exhibition of 1908 fairly reflects the fall in taste, with two undistinguished Benson pieces and an out-and-out 'Queen Anne' cabinet by Mervyn Macartney – 'a well-known purist and the author of an "Exemplar" of architectural details which is in great demand'[38] – set off by an 'Arras' tapestry reproduction of Botticelli's *Primavera*. The un-Morrisey tone of things was set by Marillier in his preface to a company catalogue of *c*.1910: 'The history of the Firm ... is written in the annals of English art ... Morris and Company undertake the entire decoration, furnishing, and lighting of houses on strictly moderate terms ... including no extra profits or commissions to middle men.'[39]

Throughout his life William Morris suffered from the fact that almost all the works of art he admired were produced in such a way that their cost, in labour and in materials, precluded general availability. People were always telling him he should be more accessible, more fashionable, to which he replied: 'They mean by this that I should spend one day over my work to two days trying to convince rich people that they care very much for what they do not care in the least.'[40] By the end he had just about given up on Morris & Co., and the direction it took after his death was clearly signposted years before: in his lacklustre invitation to Lethaby to lend a hand with Stanmore Hall (473–476), Morris dismissed it as 'a house of a very rich man – and such a wretched uncomfortable place: a sham Gothic house of fifty years ago now being added to by a young architect of the commercial type – men who are very bad'.[41] The business of house decoration obviously no longer interested him, and yet Morris remained till the end of his life, almost to the end of the century, a committed Victorian dreamer. 'I believe that art will make our streets as beautiful as the woods, as elevating as the mountain-sides', he told a group of working guildsmen, among whom he liked to be numbered. 'It is a dream, you may say, of what has never been and never will be: true ... but dreams have before now come about of things so good and necessary to us, that we scarcely think of them more than of daylight: though once people had to live without them, without even the hope of them.'[42]

413 Burne-Jones's caricature of an unwashed Morris snoring peacefully in his Madox Brown bed *c*.1860.

414

416

Early 'Morris' furniture

The only pieces of furniture Morris actually designed were those he and Burne-Jones made and painted themselves for the rooms they shared in Red Lion Square from 1856 to 1859 (none is known to survive). The first serious 'Morris' furniture was designed by Philip Webb for the Red House at Bexley Heath, into which the newly married Morrises moved in 1860; Rossetti and Burne-Jones never quite finished painting scenes from the *Nibelungenlied* on the hall settle (417); the dining room dresser was simply stained green (416). Webb's circular table (415), designed in 1860, is another typical Red House piece, its highly individual medievalism most forcefully expressed in the castellated feet.

When Morris, Marshall, Faulkner & Co. was founded in 1861, Webb continued to design furniture, including their best-selling embossed leather sideboard (414): in the same photograph is the curious oak table Webb designed for Major Gillum, probably for Oakleigh Park in 1868, its form inspired by a Japanese altar table (the embroidered panels hanging on the wall were designed by Morris for Webb's Smeaton Manor). Other commercial furniture produced by Webb for 'The Firm' included a sideboard praised at the time for its avoidance of dogma (418), and a day-bed (419) now at Kelmscott Manor, the house near Lechlade which Morris rented from 1871 until his death in 1896. The painter Ford Madox Brown also designed furniture for the Red House: a drawing room table with lockers for books and music (422), a plain green-stained trestle table (423) and a bed, washstand, towel rail and ebonized chairs since removed to an upstairs bedroom at Kelmscott Manor (424). Madox Brown produced his own studio cupboard to hold paints and reference books (421); he was also commissioned to design a suite of furniture for a working man's cottage at the Manchester Jubilee Exhibition of 1887, including this green-stained chest of drawers and mirror, made by Samuel Waddington (420).

417

415

418

419

420

421

422

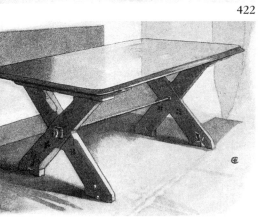

423

424

425

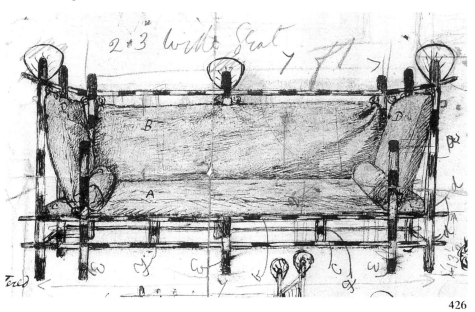

426

427

428

429

430

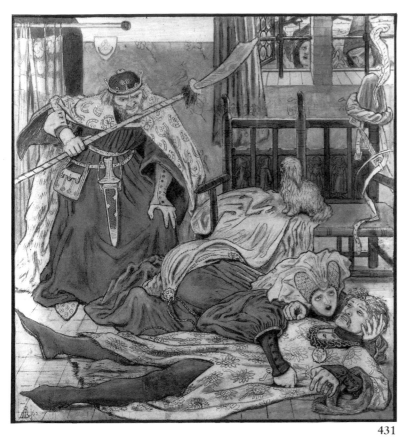

431

432

The 'Rossetti' chair

The settee Dante Gabriel Rossetti designed and painted for himself in 1862 was traditional in form (425), unlike the sofa he exhibited at the 1862 International Exhibition, known now only through a drawing (426). Rossetti lent his name to the lyre-back chair (428) made by Morris & Co. for sale alongside their revivalist 'Sussex' chairs (429) and ladder-back armchairs (430). It would be misleading, however, to suggest that Rossetti – or anyone else – was alone in inventing this type of furniture, for it appears simultaneously in different sources: for instance, Madox Brown's cartoon for *The Death of Sir Tristram* (431) and Solomon's gouache *St Cecilia* (432), both dated 1862. Godwin's so-named 'Greek' chair is similar (433), and much earlier, in 1857, Madox Brown designed this 'Egyptian' chair for Holman Hunt (434) – it is parent of a varied line of Thebes stools (427) similar to those Liberty's produced well into the 1920s. An odd ebonized chair now at Kelmscott Manor is thought to have been designed by Rossetti when convalescing there in the early 1870s (435).

433

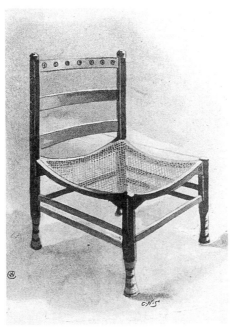

434

435

436

437

Morris & Co.

Morris, Marshall, Faulkner & Co. exhibited painted furniture at the 1862 London International Exhibition, including, it is thought, this blanket chest (**440**). Burne-Jones had already painted two important pieces: the Chaucer Wardrobe, a wedding present to Morris in April 1859 (see 407), and a sideboard for himself in 1860 (**436**). In 1867 the Burne-Joneses moved to The Grange, Fulham: in the drawing room (**438**) were two Philip Webb tables, Madox Brown's version of the 'Sussex' chair, and the Priestly piano painted by Burne-Jones with figures of 'Love' and 'Death'. In an upper room of the Morrises' Hammersmith home (**439**) the walls were hung with 'Bird', a wollen double cloth designed by Morris in 1878; the sturdy reading stand is reminiscent of the desk and settle in Burne-Jones's 1861–2 drawing of Chaucer (**437**). In 1866 the firm received two prestigious commissions: for the Armoury at St James's Palace (**441**) and the South Kensington Museum's Green Dining Room (see 402), where Webb's relief plaster decoration on the upper walls (**442**) borrows motifs from Newcastle Cathedral's fifteenth-century font. Colour was important in all their early furnishings: this bookcase (**443**), probably by Webb, has painted decoration in gold and silver, and this Webb corner cabinet (**444**) is stained green.

438

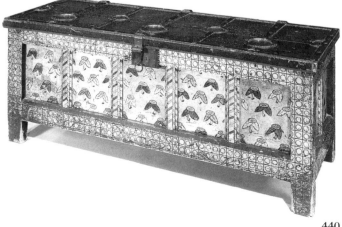

440

439

441

442

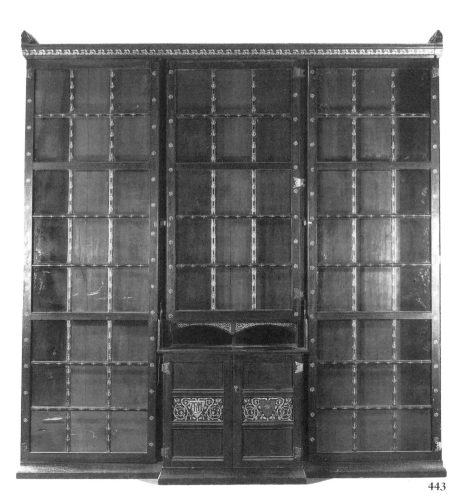

443

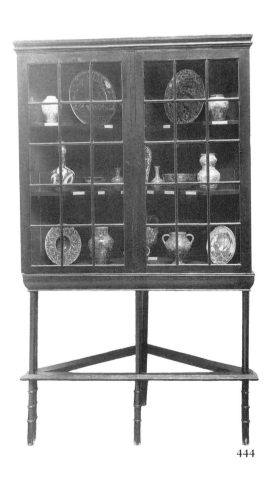

444

445

Philip Webb

446

In most of Philip Webb's architectural commissions the interior decoration was carried out by Morris & Co., beginning with Rounton Grange, Yorkshire (1872–6), for Sir Lowthian Bell. In the dining room (445) the Burne-Jones *Romaunt de la Rose* frieze was embroidered by Lady Bell and her daughters; the panelling and sideboard were made to Webb's design, but the serving table in an alcove (449) was designed by his assistant George Jack.

Webb's stylish Purbeck Marble entrance hall in the Ionides' house at 1 Holland Park (446) was added in about 1880. At the same time, Morris & Co. was decorating Old Swan House in Chelsea for Wickham Flower M.P. Two important pieces of furniture with gesso decoration by Kate Faulkner were displayed at either end of the drawing room, Webb's settle (447) and a Broadwood piano (448); in the foreground, a Rossetti chair blends with the antique furniture. The walls of Old Swan House were hung with the 'St James's' silk and the

447

448

449

450

floors were covered by two of Morris's finest carpets, giving a much more luxurious effect than Flower's country house, Great Tangley Manor, Surrey (451), rebuilt by Webb 1885–91, and carpeted with one of Morris's machine-woven Wiltons.

Standen, the country house near East Grinstead completed by Webb for the Beale family in 1894, is now owned by the National Trust. The late Morris & Co. furniture on display (450) includes two mahogany occasional tables and George Jack's 'Seville' chair, with slatted arms (the carpet was designed by Morris's chief assistant, J. H. Dearle). The Webb settle (452) at Wightwick Manor, Staffordshire – where Morris & Co. began their extensive work in 1893 – was decorated by the stained glass specialist C. E. Kempe. For Bullers Wood in Kent, the last commission on which Morris himself worked, George Jack designed in 1893 a grand piano incorporating Webb-like birds in the elaborate inlay (453).

451

452

453

454

455

Stained glass, textiles and tiles

Stained glass was another aspect of early Morris interiors in which Philip Webb was involved. In 1861 he provided lively designs for windows in the long gallery at the Red House (454) and, in 1862, this roundel for G. F. Bodley's All Saints, Selsley, Gloucestershire (455) – many of Morris, Marshall, Faulkner & Co.'s early commissions for stained glass came from Bodley, the majority for windows designed by Burne-Jones.

Burne-Jones also provided the images for Morris's major figurative textiles. 'The Pilgrim in the Garden', created in 1872, featured in embroideries executed for Rounton Grange between 1876 and 1880, and then reappeared in this tapestry made at Merton Abbey in 1901 (456). The dominant presence in much of this work is Janey Morris, *neé* Burden (457), who first modelled for Morris and Burne-Jones in Oxford 1857. *Angeli Ministrantes*,

designed by Burne-Jones in 1878 as a window for Salisbury Cathedral, was reworked by Dearle in 1894 as a tapestry (458), of which a larger version was later supplied to Eton College. Dearle also oversaw the production of carpets and rugs at Hammersmith, cleverly adapting Morris originals to new forms and colours (460).

Another Morris protégé, William De Morgan, painted the frieze panel on a Webb cabinet photographed in a corner of Mrs Lousada's drawing room in Kensington (462) – the wallpaper is Morris's 'Fruit' of 1864, one of his first three designs. Morris encouraged De Morgan into full-time production of tiles, and both Webb and Shaw used his lustre animal tiles (459) in their houses. Many of De Morgan's most impressive tile panels were produced at the Sands End Pottery (1888–98) in Fulham and have a strong Isnik influence (461).

456

457

458

459

460

461

462

Later Morris & Co. furniture

By the late 1880s neither Morris nor Webb was involved in the day-to-day management of the company's affairs. Much of the later furniture was designed by George Jack, who carved this blanket chest for himself in 1892 (463), though this Morris & Co. dining table (464) is more typical of his commercial work.

Early standards, including bobbin-turned chairs and settees (467) adapted by Webb from an eighteenth-century original and first made in 1866, were still marketed beside newer designs, such as this occasional table (468) by W. A. S. Benson, who became chairman on Morris's death in 1896. Benson designed the inlaid walnut secretaire (465) exhibited by Morris & Co. at the Franco-British Exhibition of 1908; he also combined forces with his brother-in-law Heywood Sumner to produce several music cabinets on the Orpheus theme (466). Morris & Co. furniture became increasingly revivalist: this 'Hepplewhite' sideboard (470), for example, or the 'Hampton Court' chair (469), similar to those used by Shaw in the Tabard Inn at Bedford Park. The designer of an uncharacteristically stylish group of Edwardian furniture made by Morris & Co. in ebony inlaid with silver (471 and 472), has yet to be identified.

463

464

465

466

467

468

469

470

471

472

473

474

Stanmore Hall

Morris & Co. worked on the sumptuous decoration of William Knox D'Arcy's Stanmore Hall, Middlesex, from 1888 to 1896. In the drawing room (**473**), the 'Persian Brocatel' on the walls and both carpets were designed by J. H. Dearle; George Jack's box-like secretaire (background left), bought by D'Arcy at the New Gallery in 1889, was criticized by the *Building News* as 'heavy and ungainly . . . a piece of furniture, however original, should express somewhat the purpose for which it is intended'. W. R. Lethaby designed the fireplace in the hall (**475**) and the impressively architectural table. The glazed cabinet visible in a detail of the sitting room (**474**) was exhibited by Morris & Co. at the Franco-British Exhibition of 1908; the rosewood settees, button upholstered in Morris printed silk, were, however, designed specifically for the entrance hall (**476**; the table is a Morris standard).

475

476

CHAPTER SEVEN

The Arts and Crafts Movement

477 The library, Bedales School, Hampshire, designed by Ernest Gimson shortly before his death in 1919. All the furniture is Gimson's.

fired more by the teachings of William Morris than by anything Morris & Co. itself stood for or produced, the arts and crafts movement became a recognizable force in the 1880s, enjoyed in the 1890s and the first decade of the twentieth century a reputation far beyond its narrow field of direct contact, and continues today to influence the style and ethos of conservative design. It would be wrong, however, to think of the movement as consistently coherent, for various contradictory solutions were offered to the problems of craft production at the end of a century which had witnessed a total revolution in industrial practice. Midst *fin de siècle* confusion, three themes emerged to dominate the movement: socialist concern for the plight of the 'B.W.M.' (C.R. Ashbee's cherished 'British Working Man');[1] sympathy for certain individual craftsmen's desire for isolated production; and belief in the need for stylistic unity in architecture and decoration, ordered on a human scale.

Most urban activists in the movement would have agreed with the architect-designer A. Romney Green: 'The question of the revival of our arts and crafts, as William Morris, the greatest of our modern craftsmen and revivalists knew, is obviously and almost solely a political question.'[2] For C.R. Ashbee in particular the issue was always more about people than things, and he wrote passionately and eloquently about the evils of 'wage-slavery': 'A week's work for a 15th century mason was equivalent to three sheep and a pair of shoes. An English mason now can barely earn two legs of mutton in a week, let alone the shoes.'[3] C.F.A. Voysey, like Ashbee a leading designer, not a craftsman at all, also expressed himself forcefully, though in his case about art, seldom about people. 'The intemperate indulgence in display and elaboration ... and the feverish thirst for artificial excitement', he wrote in 1894, 'are all part and parcel of our proverbial restlessness. Too much luxury is the death of the artistic soul.'[4] A lonely man, the creator of some marvellously progressive interiors, Voysey received far fewer commissions than his talents merited; emotionally he would have been better suited to the life of an isolated cabinetmaker, hewing his own wood to make plain oak furniture in a West Country barn. That sort of life, which was the other branch of the movement, is exemplified in Gimson's friend Sidney Barnsley, whose work Muthesius considered 'primitive to excess'[5] and the *Magazine of Art* castigated as 'the self-conscious baldness ... of the "rabbit hutch school"'.[6] Lethaby put it less cruelly, and more accurately too: 'Art is not a special sauce applied to ordinary cooking; it is the cooking itself if it is good.'[7]

On all sides – co-operative city workshop or one-man country craft; architect-designer or trained silversmith – by 1904 it was generally 'accepted as an article of faith ... that the finishing and furnishing of the home must be considered with the house itself, not in the scrappy fashion which has so long prevailed'.[8] In this way arguments first made by Pugin for the unified action of all the various disciplines, co-ordinated by a knowledgeable architect, were answered seventy years later in the arts and crafts movement. By then the scale of endeavour had been reduced to manageable proportions, the demand more for suburban villa than for country seat, and the merit of formal clarity widely acknowledged. The tenor of this new aesthetic was nicely caught by the architect Halsey Ricardo, William De Morgan's one-time partner: 'In one's passage through life there is a general accretion of possessions, but let us begin on a simple scale and try to keep the apparatus of life as much within bounds as possible ... There was – and still is – an idea that if the things themselves are beautiful, one cannot have too many of them; a glance into a museum ought to be enough to dispel *that* notion ... Until the house, until the room has been lived in, all looks inhuman, forbidding; it is only when the walls and their contents are redolent of human attention and human care, that the interior and its furniture can be a pride to its owner and a joy to those who see and use them.'[9]

The arts and crafts movement gained its cohesion by following John Ruskin's advocacy of the medieval guild system. Ruskin himself donated £7,000 in 1871 to found the Guild of St George, an organization whose achievements were limited to building a cottage museum near Sheffield and a few 'ideal' working men's cottages in Wales. It was left to an eager group of young architects from Richard Norman Shaw's office to set up, in 1883, their own St George's Art Society to challenge the structure of their profession and its attendant crafts. In May 1884 the Society's committee, comprising Ernest Newton, E.S. Prior, Mervyn Macartney, W.R. Lethaby, Gerald Horsley and E.J. May, decided to join forces with The Fifteen, a similar discussion group of painters and sculptors founded in 1882 under the secretaryship of Lewis Day. The resulting group was known as the Art-Workers' Guild. Pushed by the commercially energetic manufacturer W.A.S. Benson and encouraged by the call from artists like Holman Hunt for regular joint exhibitions of the fine and decorative arts, the Art-Workers' Guild founded in 1886 the Arts and Crafts Exhibition Society, with Walter Crane as its first president, a position he held until 1912 except for a three-year gap from 1893 to 1896 when the movement's grand old hero, William Morris, was persuaded to accept the post. Two assistant directors of the Grosvenor Gallery, Comyns Carr and Charles Hallé, broke away from the Grosvenor in the same year to lease their own space in Regent Street and it was here, at the New Gallery (488) in 1888, that the Arts and Crafts Exhibition Society mounted its first membership show. To compete with the Grosvenor's reputation for headline-making receptions, Hallé also arranged for Isadora Duncan to dance and William Morris to demonstrate weaving to selected 'Invitation Only' audiences.

478 Cabinet designed by C. R. Ashbee and made by the Guild of Handicraft at Essex House shortly before the move to Chipping Campden in 1901. Originally it was stained green and the openwork metal mounts were backed with red leather.

479 Wallpaper design of 1889 by C. F. A. Voysey, incorporating a self-caricature as a demon. Voysey worked for over twenty different manufacturers of wallpapers, carpets and textiles between 1883 and 1903.

480 The drawing room at Garden Corner, on the Chelsea Embankment, photographed in 1908. The interior was designed by Voysey in 1906–7 for E. J. Horniman M. P. The building contractor was F. Muntzer & Son and the furniture was made by one of Voysey's favourite cabinetmakers, F. C. Nielson. Voysey's interiors at Garden Corner were highly praised by M. H. Baillie Scott for demonstrating 'the application of serenely sane, practical and rational ideas to home-making'.

481 Clock designed by C. F. A. Voysey and manufactured in plain oak by Liberty's. It is based on an earlier, painted version designed for Voysey's own home in 1895.

482 and 483 Mahogany cabinet-on-stand with satinwood interior, designed by Charles Spooner and exhibited at the Arts and Crafts Exhibition Society in 1910. This is the finest known piece of furniture by Spooner, an influential arts and crafts figure.

484 Walnut corner hanging cabinet designed by Ernest Gimson, probably in 1890, and made by the Kenton & Co. craftsman George Bellamy (the bottom ledge is impressed 'G. Bellamy, Kenton & Co. Ltd. E. W. G.'). The fine walnut, palmwood and pewter inlay of birds in oak trees is typical of Gimson's style.

479

480

481

482

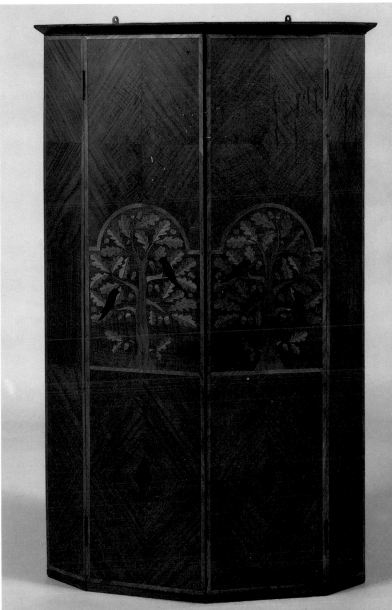

485 Design for a flat in Budapest by C. R. Ashbee, 1905. The patron for this commission was the Hungarian politician Zsombor de Szász, an admiring visitor to the Guild of Handicraft at Chipping Campden; Ashbee later dismissed him as 'an aristocrat playing with the ideals of democracy'. The furniture was of polished mahogany inlaid with holly; the electric-light fittings were hammered copper and iron. All were made by the Guild of Handicraft.

486 C. F. A. Voysey's watercolour design for the boardroom of the Essex & Suffolk Equitable Insurance Company in New Broad Street, London, on which he worked from 1906 to 1910. The tall chairs, which have the company's monogram stamped on their padded leather backs, are among Voysey's most important furniture (see 506).

485

486

487 and **488** This cabinet was designed by the Treasurer of the Arts and Crafts Exhibition Society, Lewis F. Day, and shown at their first exhibition, in 1888; the painted panels are by George McCulloch. The society's exhibitions were at the New Gallery, Regent Street, shown here in a photograph of *c.* 1890.

Whilst the New Gallery promoted public interest in the work of the movement's leaders, the Home Arts and Industries Association, founded in 1884, provided an organizational base for the host of amateur craftspeople working at home; from lace collars to pokerwork tea caddies, all their products were gathered at Carlton House Terrace in 1885 for the first of the Association's popular annual shows. By 1904 when a practical monthly manual, the *Arts and Crafts*, began publication, an editorial noted with pride that Ruskinian guilds now operated throughout the country, ranging from relatively sophisticated professional marketing units like the Mercia Guild of Handicraft in Stoke-on-Trent to the tiny South Harting Guild of Handicraft in the Hampshire village of that name. Women were always active participants in these organizations: Mrs Reynolds-Stevens, wife of the sculptor William Reynolds-Stevens, exhibited at the Arts and Crafts Exhibition Society's show of 1896 a loudly praised panel of embroidery designed by Voysey, and Mrs Walter Crane was seen 'driving herself alone in a horse and buggy to pay her visits and leave her cards, appearing in the streets in a chintz dress covered with some of William Morris' most elaborate flowers'.[10] In 1907 the Art Workers' Guild finally sponsored May Morris, William's younger daughter, and Mrs Thackeray Turner, the cabinetmaker's wife, in founding the Women's Guild of Arts.

The first of the privately run guilds was established in 1882 by the architects Arthur Heygate Mackmurdo (1851–1942) – a pupil of James Brooks – and Herbert Percy Horne (1864–1916). Their ambitions were clearly stated in their magazine, the *Hobby Horse* (489): 'The aim of the Century Guild is to render all branches of Art the sphere, no longer of the tradesman, but of the artist. It would restore building, decoration, glass-painting, pottery, wood-carving, and metalwork to their rightful place beside painting and sculpture.'[11] Mackmurdo worked in Florence for a couple of

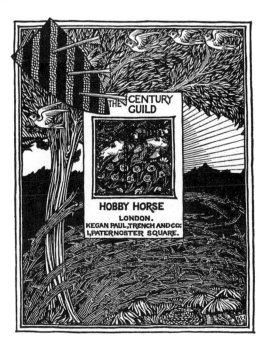

489 Mackmurdo and Horne's magazine the *Hobby Horse* was first published in 1884; the titlepage woodcut was by Selwyn Image.

490 The Fine Art Society in New Bond Street, decorated and furnished by George Faulkner Armitage in 1887.

491 C. R. Ashbee (third from left) and members of the Guild of Handicraft on an outing to Tintern Abbey in 1899.

years in the 1870s and all his furniture retained an architectural quality loosely inspired by Renaissance Italy. However, commentators have generally concentrated on the contrasting swirling linearity of Mackmurdo's decorative detail, particularly in the fret-carved back of a chair made by Collinson & Lock (514), credited by Nikolaus Pevsner as the first piece of 'Art Nouveau' furniture. That the attribution of revolutionary originality to Mackmurdo is not merely a retrospective judgement is indicated by contemporary criticism of the avant-garde aesthetics of the *Hobby Horse*; the *Magazine of Art*, for instance, deeply regretted its 'disdain . . . for the bounds of English prose and common sense'.[12] For the London International Health Exhibition of 1884 the Century Guild furnished and decorated a Music Room which was transported almost unchanged to the Inventions Exhibition in the following year (511). Instead of offering a range of products for sale, they worked solely on commission, aiming to design and produce a unique decorative ambience to fit each individual client's need, for, as a contributor to the *Builder* accurately observed, the Century Guild was 'a society of artists primarily, and a trading concern secondarily . . . an inversion of the ordinary trading method'.[13] Apart from Mackmurdo and Horne, the major Century Guild designers were Selwyn Image (1849–1930), specializing in stained glass and needlework, Harold Rathbone (1858–1929), a pupil of Ford Madox Brown and founder of the Birkenhead Della Robbia Pottery, who designed metalwork and lighting for the Guild, and Clement John Heaton (1861–1940), who also helped with the Guild's metalwork before moving first to Switzerland and then, in 1912, to the United States of America.

According to the *Studio*, much of the early Century Guild furniture was 'stained green with a touch of gold here and there, or the sparing use of an occasional copper ornament'.[14] Both in colour, therefore, as well as in form,

Mackmurdo's furniture anticipates the work of Voysey, a debt which Voysey himself personally admitted to Pevsner when they became friends in London in the 1930s. Had the Southampton Street partnership of Mackmurdo and Horne not come to an end in 1890, two years after the dissolution of the Century Guild, these highly original individuals might well have contributed more than just their one remarkable building, a modest 'modernist' house in Enfield, built between 1886 and 1887. Horne retired to Florence in 1900 and eventually left his home on the Via de'Benci and its distinguished contents to the Municipality; now known as the Museo Horne, it provides an appropriate monument to nineteenth-century England's love-affair with Tuscany. Although Mackmurdo continued in practice on his own, he spent most of the remainder of his long life studying baroque music and publishing esoteric tomes on socialist reform. Mackmurdo had no direct heirs, but his style influenced the work of George Faulkner Armitage (520), who came to the notice of the Fine Art Society at the Manchester Jubilee Exhibition of 1887 and earned a commission to decorate their Bond Street rooms (490). The fireplace Armitage designed for the Fine Art Society reappeared in many subsequent schemes in his extensive practice as an interior decorator; he also used the Mackmurdoesque chairs designed for the Fine Art Society at Stamford House, his home at Altrincham in Cheshire.

On the evidence of numbers alone, the most fanatical believer in the guild ideal must surely have been Charles Robert Ashbee (1863–1942), whose Guild of Handicraft at one time numbered a hundred and fifty working men, women and boys. After coming down from Cambridge in 1883 Ashbee joined the architectural practice of G.F. Bodley, founder of the church decorating firm Watts & Co. and designer of distinguished ecclesiastical textiles and ironwork.[15] In the Bodley office Ashbee worked alongside

Ninian Comper, creator of an impressive group of late-Gothic church interiors, but the restless Ashbee had very different interests and in 1886 he left to take up residence at Canon Barnett's Toynbee Hall in the East End of London, taking over a Ruskin reading class and dedicating himself to the cause of socialist reform through education. Following in the 1860s footsteps of Morris and Rossetti, he soon established a design class and set about redecorating the dining room (now the library) at Toynbee Hall (523). Out of this group of would-be artist-craftsmen emerged, in 1888, the Guild of Handicraft, operating for the first three years from premises further along Commercial Street, after which Ashbee moved his expanded East End family into Essex House, a half-derelict eighteenth-century property on the Mile End Road. The carpentry shop was built along one side of the house's large garden, with the smithy at the end, 'the glowing fire of which could be seen at any spring-time through glimpses of apple blossom'.[16]

Whatever the various qualities and failings of Ashbee's extensive output of designs for furniture, silver, metalwork and jewellery, and despite the eventual closure of the Guild of Handicraft in 1907, there can be no denying the merit of his social achievements. Many of the things about which he cared most deeply a century ago are now understood by a wider audience to be matters of central concern. 'Most people', he wrote, optimistically, 'are agreed that one of the greatest problems before the Country is the problem of unemployment.' Ashbee's solution was to free the craftsman from 'the precarious weekly wage-dependence' and 'to put his labour at the service of the community'.[17] He was bitterly critical of the educational system and its administrative wastage, of 'all this rigmarole, all this pishery-pashery before public money may be used in teaching . . . a village lad to use an anvil'.[18] Although the new Board Schools in London might look like 'overgrown and ill-ornamented

urinals' Ashbee noted that 'surprising results have been achieved by teachers with the right social attitudes'.[19] Ashbee himself was a great believer in the benefits of physical exercise and insisted on taking his young East End charges for regular work-outs in the swimming pools and gymnasiums of the People's Palace for East London (492). Trips into the country were even more beneficial (491): Ashbee hoped that the 'young citizen might . . . get out as often as possible into the free sunshine and enjoy the use of naked limbs in air and water'.[20] No doubt in much of this Ashbee satisfied emotional as well as ideological needs. At Cambridge he had come under the influence of the preacher

492 Ashbee used to take his apprentices to exercise in the gymnasiums of the People's Palace in Whitechapel, built by E. R. Robson and largely completed by 1888, three years before this photograph by Bedford Lemère was taken.

493 Broadwood advertisement in the *Burlington Magazine*, 1903, illustrating a typical Ashbee case made by the Guild of Handicraft.

494 A design by C. R. Ashbee for the furniture and decoration of a flat, probably for Gyula Mandello in Budapest, 1899–1900.

495 Ashbee's design for lacquered ironwork on an oak cabinet: from top to bottom, the top of a hinge, a knuckle and a drawer handle and plate. Hinges and handles were to be backed by blue leather. This drawing is dated *c*.1898.

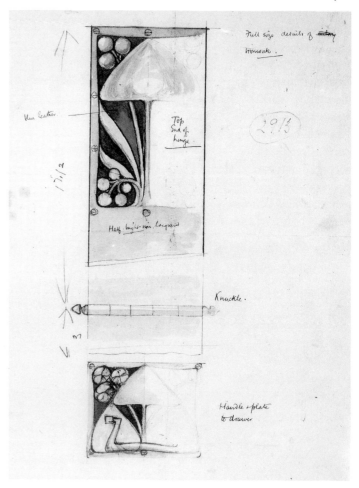

of social and sexual reform Edward Carpenter and although his unconventional marriage eventually produced four daughters, Ashbee always yearned for what Carpenter termed 'homogenic love', a non-physical homosexual creed of comradely love of the kind he shared with apprentices like Sammy, 'a veritable cock-sparrow of a boy with a touch somehow – a far off touch, I don't know why, of the aristophanic Athenian'.[21]

The Guild of Handicraft was slow to develop proficient production of furniture, partly because of the ponderous inadequacies of the early designs supplied by Ashbee and the ubiquitous architect and teacher Charles Spooner, which resulted, according to the normally supportive *Studio*, in 'simplicity carried dangerously near triteness'.[22] By 1894 the furniture workshop at Essex House had expanded to employ ten people, and a certain freedom of expression was achieved by Ashbee's insistence on one craftsman executing every part of each individual piece. Liberation came, however, both for Ashbee and his cabinetmakers, with the commission from M.H. Baillie Scott in 1898 to make all the furniture for the Duke of Hesse's palace at Darmstadt (628). After this experience furniture designed by the Guild became lighter and altogether more adventurous in decorative detail.

With the help of his able assistant Charles Holden, Ashbee also maintained a small architectural practice, and built a number of mildly eccentric houses in Chelsea, including, in 1893–4, one for his mother at 37 Cheyne

Walk. Three years earlier Mrs Ashbee had finally left her outwardly respectable City merchant husband, Henry Spencer Ashbee, otherwise known as 'Piranus Fraxi', the famous collector of erotica, numbered amongst which was a volume of drawings bound, it was alleged, in human skin brought back for him from Africa by Sir Richard Burton. Noting that his father 'just passed as morning sunlight'[23] out of their lives, Ashbee settled down to creating a home that was always intended to be as much his as his mother's and to which he brought his wife, Janet, on their marriage in 1898. Called the Magpie and Stump after a sixteenth-century inn on the site, the Ashbee house was full of experimental decorative detail, some of which, like the red and green enamel fireplace in the hall, was removed to the Victoria and Albert Museum in 1968 when the building was bulldozed by developers. Romantic, certainly, and even sentimental – though seldom nostalgic – Ashbee believed in taking full advantage of scientific progress and he encouraged his excellent metalworkers at the Guild into adventurous experiment with electric light fitments, the bulbs of which he veiled in silk bags, decorated with 'little glinting coloured beads of coral and gemstones'.[24] In the dining-room at Cheyne Walk (522), he labelled a frieze of painted peacocks 'Fop and Fashion Peacocking', a parody of the life-style in artistic Chelsea from which he bicycled away every day to his workshops in the Mile End Road. Tirelessly energetic, Ashbee bought much of the Kelmscott Press printing equipment when Morris died in 1896 and set up his own Essex House Press. In 1899 the Guild opened its own shop in Dering Yard, round the corner from the Dering Street retail warehouse operated by W.A.S. Benson since 1890.

Inspired by the success of group visits to the country and seduced by late-nineteenth-century dreams of idyllic rural craftsmanship, at a meeting in Essex House on 6 December 1901 Ashbee persuaded the guildsmen to vote in favour of

496–498 Halsey Ricardo's two designs (*above*), dated January 1899, of cast-iron grates for the founders Longden & Co. are closely comparable to W. R. Lethaby's for Coalbrookdale. C. R. Ashbee designed a similar series of grates for the Falkirk Iron Company: they were illustrated in the *Studio* in 1898 (*below*), where Ashbee claimed to be 'avoiding all sharp lines that might suggest an origin in woodwork'.

permanently moving the workshops to the old silk mill in the Cotswold town of Chipping Campden. Moving in stages to their new homes throughout 1902, the East Enders and their families were joined by skilled craftsmen from other parts of the country until, by the end of the year, the Guild of Handicraft employed seventy-one men. From the social point of view the venture was broadly successful, especially for Ashbee, who adored close communal life – evening discussions, mass bicycle rides, seasonal theatricals – and delighted in the increased physical well-being of young and old alike. In the Guild of Handicraft's 'Memorandum and Articles of Association' Ashbee had declared his intention 'to do good work and to do it in such a way as shall best conduce to the welfare of the workmen'.[25] This included providing pensions for all the retired craftsmen, such as Dick Read, who had been to prison in 1875 in defence of trade unionism and died in 1908 a closely cared-for eighty-three-year-old. The Guild's social achievements were much admired, and droves of influential visitors were drawn to Chipping Campden by Ashbee's magnetic enthusiasm.

Financially, however, the move to the country put an enormous strain on the Guild's resources and after three successive years of serious commercial depression, in 1907 the Guild of Handicraft, by then a limited company, was abandoned by its shareholders. Many of the craftsmen continued to work independently in Chipping Campden, and the Essex House Press survived for a few more years under Ananda Coomeraswamy who moved into The Norman Chapel, the Ashbees' old home in Chipping Campden. Back home in London, analysing the experience, Ashbee warned future dreamers: 'It is not sufficiently observed how the complexity of modern business methods is coming in itself to be more and more a tax on labour.'[26] In London his skilled craftsmen could easily obtain 'inferior

work ... in the ordinary commercial shops'[27] to tide them over hard times, but in Gloucestershire there was no alternative but to continue in the production of goods which sold for less than they cost to make. It was the inequitable economic structure of society itself which had defeated them, a world in which the admired Essex House Prayer Book was retailed by entrepreneurs in America for £300 when still printing in Campden at the published price of £30. Disillusioned, Ashbee bowed out of the arts and crafts movement, leaving the field to 'lady amateurs' from the Home Arts and Industries Associations, jokingly referred to in happier days at the Guild as the generic 'Dear Emily', whose livelihood need never depend on their own labour.

Privately run craft organizations had a high failure rate: the respected Kenton & Co. survived for barely two years after its formation in October 1890. Its key figures were William Richard Lethaby (1857–1931), a founder of the Art-Workers' Guild, and Ernest Gimson (1864–1919), a protégé of William Morris's; these two (500), together with their architect friends Mervyn Macartney, Reginald Blomfield – nephew of Sir Arthur W. Blomfield – and Sidney Barnsley, with a Colonel Mallet as contacts-man, each subscribed £100 to set up workshops in a mews off Kenton Street, on the eastern fringes of Bloomsbury. Seven cabinetmakers were employed producing furniture exclusively to the design of the five architect partners. Their first exhibition, held at Barnards Inn, Holborn, in December 1891 (533), was both a critical and financial success, with sales of over £700. At the Arts and Crafts Exhibition Society show in 1890 Lethaby's severely rectilinear veneered walnut cabinet, made by Marsh, Jones & Cribb of Leeds, had been praised by the progressive critic Lawrence Weaver as 'an exemplar' of modern design,[28] and by Gimson as 'wonderful furniture of a commonplace kind'[29] – very different from the 'carpenter's furniture'[30] Lethaby exhibited at Barnards Inn. The back of Lethaby's throne-chair was inlaid with sheep grazing amongst flowers; the uprights were boldly chip-carved in the manner favoured by Gimson and derived from the decoration of farm carts, the solid members of which were worked in this way to reduce weight without loss of strength. When the company disbanded a year later the partners divided the unsold pieces between them, Lethaby ending up with a Gimson walnut cabinet, a Blomfield cabinet, Barnsley's table, the Macartney revolving bookcase and an oak chair of his own: 'After all, these five pieces with all the fun and some experience gained were not a bad return for £100 down.'[31]

Lethaby had won the Soane Medallion at the Royal Academy in 1879 and, having been turned down by Butterfield, was promptly recommended to Richard Norman Shaw by Maurice B. Adams, editor of the *Building News*. Although older men like Macartney and Horsley were already ensconced in the office, Shaw appointed Lethaby his chief assistant. As Beresford Pite, another assistant, confirmed: 'Shaw loved and valued Lethaby and gave him a liberty in dealing with his work [which] was the real

499 A rosewood desk-box inlaid with mother-of-pearl, one of a series of relatively expensive 'miniatures' designed by Ernest Gimson after his move to Gloucestershire in 1893.

estimate of his quality.'[32] Even when Lethaby set up in independent practice in 1889 he still came into Shaw's office to help on three days a week and this long association inevitably influenced his architectural style: 'Vive La Renaissance' was inscribed on some of his drawings. After Lethaby moved office in 1891 to Gray's Inn Square, Shaw's classical influence was balanced by the sterner aesthetic of Philip Webb, Lethaby's admired new neighbour, and he went on to produce some of his best architecture and furniture within a prolific five-year period from 1898 to 1903: Melsetter House, an imaginative project of reconstruction on the island of Hoy in the Orkneys; High Coxlease, Lyndhurst, Hampshire, for Eustace Smith, a Tyneside ship-repairer whose mother and sister had both been implicated in the Dilke scandal; the ancient-seeming chapel of SS Colm and Margaret on Hoy; the sensationally massed All Saints, Brockhampton, near Ross-on-Wye; and his unexecuted masterpiece, the Liverpool Cathedral competition drawings and model, partly inspired by his trip to Turkey in 1893. Lethaby's creative achievement during this period is all the more remarkable as it coincided with the foundation of the Central School of Arts and Crafts, of which he was joint director (with the sculptor George Frampton) from 1896 to 1900, and sole principal from 1900 to 1912. Like Webb before him, Lethaby declined the RIBA Gold Medal, dismissing this coveted award as 'a lot of nobodies giving themselves "distinctions"'.[33]

Of the other Kenton & Co. partners, Macartney subsequently wasted too much time on health cures in Colorado Springs and Blomfield deserted the craft cause in favour of a lucrative career designing country houses in the grand manner, leaving Grimson and Barnsley to salvage what they might from the experiment.

Ernest Gimson had first met the Barnsley brothers when he came down to London from Leicestershire in 1886 to work as an architectural draughtsman in the office of J.D. Sedding, next door to the Oxford Street showrooms of William Morris, by whom he had been introduced to Sedding. Coming from a well-connected family of Birmingham builders, with close ties to J.H. Chamberlain, the elder Barnsley brother, Sidney, was articled to Shaw and the younger, Ernest, to Sedding. The metalworker Henry Wilson wrote of Sedding, who had been his teacher: 'It was not what he did … but what he made others do … He was a radiant centre of artistic activity; a focus of creative fire; a node of magnetic force.'[34] The other important influence on their lives was Philip Webb, Gimson's neighbour in Gray's Inn and a respected figure at meetings of Morris's Society for the Protection of Ancient Buildings, which they regularly attended. A founder committee member in 1877 of the S.P.A.B., Webb continuously emphasized the relevance to modern design of preserving traditional craftsmanship through architectural conservation. When Gimson and the Barnsleys left London in 1893 for Ewen, Gloucestershire, there were hopes that Webb himself would make the journey too, for he shared their ambition 'to get

500 W. R. Lethaby (standing) and Ernest Gimson, a photograph probably taken in 1889 during a holiday they spent together in a farmhouse near Fountains Abbey.

hold of a few capable and trustworthy craftsmen and eventually have workshops in the country where we should all join together and form a nucleus around which in time others would attach themselves'.[35]

The etcher F.L. Griggs, who lived in Chipping Campden but much preferred Gimson's company to Ashbee's, wrote that 'Ernest Gimson was in all he did a very English genius'.[36] The origins of his architectural and decorative style are indeed to be found exclusively in rural England: when D.S. McColl, William Morris's biographer, discovered in 1888 a chairmaker called Philip Clissett still working the pole-lathe to produce ladder-back chairs that were 'strong, light, shapely and entirely right' (503),[37] Gimson went off to work with him in Bosbury, Herefordshire. Plastering was another traditional skill Gimson acquired, which led to commissions from several architect friends: for Lethaby at Avon Tyrrell, Hampshire, for instance, and for Halsey Ricardo at Sir Ernest Debenham's house in Addison Road, London. According to Lethaby, Gimson's plasterwork was 'as good, every bit, as old work and yet simple as a piecrust'; he also 'drew beautifully, in a tender Ruskinian way'.[38] The

501 Ernest Gimson's simple sitting room at Sapperton in Gloucestershire. The chair on the left, by W. R. Lethaby, dates from Gimson and Lethaby's collaboration in Kenton & Co., 1890–2.

cottage Gimson built for his brother at Markfield in Leicestershire (with the architect Detmar Blow as clerk of the works), and his hall and library at Bedales School, Petersfield, Hampshire (477), have the look almost of rural re-creations, although direct plagiarisms in his work are rare; one of the few discernible from his sketchbooks is the transposition of a fourteenth-century fresco at Berkeley church, Gloucestershire, into the floral inlay of a cabinet.

In the summer of 1894 Gimson and the Barnsleys moved from Ewen to Pinbury, an idyllic enclosed Gloucestershire valley which Sidney's son Edward has described as 'a very

happy set-up indeed, with all three men working together in the workshop and sharing ideas'.[39] Forced by their landlord, Lord Bathurst, to move to nearby Sapperton in 1902, Gimson and Ernest Barnsley briefly operated in partnership, establishing a business which was continued by Gimson with the help of the Dutch cabinetmaker Peter Waals. In June of that year Gimson wrote optimistically to Philip Webb: 'As to manufacture . . . things look quite cheerful, the difficulty now being to complete the orders we get and so we are launching out as businessmen'.[40] Lord Bathurst loaned them a fine sixteenth-century manor, Daneway

502 From 1902 Lord Bathurst loaned sixteenth-century Daneway House, near Sapperton, to Gimson and Barnsley for use as a showroom. The furniture on display is (from left to right) a mahogany cabinet, a variant of one of Gimson's earliest designs; a bobbin-turned ash chair of the type made for Gimson by Edward Gardiner; a dark oak settee by Gimson, on sale in 1905 for £13 10s; a corner cabinet designed and made by Sidney Barnsley; and another rush-seated armchair.

503 Sidney Barnsley's parlour in the house he built for himself in Sapperton 1902–3. Against the back wall is one of the ladder-back chairs made by Philip Clissett to Gimson's design; in the foreground is Barnsley's own chunky desk, exhibited at the Arts and Crafts Exhibition Society in 1903.

House, in which to display the work (502), and visitors began to arrive in numbers, including Eric Gill, Romney Green and others of the next generation of artist-craftsmen. Direct sales complemented commissions given to Gimson by architect-friends such as Robert Weir Schultz, W. Curtis Green, E.S. Prior and F.W. Troup to furnish houses they were building for clients. Whilst Gimson soon gave up all practical craftsmanship to concentrate on design, Sidney Barnsley went in the opposite direction and set up a workshop in which he laboured alone on his own furniture, even hewing his own wood. In a letter of 1904 to Webb he described his new Sapperton workshop as 'much better lighted and being thatched warmer and drier, and from the end window I have a most wonderful view across the valley to the hanging wood you would remember'. On quitting the Gimson partnership Ernest Barnsley had returned to architecture and ended up working almost exclusively for the Society for the Protection of Ancient Buildings. Both brothers died in 1926.

Eschewing Ashbee's crusader histrionics, Gimson founded a community of rural craftsmanship which long outlived the Guild of Handicraft and can boast direct descendants today in the workshops of Edward Barnsley (b. 1900), Oliver Morel (b. 1916) and Hugh Birkett (b. 1919). Gimson's communal instincts were strong: just before the First World War he purchased a parcel of land near Sapperton to which he brought the mains water supply in preparation for building a craftsman's village. The war and Gimson's ill-health prevented significant progress, however, and on 12 August 1919 Gimson died. Known to present-day collectors by his superb designs for furniture and metalwork (560–563), he was remembered by West Country friends equally as a countryman: to quote Ernest

Barnsley's son-in-law, the architect Norman Jewson, he was 'a man entirely at peace with himself and all the world'.[41] In his contribution to *Ernest Gimson: His Life and Work*, a privately subscribed memoir edited by Lethaby, Griggs wrote in admiration of the quiet confidence of Gimson's belief that 'the work could be left to itself to secure all the notice and influence it deserved', work which Griggs considered 'as much beyond praise as beyond criticism'.

The last leading architect-designer of the arts and crafts movement, C.F.A. Voysey (505), was a very different character: an intense visionary, whose chronic conviction of his own infallability resulted in difficulties with clients and a tantalizingly small body of immensely impressive work (566–575). The son of a de-frocked clergyman, Voysey received his architectural training in the offices first of J.P. Seddon and then of George Devey, before setting up in independent practice in London in about 1882. His first recorded furniture design, for the 'Swan' chair, came in the following year. It revealed a keen admiration of Pugin, and although Voysey's mature furniture of the period 1895 to 1910 displays no such direct visual debt, he always saw himself as an heir to Pugin rather than a founder of the modern movement, as many admirers suggested. When tyroes like Lutyens praised the 'absence of accepted forms' in his work,[42] Voysey replied (in his last public lecture, in 1934): 'Modern architecture is pitifully full of such faults as proportions that are vulgarly aggressive, mountebank eccentricities of detail and windows lying down on their sides . . . This is false originality, the true originality having been, for all time, the spiritual something given to the development of traditional forms by the individual artist.'[43] Like Pugin, Voysey was driven by an overtly religious image of the artist's role; like Pugin too, he drew every last detail of his

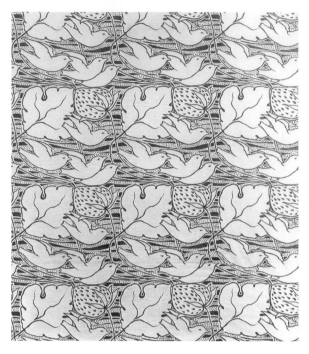

504 A reversible roller-printed cotton designed by C. F. A. Voysey *c.*1895 for Newman, Smith & Newman.

505 Harold Speed's portrait of Voysey in 1905.

506 One of the chairs designed by Voysey for the Essex and Suffolk Equitable Insurance Company, 1906–10.

commissions himself, and even in the age of the typewriter continued to hand-write all his own business letters. As the *Studio* noted as early as 1896, Voysey 'never coquetted with the passing taste',[44] but campaigned passionately against the evil of ugliness in modern society. 'Cold vegetables', he wrote in his slightly mocking, ironical tone, 'are less harmful than ugly dish covers. One affects the body and the other affects the soul.'[45]

Voysey worked most consistently as a flat-pattern designer (504). He produced his first wallpaper in 1883 for Jeffrey & Co., and was still well enough known in 1920 for Essex & Co. (575) to promote him in advertisements as 'the Genius of Pattern'.[46] As well as wallpapers (479), he designed tiles, carpets, rugs, curtains and quantities of furnishing fabric (576). Some of the later work may be rather too busily figurative, but the majority of his patterns were brilliantly inventive and much admired in Europe – the Belgian architect Victor Horta used Voysey papers in 1896 in the Hôtel Tassel, Brussels, a blueprint for *L'Art Nouveau*, and again in the Hôtel Solvay. The *Magazine of Art*, however, criticized Voysey's carpets in the Arts and Crafts Exhibition Society show at the New Gallery in 1896 for only working when viewed from one direction: 'always happy in colour [they] are not equally admirable in design'.[47] For the simplicity of style which Voysey demanded of himself – 'simplicity in decoration is one of the most essential qualities without which no true richness is possible'[48] – one must turn to his furniture, on drawings for which the cabinetmakers' names most frequently seen are F. Coote, F.C. Nielsen and B. Thallon (occasionally also C.H.B. Quennell, J.S. Henry and A.W. Simpson). The collector Charles Handley-Read, who purchased in 1967 for £57 all the available Voysey pieces in the New Broad Street offices of Chase, Henderson and Tennant, previously the Essex and Suffolk Equitable Insurance Company (486 and 569), felt that 'his furniture nearly always suggests what might be called Quakerly moderation – low living and high thinking'.[49] Mostly made in 'oak lightly oiled'[50] Voysey furniture is deceptively simple in appearance, the subtle tapers and rounded chamfering easily misinterpreted by commercial manufacturers (568).

Despite failing to secure a single major public commission, Voysey designed, decorated and entirely furnished five small but distinguished houses. Best known perhaps is The Orchard in Chorleywood, Hertfordshire, which he built for himself and his family in 1899 (566). The interiors of The Orchard are endowed with a stylistic unity matched in Britain for originality only by those of Charles Rennie Mackintosh. A committed architectural colourist, Voysey used startling yellows and blues for the exterior of many of his buildings. Inside The Orchard, although the ground-floor woodwork and walls were enamelled white, he placed a peacock blue rug in the hall, a grey-green carpet up the stairs and hung bright red turkey-twill curtains throughout. As usual with Voysey's interiors, the furniture was made of oak, 'the wood in its natural colour which every day grows more pleasant to look at'.[51]

The same year Voysey designed a house for H.G. Wells near Folkestone, with a heart-shaped letter plate which he was obliged to transform into a spade, for Wells refused 'to wear his heart on his front door'.[52] Voysey created some of his most adventurous furniture for the Ward-Higgs's house at 23 Queensborough Terrace, Bayswater, in the late 1890s; for C.T. Burke's Hollymount, Beaconsfield, in 1905 (571); for The Homestead at Frinton-on-Sea, designed 1905 to 1906; and, in the following year, for Garden Corner, Chelsea, home of the tea-merchant turned politician E.J. Horniman (480). Horniman was evidently a man of advanced tastes for he and the architect Charles Harrison Townsend were already responsible for the most dazzlingly un-English building of the period, a 'Byzantine' museum in south London, designed in 1896 to house the M.P.'s collection of ethnographica. Voysey's alterations to Garden Corner, designed by Edward l'Anson in the 1870s, also have a distinctly Continental flavour, recorded in a stylish series of photographs published in the *Studio* in 1908. However, although Voysey designed his furniture to minimize production costs, it seldom reached the popular market and he, like other arts and crafts designers, was blighted by exclusivity, a point well-made by the *Studio*: 'If few people can afford to have furniture specially designed for them, there are still fewer who, having the means, possess the taste to put the idea into execution and courage enough to face the result.'[53]

Isolated in his working practice, and incomprehensibly convoluted in his theoretical writing, Voysey had only one direct disciple, Arthur Simpson. In 1886 Simpson set up his own business in Finkle Street, Kendal, and from 1896 regularly executed furniture for Voysey's northern commissions (573). He also worked successfully on his own designs in the Voysey idiom (574), but nevertheless turned to Voysey in 1909 for a new house for himself, Littlehome in Kendal, which has one big 'living-room', a term thought to have been first used by Voysey. There is a Voysey link also with another furniture designer well-known in his time but largely ignored today, Charles Spooner (1862–1938), secretary of the Wood Handicrafts Society, in whose name both he and Voysey exhibited significant pieces at the Arts and Crafts Exhibition Society show of 1893. Spooner ran his own workshop in Hammersmith, taught first at the Guild of Handicraft, then at the Central School of Arts and Crafts, and in 1908 was named by Ashbee alongside Lethaby, Gimson and Barnsley as one of the four people 'with whom the Arts and Crafts movement is identified' (482 and 483).[54] C.H. Spooner and 'that excellent designer'[55] C.H.B. Quennell, whose furniture was produced by J.P. White of Bedford, were both lionized by Muthesius, although, on the evidence of illustrations in contemporary periodicals, much of their work was depressingly derivative. As Spooner himself put it: 'the great bulk of furniture made at the present time is entirely without art'.[56]

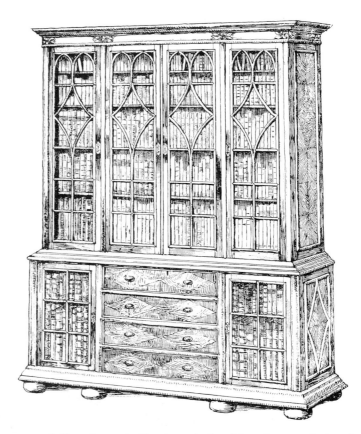

507 A Georgian revival bookcase in Spanish mahogany, designed by Charles Spooner, *c.*1905.

508 Murals and furniture by Frank Brangwyn in the dining room at Casa Cuseni, Taormina, 1909.

Few of the other leading architects of the movement designed furniture in any quantity. Walter Cave (1863–1939), an Old Etonian county cricketer, ran a successful architectural practice and designed a limited range of furniture (576–577), metalwork and wallpaper. The eccentric Old Harrovian E.S. Prior (1852–1932) only 'really enjoyed being in a minority of one';[57] he designed a house at Harrow and the music school at Winchester, and believed that 'the saviour of his art to the architect is ... in experiment in the devices of craftsmanship'.[58] No furniture by either Prior or another Shaw pupil, 'our comic friend'[59] Arthur Beresford Pite (1861–1934), has yet been located, though some Pite furniture must surely exist, possibly in Uganda, where he built Kampala Cathedral. Yet another architect from Shaw's office, Robert Weir Schultz (1860–1951), also established a flourishing independent career, working from 1891 for Burges's patron the 3rd Marquis of Bute, for whom he designed furniture for St John's Lodge, Regent's Park, and for the House of Falkland on the Isle of Bute. For the 4th Marquis Schultz worked with Gimson in furnishing Old Place, Mochrum, and he again employed Gimson to design the wonderful bone-inlaid choir-stalls in St Andrew's Chapel, Westminster Cathedral. Schultz designed his own choir-stalls, however, for Khartoum Cathedral.

Other important designers of arts and crafts furniture, such as Romney Green and Gordon Russell, made their names after the First World War and their work therefore falls outside our period. Many designs for the decorative arts by the painter Frank Brangwyn (1867–1956) were, however, executed before 1915 (579–580). Of his textiles Muthesius wrote: 'Brangwyn is the only artist who has

509 Two rush-seated ladder-back chairs designed by Edwin Lutyens for Little Thakeham, Sussex, as illustrated in W. Shaw Sparrow's *Hints on House Furnishing* (1909).

510 A decoration by C. R. Ashbee for the text of his lecture delivered to the Edinburgh Art Conference of 1889, in which he declared that 'from the obscene bulb of the plutocracy, sprang the tulip of the new civilization'.

designed really modern carpets in the present-day continental sense. His patterns have a mysterious ambiguity which is extremely attractive ... the colour is fresh without being startling, lush without becoming brutal'[60] – a compliment to William Morris, who had employed Brangwyn as a draughtsman in 1882, when he was aged only fifteen. His major extant domestic commission is the dining room at Casa Cuseni in Taormina, for the watercolourist Robert Kitson (508); the furniture was made in 1909–10 by local craftsmen. The importance of the scheme was pointed out to the owner by Charles Handley-Read in the 1960s. She responded: '[As the] house suffered from three occupations during the war ... it is a bit of a miracle that everything survived ... I am unexpectedly grateful to you for making me realize that it is urgently required to do some upkeep.'[61] Handley-Read offered to buy the furniture if she 'ever felt driven to dismembering the interior'. 'Do forgive these business-like asides', he added.[62]

The work of Edwin Lutyens (1869–1944) has only recently attracted the attention of furniture collectors – Handley-Read had no interest, it would seem, in owning any, and other collectors have tended to follow his example. This is partly explained by the fact that Lutyens designed furniture only as an adjunct to specific architectural commissions, never as an independent exercise; also, the furniture he did design was very varied both in style and quality, and cannot consistently be placed into any particular art-historical pigeon-hole. Lutyens trained in the office of Ernest George and Harold Peto, where his personal preference for antique furniture was fostered. It was a taste shared by many of the clients attracted to the busy independent practice he set up in 1889. In the 1890s

Lutyens's architecture would have been thought of as 'arts and crafts', especially the cottage at Munstead Wood, Surrey, that he built for the garden designer Gertrude Jekyll, and Deanery Garden in Sonning, Berkshire, for Edward Hudson, founder of *Country Life*. Hudson was a discerning collector of antiques, Jekyll an admirer of tough country-made furniture, and neither therefore needed any furniture by their architect. The few pieces Lutyens did design before 1915 are in various styles. There was arts and crafts furniture: the rush-seated ladderback chairs photographed in the hall at Little Thakeham, Sussex, and illustrated by W. Shaw Sparrow in *Hints on House Furnishing* (1909); eighteenth-century revivalist furniture in the Richard Norman Shaw tradition – 'anything but modern', according to Muthesius;[63] and the Renaissance-style unstained oak furniture designed for his own house at 29 Bloomsbury Square, which included an exotic casket covered in gilt-tooled leather which he gave to Lady Emily Lytton in 1896, a year before their marriage – the base resembles a safe designed for Marshcourt, Hampshire, in 1901 (578).

The stylistic inconsistency of Lutyens's furniture and interiors is a problem which concerns the whole of the arts and crafts movement. On the one hand there were artist-craftsmen such as Sidney Barnsley who retired to the country to practise traditional rural crafts. On the other were designer-architects such as Voysey whose work was hailed on the Continent for its modernity in enthusiastic articles by the progressive Dutch architect Henri van de Velde in *Art Moderne* (1894) and in the first volume of *Dekorative Kunst* (1897). Whatever the stylistic origins or directions of its aesthetic, the best English furniture of this period is, however, of lasting quality and interest.

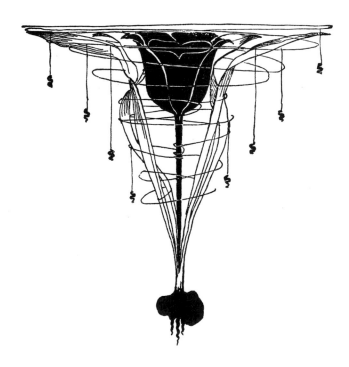

511

The Century Guild

A CENTURY GUILD FIRE DOG

512

The Century Guild first exhibited publicly at the International Health Exhibition in 1884, and moved its stand virtually unchanged to the Inventions Exhibition the following year (**511**). The Guild's furniture (**513, 517** and **518** – illustrated in the *Building News* in 1880) was designed by A. H. Mackmurdo, often with avant-garde architectural detail; his best-known chair (**514**), however, is relatively conventional in form, except for the swirling fretwork of its back, which anticipates Art Nouveau.

The Guild worked on commission, calling mainly on Herbert Horne for the design of textiles, on Selwyn Image for stained glass, and on Harold Rathbone, Clement John Heaton and Kellock Brown for decorative metalwork (**512**). The Guild's stand at the Liverpool International Exhibition of 1886 (**515**) included a tall

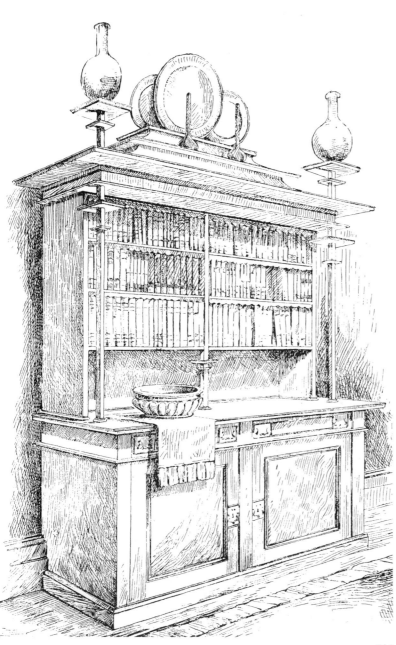

513

514

515

516

mahogany buffet by Mackmurdo, made by
E. Goodall & Co. and bought by the
Manchester brewer Henry Boddington for
his Wilmslow home Pownall Hall, the
decoration of which he then handed over
entirely to the Guild. Much of the Guild's
work was in the Merseyside area, including
the furnishing of Rainhill (516), a house
designed by Harold Rathbone's brother
Edmund.

In 1888 the Guild was disbanded and
Mackmurdo turned his attention away from
furniture. The octopus-like table (519)
designed by Charles Edward Horton and
exhibited by Lamb's at the Manchester
Jubilee Exhibition of 1887, a desk designed
by George Faulkner Armitage (520) and
some early Voysey furniture are amongst
the few pieces directly modelled on
Mackmurdo's progressive inventiveness.

517

518

519

520

C.R. Ashbee and the Guild of Handicraft

C. R. Ashbee founded the Guild of Handicraft in 1888 when living and working at Toynbee Hall, an educational charity in the East End of London. The Guild's decoration of the dining room at Toynbee Hall has been restored (**523**); the room now houses the piano Ashbee designed in 1900, painted for him by Walter Taylor with 'City of the Sun' imagery. Most of the furniture made in the Guild workshops was designed by Ashbee: the often clumsy proportions of his early designs (**528–531**, illustrated in the *Studio* in 1898) were replaced by angular elegance (**525**), excellent geometric inlay (**526**), and – in a cabinet illustrated in 1904 in the magazine *Art and Crafts* (**524**) – imaginative metalwork.

Ashbee, who continued to run an independent architectural practice, designed for his family a house in Chelsea, The Magpie and Stump. For the drawing room (**521**) Roger Fry frescoed the chimney and the Guild made an ebony and holly cabinet (1902); for the dining room (**522**) the Guild craftsmen produced a narrow trestle table and some ebonized eighteenth-century-style chairs with rush seats, similar to Gimson's, Morris & Co.'s and Liberty's.

The work of the Guild of Handicraft was greatly admired on the Continent and fifty-three pieces were exhibited at the Vienna Secession in 1900: Ashbee's cabinet was displayed in a prominent position in the central hall (**527**). The Guild moved to Gloucestershire in 1902 and by 1905 had completed the library at Madresfield Court (**532**): designed by Ashbee, the magnificent carving was executed by Alec Miller. Despite such successes financial pressure forced the Guild of Handicraft into liquidation.

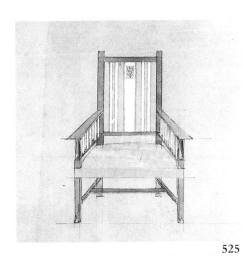

525

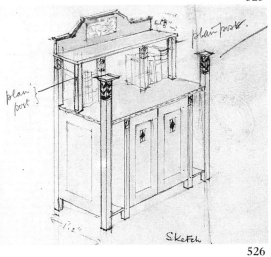

526

527

528–531

532

W.R. Lethaby and Kenton & Co.

Kenton & Co. was founded in 1890 by W. R. Lethaby, Ernest Gimson and four friends to make one-off pieces of furniture designed only by themselves. The furniture displayed at their exhibition at Barnards Inn, Holborn, in 1891 included, from left to right (**533**): the bishop's throne designed by Lethaby (now at St John the Baptist, Aldenham, Herts.); a Lethaby blanket chest; a serpentine secretaire by Mervyn Macartney; a walnut-veneered cabinet by Reginald Blomfield; Lethaby's hexagonal workbox (on an unidentified chest); Macartney's walnut chair, behind a gate-leg table by Sidney Barnsley; Gimson's sideboard, with his inlaid mirror above, and Macartney's revolving bookcase. The *Builder* described the Gimson inlaid cabinet (**534**) made by the Kenton & Co. foreman A. H. Mason for the exhibition at Barnards Inn as 'a really fine thing, full of character'. Macartney's more slavish interest in the eighteenth century is illustrated in this later cabinet (**535**), larger in scale than his Kenton & Co. pieces.

W. R. Lethaby worked for more than a decade as Richard Norman Shaw's chief assistant, contributing numerous important architectural details to the office commissions: in 1885 he designed the panelling and complex ceiling in the tapestry room at 49 Princes Gate (**536**), the last of the rooms to be redecorated there; he was also responsible for the sculptural detail on the monumental marble fireplace Shaw erected in the drawing room at Cragside between 1883 and 1888 (**537**). By 1888, a year before he set himself up in independent practice, and the year of this unexecuted design (**538**), Lethaby had already developed a highly personal style. Similar chimney-pieces, in onyx and marble, were made by Farmer & Brindley, both for general retail and for installation in Lethaby's buildings, notable the hall at Avon Tyrrell, Hampshire. Lethaby's design for the inlay on the staircase at Stanmore Hall, shown in a drawing for William Morris of 1891 (**539**), is reflected in the sideboard he exhibited at the Arts and Crafts Exhibition Society in 1896, known now only in a damaged photograph (**540**).

535

536

537

538

539

540

Ernest Gimson

The chairs made to Gimson's design by his craftsmen at Sapperton in Gloucestershire (**541–549**) look back beyond the machine-age to eighteenth-century English traditions, and earlier. On moving from London to the Cotswolds in 1893 Gimson made a close study of rural crafts and was continuously adapting traditional forms and decoration: the 'hay-rake' stretcher and the running decoration simply executed with a rounded chisel on this solid oak table (**551**), for instance. The standard of craftsmanship in his workshops was uniformly high, as wonderfully illustrated in the butterfly joints on the top of a figured mahogany dining table photographed in the Daneway Workshops at Sapperton *c.*1905 (**550**).

Gimson's craftsmen were capable of sophisticated, even luxurious, work too, such as the holly and ebony cabinet with silver mounts shown at a special exhibition at Debenham and Freebody's in 1907 (**552**); the ebony stand has disappeared, but the cabinet is now part of the impressive Gimson collection at Cheltenham Museum. A large walnut secretaire bookcase (**553**) presents another favourite Gimson decorative motif, chequer banding in holly and pear. Gimson died in 1919, but the contrasting use of walnut and ebony in this cabinet (**554**) and the linearity of his java teak wardrobe (**555**) anticipate Continental Art Deco of the 1920s.

541–549

550

551

552

553

554

555

556

558

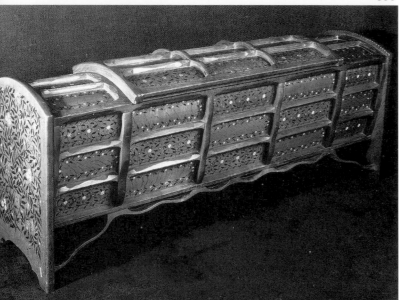

557

Cotswold craftsmen

Gimson's companions in the move to Gloucestershire were the architect brothers Sidney and Ernest Barnsley. Unlike the other two, Sidney Barnsley himself made all the furniture he designed, often also cutting his own wood. Typical of his early work is the large sideboard photographed at his home in Pinbury (**559**) shortly before the move to Sapperton in 1901. When it was shown at the Arts and Crafts Exhibition Society in 1899 the *Builder*. commented: 'The object now seems to be to make a thing as square, as plain and devoid of any beauty of line, as is possible, and call this art.' The desk Barnsley made for himself in about 1915 was more sophisticated in design (**556**).

Alfred Powell, a colleague of Gimson's in J. D. Sedding's architectural practice, also migrated to Gloucestershire, where he and his wife Louise specialized in the painted decoration of pottery and furniture (**558**); they occasionally decorated Sidney Barnsley's furniture too, such as the coffer (**557**) made in about 1905 but not exhibited till 1910.

559

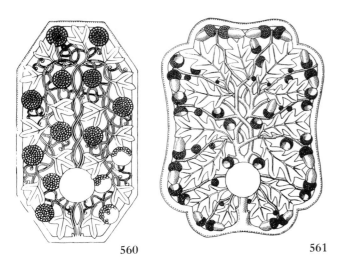

560   561

562–563

In 1903 Gimson met the metalworker Alfred Bucknell, son of
the village blacksmith at Tunley, and set up a workshop for him in
Sapperton. Gimson produced delicate designs for wall-sconces
(**560** and **561**) made by Bucknell in brass, copper and steel; these
Bucknell fire-dogs, in brilliantly cut and polished steel, were
designed by Gimson in 1904 (**562** and **563**).

The Dutchman Peter Waals joined Gimson as a cabinetmaker
in 1900 and became manager of the workshops in 1902. He was
responsible for the execution of these Gimson candlesticks, casket
and secretaire (**565**). After Gimson's death Waals re-employed
many of the craftsmen in the cabinet workshops he opened nearby
at Chalford; his own furniture design – this cabinet (**564**), supplied
to the Goddard family of Leicestershire in 1929, for instance –
directly imitated Gimson.

564

565

566

C.F.A. Voysey

Voysey's most avant-garde furniture and interiors were designed between 1895 and 1910; they include The Orchard in Chorleywood, Hertfordshire, the house he built for himself and his family in 1899. The uncompromising simplicity of the furniture in the ground floor sitting room at The Orchard (566) contrasts with the awkward proportions of an earlier cabinet, illustrated in the *Studio* in 1896 (567). The subtly designed detail of Voysey's furniture is illustrated by comparing the pieces made for him by F. C. Nielsen from 1906 to 1910 for the Essex and Suffolk Equitable Insurance Company (569) with the Voysey-style furniture marketed, with his permission, by Liberty's (568).

Voysey's work was admired on the Continent, where this clock of 1906 (570) and the crab-like tables designed in 1905 for Hollymount in Beaconsfield, Buckinghamshire (571 and 572), would have been enjoyed for their modernity – more of these tables were installed by

567

568

569

570

571–572

Voysey the following year in Garden Corner on the Chelsea Embankment. For his Northern commissions, Voysey frequently turned to Arthur Simpson of Kendal: Simpson made this Voysey table (**573**) in 1898–9 for Moor Crag, a house by Lake Windermere; the furniture manufactured to Simpson's own design (**574**) reflected his admiration of the Voysey idiom.

Voysey was also a prolific designer of textiles and wallpapers. From 1893 he worked on contract to the decorating firm of Essex & Co.: Bedford Lemère's 1897 photograph (**575**) of their showrooms in Victoria Street, London, shows a Voysey wallpaper on display on the right; he also designed the square chair, the table in the centre and probably the fireplace and the booths.

573

574

575

576

577

Walter Cave, Edwin Lutyens and Frank Brangwyn

A settle designed by Walter Cave in 1894, and painted by his wife with scenes from the *Morte d'Arthur* (**577**), was shown at the Arts and Crafts Exhibition Society in 1896. Cave's furniture, though stylistically varied, was unoriginal: his typically 'Art Nouveau' settee for Liberty's (*c*.1905) was covered in Voysey fabric (**576**).

Frank Brangwyn and Edwin Lutyens operated only on the fringes of the arts and crafts movement; indeed, Lutyens castigated 'that most-to-me distasteful Ashbee, now artist – and furniture freakist'. As with architecture, so with furniture Lutyens worked in a variety of styles: this oak safe (**578**), one of his more adventurous surviving pieces, is from Marshcourt in Hampshire, built 1901–04. Brangwyn was commissioned to design the interiors of the British pavilions at the Venice Biennales of 1905 and 1907; his pre-war commercial furniture was made and marketed by the London cabinetmakers Normans & Stacey (**579**), J. S. Henry & Co. (**580**) and Paul Turpin.

578

579

580

CHAPTER EIGHT

The 'New Art'

581 Detail of inlay designed by M. H. Baillie Scott for a Broadwood 'Manxman' piano, 1897.

The British leaders of Art Nouveau, Charles Rennie Mackintosh (1868–1928) in Scotland and M.H. Baillie Scott (1865–1945) in England, were reviled by popular critics. H.J. Jennings, for instance, referred to 'the Scotto-Continental "New Art"' in *Our Homes and How to Beautify Them* (1902) as '"Hooliganism" ... a blasphemy against art'.[1] The language of professional designers may have been more refined but it was no less vituperative. Distancing himself from a movement of which he might otherwise have been hailed a leader, Voysey wrote in 1904: 'I think the condition which has made *L'Art Nouveau* possible is distinctly healthy, but at the same time the manifestation of it is distinctly unhealthy and revolting.'[2] Lethaby warned students in Birmingham that 'the frantic contortions of the so-called Art Styles' sprang from 'a repulsive sort of demi-monde idea'.[3] Even the sculptor Alfred Gilbert, whose tomb for the Duke of Clarence at Windsor is as sinuously seductive as any Art Nouveau monument, called the style 'absolute nonsense ... [a] mud mountain of rubbish daily and yearly heaped up by the incompetent, social, amateur ass'.[4]

On the Continent, however, Mackintosh and his Glaswegian colleagues were treated as heroes. Hermann Muthesius rightly claimed that 'an unbreakable bond was forged between them and the Vienna movement over England's head', leaving arts and crafts addicts 'still content to trot out little boxes, embroidery ... metalwork and furniture as before'.[5] Returning to Berlin after seven years with the German embassy in London, Muthesius published the three-volume *Das Englische Haus* (1904–5), in which Mackintosh was allotted god-like status, his interiors seen as 'milestones, placed by a genius far ahead of us to mark the way to excellence for mankind in the future'. 'Mackintosh's rooms', Muthesius wrote, 'are refined to a degree which even the artistically educated are still a long way from matching. The delicacy and austerity of their artistic atmosphere would tolerate no admixture of the ordinariness which fills our lives.'[6] In England only the *Studio* placed itself solidly behind the Glasgow School – 'No artist owes less to tradition than does Mackintosh; as an originator he is supreme'[7] – indeed, this progressive magazine, founded in 1893 by one of Christopher Dresser's old backers, Charles Holme, remained a staunch and influential defender of experiment in all areas of the decorative arts. As Baillie Scott, another of their favourite sons, said: 'It must never be forgotten that all the old work we admire so much was new once, and when it first appeared it must have been as startling in its novelty as many of the products of the "New Art" of our day.'[8]

Father-figure of what is generally referred to as 'The Glasgow Style' was Francis ('Fra') Newbery, from 1885 headmaster of the Glasgow School of Art, where in 1892 he set up the influential Technical Arts Studios, open to graduates in Design and Decorative Art. It was he who taught young Charles Rennie Mackintosh and his friend from the architectural office of Honeyman & Keppie,

Herbert MacNair (1868–1955), when they attended night classes at the School of Art; he also introduced them to the two Macdonald sisters. MacNair married Frances Macdonald in 1899 and Mackintosh Margaret in 1900; they were known for their design work as 'The Four'. Another distant but significant early influence was J.D. Sedding, a quotation of whose Mackintosh adapted as the Glasgow designers' motto, their summons to radical invention: 'There is hope in honest error: none in the icy perfection of the mere stylist.'[9] Having guided Mackintosh to the Glasgow Institute of Architects' Alexander Thomson travel scholarship in 1890, Newbery then took the brave decision in 1897 of commissioning the twenty-eight-year-old for his school's new buildings in Renfrew Street. By the time the second stage had reached completion in 1909 (584), Mackintosh's Glasgow School of Art was already recognized by some as a masterpiece of modern architecture.

Mackintosh was fortunate early on in his career also to find a devoted private patron, Kate Cranston, daughter of a Glasgow tea-importer and hotelier. Miss Cranston opened her first tea room in 1884 in one of her father's properties, the Aitkins Hotel in Argyle Street; after acquiring the whole of the building for herself and renaming it the Crown Lunch and Tea Rooms, in 1896 she commissioned Mackintosh to design new furniture and his friend George Walton to provide the decoration (604). Earlier in the same year these roles had been reversed in the Cranston Tea Rooms in Buchanan Street, where Mackintosh designed the stencilled wall decoration (618) and Walton was responsible for the furniture, some of which he brought in from commercial manufacturers, the rest being made to his own design. Mackintosh went on to furnish for Miss Cranston – as she preferred to be called in business, even after her marriage in 1892 and widowhood in 1917 – the Ingram Street Tea Rooms in 1900, her home Hous'hill at Nitshill in 1903–4, the Willow Tea Rooms in Sauchiehall Street, the grandest of her rooms, in 1903–5 (606), and the addition of the Cloister and Chinese Rooms to Ingram Street in 1910–11. Meanwhile Mackintosh had received domestic commissions from two other important Glasgow patrons, William Davidson Jnr (609) and Walter Blackie (592 and 607–608). The Blackie commission came through Talwin Morris, the book illustrator, who had moved to Glasgow in 1893 to work for the publishers Blackie & Sons. Morris's bizarre decoration of the outhouse of a ruined castle on the Clyde in which he lived had impressed Mackintosh, and the fine bookbindings, metalwork, stained glass, jewellery and occasional pieces of furniture exhibited by Morris until his sudden death in 1911 played a significant part in the creation of 'The Glasgow Style'.

A recognizable style in interior design had first emerged in Glasgow in the mid-1890s with furniture made by Guthrie & Wells to designs by both Charles Rennie Mackintosh and Herbert MacNair. Their work was first seen in London at the Arts and Crafts Exhibition Society show of 1896, where Mackintosh's poster for the Scottish

582 and **583** Charles Rennie Mackintosh
and his wife, Margaret Macdonald,
photographed *c.*1900, at the zenith of their
careers, shortly after their marriage.
Margaret is seated in front of her own desk,
for which she made the beaten brass panels.

584 The library in the Glasgow School of
Art, designed by Mackintosh and
completed in 1909. The chairs at the
periodical desk in the centre were made for
the Ingram Street tea rooms, 1910–11; the
desk in the background has been moved
into the library from the Master's Room.

Musical Review was considered shockingly decadent: 'the bones of men and animals have been pressed into service, and a goulish sort of ornament has been founded on them'.[10] In fact, a poster of the same date designed by MacNair and the two Macdonald sisters for the Glasgow Institute of Fine Arts is stylistically indistinguishable from Mackintosh's and the development of what became known, derogatorily, as 'the Spook School' may be credited more or less equally to all members of 'The Four'. Although MacNair left Glasgow in 1898 to take up an appointment at the School of Architecture and Applied Art at Liverpool University, he and his wife continued to work in tandem with the Mackintoshes. They exhibited together at the Vienna Secession in 1900 and again in Turin in 1902. Muthesius, who was friendly with all four of them, admired 'the lofty, rather mystical spirit of their art ... a lovely fairy-tale world'.[11]

Fêted in Vienna by Josef Hoffmann and the other Secessionists, the Glasgow designers were awarded in 1901 the whole of a *Ver Sacrum* issue to themselves. The following year Mackintosh was commissioned by Fritz Wärndorfer, financier of the Wiener Werkstätte, to design his music room, and in 1905 the furniture dealer A.S. Ball ordered a dining room from Mackintosh for a special exhibition in his Berlin showrooms of furniture by leading international architects. At this stage there must have seemed no limit to future possibilities, and yet by 1914, disillusioned and neglected, a near-alcoholic, Mackintosh had left Glasgow for good. In 1916 he settled in London, and from there worked for his only significant post-war client, the Northampton model manufacturer W.J. Bassett-Lowke. In 1923 the Mackintoshes went to live in France, where Charles died of cancer in 1928. Rehabilitation of Mackintosh's reputation came just too late: in 1933 the McLellan Galleries mounted the 'Charles Rennie Mackintosh, Margaret Macdonald Mackintosh Memorial Exhibition' (610) and in 1936 Nikolaus Pevsner, describing the Glasgow School of Art, said of Mackintosh that 'building in his hands becomes an abstract art, both musical and mathematical'.[12]

Admirably progressive though Mackintosh's architecture and interior design often are, it would be a mistake to think of all his furniture as an integral part of twentieth-century functionalism, for his initial streamlining of traditional forms sprang not from any sympathy with modern design theory but from a passion for visual imagery. Although Mackintosh quickly formulated his own personal style, the early furniture, with overhanging cornices and tall freestanding shafts, followed paths laid out by William Morris, who lectured regularly in Glasgow from 1884 onwards. Unlike Morris, however, Mackintosh was not remotely interested in craftsmanship *per se*, and much of his furniture was not only badly made – by a variety of Glasgow firms – but was also structurally ill-designed. The key to his aesthetic lay in the inspired use of organic forms, first in the furniture itself and then in the total decorative ambience, which was often enlivened by the addition of strongly coloured stained glass and prominent metalwork. His wife made an important contribution with her large gesso panels, symbolist in style; her refined wirework-and-linen vases of flowers also featured prominently in the classic Mackintosh interiors, which are intense expressions of a painterly dream in three-dimensional reality. In his later commissions – notably the Bassett-Lowkes's house at 78 Derngate, Northampton, furnished and decorated between 1916 and 1920 – Mackintosh experimented very successfully with pure geometric forms, a stylistic development which is often compared with the Dutch painter Piet Mondrian's contemporary move from naturalism to abstraction.

Three of the other leading furniture designers of the Glasgow School, George Logan (1866–1939), John Ednie (1876–1934) and Ernest Taylor (1874–1951), all worked for Wylie & Lochhead (613–616), a large firm of coachbuilders and cabinetmakers that had made its name maunufacturing coffins in the 1832 cholera epidemic and developed its reputation in the 1870s with omnibuses and ocean-liners. Wylie & Lochhead dominated the 1901 Glasgow International Exhibition, commissioning individual room settings from each of their three main designers, and it was they rather than Mackintosh who finally took a diluted Glasgow style south by means of a permanent retail outlet in London. The firm also brought London design north by retailing in Glasgow the products of J.P. White, J.S. Henry and Liberty's, and by commissioning special designs from Ashbee and from the Silver Studios, amongst other English designers.

George Logan trained not as an architect but as a cabinetmaker, joining Wylie & Lochhead in about 1882 and remaining continuously in their employment until retirement in 1937. Logan also produced freelance designs for the Greenock Cabinetmaking Company, during its brief ten years of existence an influential outfit (it manufactured some of Mackintosh's furniture on contract and ran its own shop off London's Oxford Street from 1902 until the firm's closure in 1904). A fine watercolourist and cultivated musician, Logan launched one of his daughters on a career as an opera singer; defending the scheme of decoration in his 1905 music room (593), he wrote: 'The secret of colour harmonies is with those whose hearts are betrothed to nature ... creations of the great Master-worker.'[13] Even the *Studio*, a committed supporter, was forced to admit that 'not all the furniture designed by Mr Logan appears to us to fulfil the first essential of absolute comfort'.[14] John Ednie was rather more conventional. Trained by the Edinburgh decorators Scott Morton before joining Wylie & Lochhead in 1900, he first gained public notice with his dining room at the Glasgow International Exhibition in 1901. Ednie worked full-time for Wylie & Lochhead till 1906, after which he continued to design for them and for Garvie & Son of Aberdeen on a freelance basis. Two of his most important interiors were for his own house in Ashley Terrace, Edinburgh, and for Huntly Gardens in Glasgow.

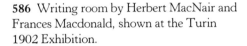

585 Settle designed by Mackintosh and exhibited at the Arts and Crafts Exhibition Society in 1896.

586 Writing room by Herbert MacNair and Frances Macdonald, shown at the Turin 1902 Exhibition.

The third of the trio, Ernest Taylor, joined Wylie & Lochhead as a trainee draughtsman in 1893 or 1894. His major interior commissions included 32 Radnor Road, Handsworth, Birmingham (for Robert Coats), and Douglas House, Pollokshields, for Lord Weir of Cathcart. In 1906 Taylor went to live in Manchester, where there is no record of any further activity in furniture design, although he did produce over one hundred stained glass cartoons for George Wragge & Company. Taylor's wife, Jessie M. King, was a more consistent performer in the Glasgow style, contributing gesso panels, book covers, illustrations, interior decoration, jewellery and silver. From 1911 to 1914 the Taylors ran a combined decorative and fine arts gallery in Paris.

The two Scottish architect-designers best known in England at this time were Robert Lorimer (1864–1929) and George Walton (1867–1933). Lorimer trained for a short period in the office of G.F. Bodley in London before settling to his own practice in Edinburgh in 1893. A traditionalist, he worked in the arts and crafts style (617), specializing in restoration projects like that at Marchmount, the McEwan family's home in Berwickshire, a well-documented undertaking for which all the furniture was supplied in 1914 by Whytock & Reid, Lorimer's favoured cabinetmakers. Lorimer exhibited furniture at several Arts and Crafts Exhibition Society shows in the 1890s; he also designed textiles, stained glass, ironwork and, in 1915, the Shanks Remirol water closet (the name is 'Lorimer' spelt backwards).

Except for the occasional evening class, George Walton had no design experience when in 1888 he established himself in business as an 'ecclesiastical and house decorator'[15] at 152 Wellington Street, Glasgow. Neverthe-

less, in 1892 he received a major commission for redecoration at the collector William Burrell's house in Devonshire Gardens, a scheme which included the surviving stained glass window 'Gather Ye Rosebuds While Ye May', an early amalgam of many standard Glasgow School emblems. Despite profitable contracts with Miss Cranston (618–620), Walton journeyed south to London in 1898 to follow up his working relationship with George Davison, European head of Kodak (621), though he still maintained his cabinet workshop in Glasgow. Through Davison, Walton met the photographer J.B.B. Wellington and built for him The Leys at Elstree, a large suburban house dominated by a centrally placed double-height billiard room. Photographs of Walton room settings published in the *Studio* (623) and a sketchbook now at the Royal Institute of British Architects illustrate the derivative nature of Walton's furniture, over-generously commended by Muthesius for its 'charm, reserve and simplicity'.[16] Walton regularly adapted earlier designs to subsequent commissions; his chairs for the Buchanan Street Tea Rooms, for instance, reappear with green leather upholstery as the 'Abingwood'.[17] Some attractive Walton designs for Liberty's (626) are counterbalanced by the dull commercialism of his 'Castle' and 'Lancelot' suites. During the First World War, as assistant architect to the Central Liquor Traffic Control Board, Walton surveyed and refurbished pubs and canteens from an office in Carlisle.

The only English 'New Art' designer with a Continental reputation comparable to Mackintosh's was Mackay Hugh Baillie Scott, who worked as an assistant to the Bath City Architect C.E. Davis before settling in 1889 in Douglas in the Isle of Man. Baillie Scott's first foreign commission, from the Grand Duke of Hesse in 1897, was to design new furniture for the dining-room and drawing-room in the ducal palace at Darmstadt. Largely as a result of this, the Darmstadt-based magazine *Zeitschrift für Innen-Dekoration* awarded him the highest prize in the 1901 competition to design a 'House for an Art Lover'. This was followed by the publication of his work in Alex Koch's *Meister der Innenkunst* and commissions to design furniture, tapestries and interiors for the Deutsche Werkstätten, for Karl Schmidt's Dresden Werkstätten, and for Wertheimer in Berlin. In addition he managed to secure a contract from Queen Marie of Romania to decorate her forest retreat, Le Nid. In a *Studio* article of June 1898 on his Darmstadt furniture, Baillie Scott expressed particular pride in the brightly painted interior of a music cabinet, a style of decoration he long maintained (630). The Darmstadt furniture was made by Ashbee's Guild of Handicraft and Baillie Scott admitted that one of the chairs 'shows a modification of a design by Mr Ashbee which formed such a notable feature at a recent Arts and Crafts exhibition'; another chair (628) directly acknowledged his admiration of the Burne-Jones Merton Abbey tapestry 'The Knights of the Round Table Summoned to the Quest by the Strange Damsel' (627).

While living in Douglas, Baillie Scott designed for John Broadwood the first Manxman cottage piano, exhibited with success at the Arts and Crafts Exhibition Society of 1896. In 1901 he moved to Bedford and the same year J.P. White issued a catalogue of 'Furniture made at the Pyghtle Works Bedford ... Designed by Baillie Scott'. In a passionate preface Mr White advised clients to throw out all the furniture of the previous generation and not 'perpetuate the memory of the departed in preserving these gloomy and silent witnesses of their bad taste'. The resulting nakedness was to be clothed in a modern decor united by some simple leitmotif, such as the daisy inlay of a Baillie Scott dresser, which could be repeated in the wallpaper, the carpet, even the table cloths. Much of the advertised appliqué work was executed by Baillie Scott's wife, Florence, whilst White himself ordered the special rugs to set off the bronze-green furniture. Despite Baillie Scott's preference for painted furniture, most of the pieces made at the Pyghtle Works were of inlaid oak, such as the typical settle illustrated (629), which retailed in 1901 for 10 guineas. Although Baillie Scott occasionally descended to dreary commercial design for Story & Co. of Kensington, Muthesius described the overall character of his work as 'tender and intimate but refreshingly healthy pastoral poetry'.[18]

With the rise in popularity on the continent of *L'Art Nouveau* – or *Jugendstil* – adventurous London furniture manufacturers turned their attention from the Edwardian fashion for sturdy Georgian reproductions to newer, lighter forms, still made in mahogany but with stylish novelty in the use of inlays and stained glass. J.S. Henry & Co. of 287–91 Old Street in Shoreditch, the late-Victorian centre of the commercial cabinet trade, produced smart little

587 Inlaid oak mantel-clock similar to Baillie Scott designs in J. P. White's 1901 catalogue of furniture made at the Pyghtle Works, Bedford.

catalogues of such furniture, laying claim to 'the experience and intuition necessary ... to adapt the various classical styles in decoration and furniture to the requirements of everyday life, in which comfort and refined surroundings form such an important part'.[19] Much of the best J.S. Henry & Co. furniture was designed by George Montague Ellwood (595, 633 and 636), whose first recorded work for the company was shown on their acclaimed stand at the Paris Exhibition of 1900. Ellwood (1875–c.1960) also designed for Trapnell & Gane of Bristol and for the Bath Cabinetmakers Company, and was a founder member in 1899 of the Guild of Art Craftsmen, a group of artists each working in several disciplines, including the carver J. Osmond and the sculptor Richard Garbe, who gave annual exhibitions at their Camden Square premises until 1905. After the First World War the soft, curved lines of Ellwood's designs were replaced at the Bath Cabinetmakers Company by the harsher, angular style of H.D. Richter.

Writing in the *Studio*, the historian Aymer Vallance stated that the origin of W.J. Neatby's style lay in his native Yorkshire, although there is little evidence of this in the stylish 'New Art' pieces known to us today (597). In any case, Neatby (1860–1910) is best remembered as a designer of tiles, first for Burmantofts in Leeds and then for Doulton's of Lambeth, where he was appointed head of the architectural department in 1890. Amongst many important decorative commissions, Neatby designed the extravagant tile panels in the Meat Hall of the new building which Harrods began to construct on their Brompton Road site in 1894 (its facade famously cased in Doulton terracotta by the architect C.W. Stephens). Neatby also designed frescoes, including 'My Love is like a Red Red Rose', commissioned

588 Mahogany music cabinet designed by A. H. Mackmurdo and made by E. Goodall of King Street, Manchester, *c*.1886. The painted panels were probably designed by Selwyn Image, a close associate of Mackmurdo's Century Guild.

589 Mahogany hall table with herring-bone inlay and brass feet designed by W. R. Lethaby. It was made – probably by Kenton & Co. – for Avon Tyrrell, Hampshire, Lethaby's first building, commissioned in 1890 by Lord Manners. The table originally stood in the hall, opposite a Farmer & Brindley fireplace and beneath a plasterwork ceiling executed by Ernest Gimson.

588

589

590 Clock with 'domino' numerals, designed in 1917 by Charles Rennie Mackintosh. Made of ebony inlaid with ivory and coloured Erinoid (an early form of plastic), its progressive form anticipates Art Deco.

591 Table exhibited by Mackintosh in Moscow in 1903. It is identical to one he had installed the year before in the music room in Vienna that he designed for Fritz Wärndorfer.

592 Clock (of stained pine and painted metal) and wall decoration in the entrance hall of The Hill House, Helensburgh, designed by Mackintosh in 1903 for the publisher Walter Blackie. The severely rectilinear hall furniture dates from 1904 and remains *in situ*. The house is now owned by the National Trust for Scotland and is open to the public.

590

591

592

593 Design for a music room, 'The White Boudoir' (1905), by George Logan, who worked for the Glasgow decorators Wylie & Lochhead.

594 'The Rose Boudoir', designed by Mackintosh and his wife, Margaret Macdonald, for the Scottish section of the Turin Exhibition of 1902. The chairs are a development of those designed the year before for the redecoration of 14 Kingsborough Gardens, Glasgow, for Mrs Rowat; they were given further refinement for the Room de Luxe of Miss Cranston's Willow Tea Rooms, completed in 1904. The gesso panels, based on Maeterlinck's *Seven Princesses,* were among Margaret Macdonald's finest work.

595 Inlaid mahogany cabinet designed by George Montague Ellwood for J. S. Henry & Co. It is part of a suite of furniture commissioned by James Cook in 1904 for Mount Harry, Sevenoaks, Kent.

593

594

596

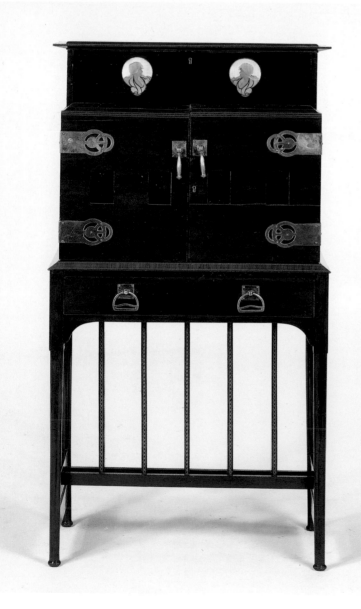

596 Watercolour design by M. H. Baillie Scott for the music room in a house in Crowborough, Sussex, illustrated in the *Studio* in 1902. Baillie Scott is one of the heroes of *Das Englische Haus* (1904–5), in which Muthesius notes that in England 'all ideas of domestic comfort, of family happiness, of inward-looking personal life, of spiritual well-being centre round the fireplace'.

597 An inlaid mahogany writing cabinet designed by W. J. Neatby in 1903 in a style that imitates Continental Art Nouveau.

597

598 The Giraffe Cupboard, a Cubist design by Roger Fry sold through the Omega Workshops to Lady Tredegar; it was made in 1915 or 1916 by J. J. Kallenborn & Sons of Stanhope Street, close to Omega's Fitzroy Square premises.

599 'Living Room in a Country House', a typical Liberty's interior illustrated in the *Studio* in 1907. The artist was Leonard F. Wyburd, founder in 1883 of The Liberty Furnishing & Decoration Studio and the principal in-house designer of their heavy fumed-oak furniture.

598

599

by the decorators John Lines & Co. for their stand at the Franco-British Exhibition of 1908. H.C. Marillier, by then managing director of Morris & Co., described Neatby as 'a clever artist ... not exactly a Gozzoli or Carpaccio, but a deserving artist with a better sense of decoration than most of the men in his line of business'.[20]

Sadly, very little furniture by the progressive Lancashire architect Edgar Wood (1860–1935) has yet been rediscovered. Wood opened an office in Oldham in 1889, moved in 1893 to Manchester and three years later became a founder member of the Northern Art Workers' Guild. His fitted interiors, unified by clever geometric decoration, gained Wood a high reputation on the Continent, where his work was extensively illustrated in *Moderne Bauformen* in 1908, the year in which he also designed the Brussels exhibition stand for the glass and pottery manufacturers Pilkington's, with a floor and fireplace of coloured marbles beneath a glittering Byzantine dome. Pevsner praised Wood's 1903 Christian Science Church in Victoria Park, Manchester, as 'a pioneer work ... of Expressionism, half way between Gaudí and Germany about 1920'.[21] From 1904 Wood practised in partnership with James Henry Sellers (1861–1954), who seems to have been responsible for most of their furniture (632), apart from a remarkable series of painted geometric designs Wood sent back from retirement in Italy. Charles Handley-Read tracked down the heirs of Wood's neighbour Inglis Sheldon-Williams, purchasing from them a mirror; he also acquired a photograph of the front door of the architect's house, one half of a monastery called Monte Calvino, perched high above Porto Maurizio. Sheldon-Williams objected to the unfriendly way Wood shut himself away alone 'on his hilltop which might be at the South Pole ... his conceit is so amazing'.[22]

Another northern architectural partnership, Barry Parker and Raymond Unwin, followed in their friend Edgar Wood's footsteps in dismissing 'furniture which can be considered apart from the building it furnishes'.[23] Unlike Wood, however, Parker and Unwin were committed socialists, aiming to provide simple affordable housing with interiors designed on an open-plan system which need not be 'completely smothered in lifeless and meaningless fuss of pattern, moulding, knick-knack, flourish and convention'.[24] Their work from 1902 onwards for the First Garden City Company at Letchworth (640) and for Henrietta Barnett at Hampstead Garden Suburb, begun in 1906, belongs both stylistically and philosophically to the post-War period, as do the very different productions of the Omega Workshop (598, 637 and 639), founded in 1913 by Roger Fry (1866–1934). Fry and his Bloomsbury friends were amongst the first to appreciate and to practice Post-

Impressionism; their aim at Omega was to carry this appreciation into interior design and 'to keep the spontaneous freshness of primitive or peasant work while satisfying the needs and expressing the feelings of modern cultivated man'.[25] Most of their marquetry furniture was made around the corner from their Fitzroy Square premises, in the Stanhope Street workshops of J.J. Kallenborn & Sons (598). Other Omega furniture was manufactured by Dryad, an interesting firm founded in 1907 by the bookseller Harry Peach at the instigation of Benjamin Fletcher, headmaster of Leicester School of Art. The Dryad experiment began with an attempt to revitalize the local craft of basket weaving, based on the ready supply of fine willow from the Trent Valley. With Fletcher as designer and Charles Crampton as technician, Dryad soon set about producing cane furniture modelled on German prototypes (638); the company prospered, employing 200 people by 1914 and competing successfully in the American and European export markets.

The directors of Dryad themselves noted that their angular chairs did not 'commend themselves to British notions of comfort or fit the homely reserve of the English house'.[26] In fact, the work of Benjamin Fletcher at Dryad, like that of Edgar Wood and other genuinely progressive English designers, was much 'newer' than Baillie Scott's self-styled 'New Art'. For all his Continental fame, Baillie Scott's colourful interiors, with their inglenooks and cottage pianos, remained firmly rooted in the English nineteenth-century tradition of Morris and Shaw. This safe, essentially middle-class ethos was echoed by the minor architect and critic John Cash, who wrote in 1904: 'How comfortable a retreat the fireplace may be is realized only by those who have whiled away an hour or two in some deeply recessed ingle, on a broad cushioned seat with high, restful sloping back, and close at hand a few shelves of books. Away from draughts, in a pleasant gloom, the light falling from behind through some tiny window on the printed page, the fireplace is an encouragement to a sweet idleness that invigorates the mind and body for further effort.'[27]

600 'A sitting room in a London flat', designed by Ambrose Heal in 1915.

601 Sitting room with furniture designed by W. J. Neatby, illustrated in the *Studio*, 1905.

602

Mackintosh interiors

603

The great distinction of Charles Rennie Mackintosh's domestic interiors is their stylistic unity: his furniture, fabrics, lights, architectural details and decoration are all conceived of as a single whole. This quality is illustrated by the transformation he and his wife, Margaret Macdonald, wrought in 1900 on their Glasgow flat at 120 Mains Street (**602**, **603** and **605**). On moving in 1906 to Southpark Avenue they took with them most of the fixtures and fittings, including the remarkable gas-light chandeliers, and even the fireplace.

Mackintosh was fortunate in the public patronage of Miss Kate Cranston, who asked him in 1896 or 7 to furnish the Crown Lunch and Tea Rooms in her father's Aitkins Hotel, Argyle Street, Glasgow (**604**); usually referred to as the Argyle Street Tea Rooms, the wall decoration and fixed furnishings are by George Walton. Mackintosh was solely

604

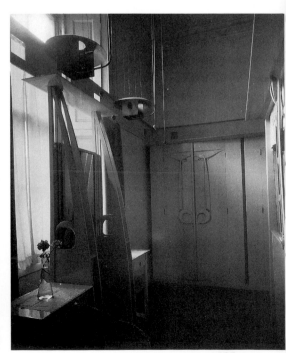

605

606

responsible for many other of Miss
Cranston's interiors, notably the Willow
Tea Rooms in Sauchiehall Street, Glasgow's
main shopping street: a promotional
photograph taken in 1903 shows the Front
Saloon through the glazed screen on the
staircase (606).

One of Mackintosh's earliest domestic
commissions was for the furniture at
Windyhill, Kilmacolm, made between 1899
and 1901 by Alexander Martin's Glasgow
firm of wholesale cabinetmakers and
upholsterers (609). In 1902 he received a
significant commission from the publisher
Walter Blackie to build a new house looking
out onto superb views of the Firth of Clyde:
the furniture in the hall (607) and bedroom
(608) at The Hill House yet further
developed the themes of Mains Street and
Windyhill. Mackintosh's Hill House
furniture, almost oriental in its refinement,
is incomparably original.

607

608

609

Scottish furniture

The Mackintosh Memorial Exhibition in Glasgow in 1933 gathered an important group of his furniture (**610**). From left to right: lattice chair from the Ingram Street Tea Rooms (1909); desk with panels by Margaret Macdonald (1900); crescent chair from the Glasgow School of Art (1899); and the Mackintoshes' own tub chair (1900). The Mackintoshes collaborated on a pair of white cabinets (**611**) for Kingsborough Gardens in 1901.

The other main furniture designers of 'The Glasgow School' were George Logan (**613**), John Ednie (**614** and **616**) and Ernest Taylor (**615**), who all worked for the influential Glasgow cabinetmakers Wylie & Lochhead. The principal Edinburgh cabinetmakers of the period were Whytock & Reid, much of whose best furniture was designed by Robert Lorimer. This inlaid buffet (**617**), similar to one Lorimer sent to London for the Arts and Crafts Exhibition Society show of 1896, was designed between 1890 and 1892 for the refurnishing of Earlshall, Renfrewshire. A sturdy Lorimer table of *c.*1900 (**612**) is here shown with a Doulton Chang Ware vase by Charles Noke.

610

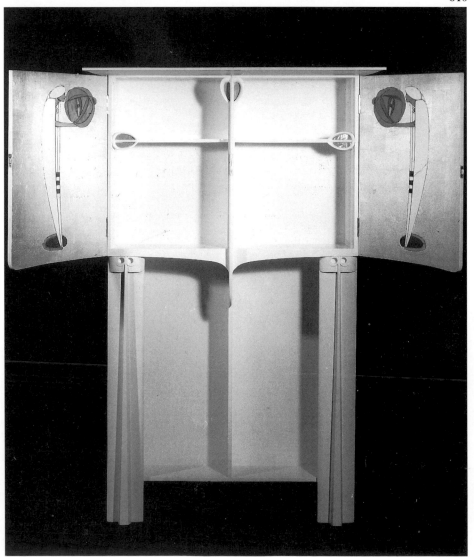

611

612

613

614

615

616

617

618

619

George Walton

In 1896 Miss Cranston commissioned the self-taught Glasgow decorator George Walton to refurbish her Buchanan Street Tea Rooms. He handed over the wall decoration of the Ladies' Tea Rooms (618) to Mackintosh, who produced the most dramatic of his 'Spook School' stencilled designs, complementing Walton's ladder-back chairs. In the Smoking Gallery (619) the decoration was again Mackintosh's, the furniture bought in by Walton from commercial manufacturers. Only for the Billiard Room (620) did Walton design furniture of any significance at Buchanan Street; the ash chairs were subsequently reproduced in oak by Liberty's.

In 1897 Walton designed the Photographic Society's London Exhibition, as a result of which the European head of Kodak, George Davison, commissioned him to redesign Kodak shops in Glasgow, Brussels, Milan, Vienna, Leningrad, Moscow and London. Decoration of the Brompton Road premises was completed in 1900 (621): the furnishings included Walton's

white-painted caned chairs, later examples of which are usually ebonized (622 and 624).

On moving to London in 1898 Walton also began to practise as an architect, building two houses for Davison, Plas Wernfawr (623), near Harlech, and The White House at Shiplake. Both these interiors revealed Continental influences, particularly that of the German architect Peter Behrens, in contrast with most of Walton's surviving watercolour designs for furniture, which rely on seventeenth- and eighteenth-century English precedent. Walton ran his own workshops and retail premises in both London and York and his furniture was extensively illustrated in the *Studio* (625). He retained something of the Glasgow influence – the curtain fabric in a bedroom he furnished for Liberty's (626) is identical to his wall stencilling in the Dining Room at Buchanan Street – but, as Hermann Muthesius pointed out, Walton's style was 'more down-to-earth' than Mackintosh's.

620
621

622

623

624

625

626

627

628

English 'New Art' furniture

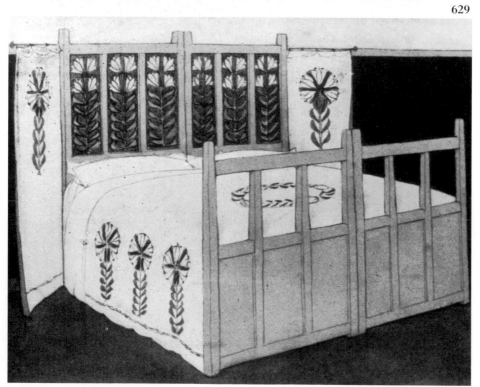

629

M. H. Baillie Scott was commissioned in 1897 to furnish the ducal palace at Darmstadt; he admitted basing this tub chair (**628**) on Burne-Jones's design for the Holy Grail tapestries woven for Stanmore Hall in 1893 (**627**). His best inlaid oak furniture was made by J. P. White of Bedford: this settle (**629**), branded 1901, was marketed at 10 guineas. Baillie Scott's painted furniture (**630**) seems dully traditional in form compared to furniture by the Omega Workshops, such as this dressing-table mirror (**631**) decorated in 1914 by Vanessa Bell.

Surviving furniture by the avant-garde architectural partnership of Edgar Wood and J. H. Sellers is disappointingly revivalist: this typically Neo-Georgian mahogany bookcase (**632**) was made in 1912 by Henshall & Sons of Oldham. J. S. Henry & Co. were amongst the most adventurous of commercial manufacturers of 'New Art'. Although G. M. Ellwood was Henry's principal designer (**633** and **636**), George Walton designed their 1903 Arts and Crafts Exhibition Society stand, including, it is thought, these chairs (**634** and **635**).

630

631

632

633

634

635

636

637

638

Omega and others

At the official opening of the Omega showrooms at 33 Fitzroy Square on 8 July 1913 (**637**), the screen displayed on the right was painted by Wyndham Lewis; the screen in the room beyond is by Duncan Grant, who also designed the textiles. Other artists working there included Vanessa Bell, Frederick Etchells, Cuthbert Hamilton, Henri Doucet and Nina Hamnett. *The Times* commented: 'What pleases us most about all the work of these artists is its gaiety.'

In 1914 the Omega Workshops were commissioned to furnish and decorate the Cadena Café at 59 Westbourne Grove, Bayswater (**639**): rugs, tablecloths, pottery, even the waitress's clothes were designed by Omega artists. The chairs were made for them by Dryad, a company founded in 1907 to foster the Leicestershire craft of basket-weaving. By 1914 Dryad employed two hundred people in the manufacture of cane furniture such as this chair, called 'Eve's cushion' (**638**), designed in 1908 by Benjamin Fletcher, headmaster of Leicester School of Art.

Some of the socially most progressive interiors of the period were created by the architectural partnership of Barry Parker and Raymond Unwin. Their 'Open-Air Bedroom' (**640**) at Crabby Corner, Letchworth, was illustrated in the *Studio Year-Book of Decorative Art* of 1917.

639

640

CHAPTER NINE

Heal's and Liberty's

641 Inlaid oak armchair commissioned from Heal's by Christine Angus (later Mrs Walter Sickert) as a present for her sister Joan, 1901–2.

At the same time as criticizing the establishment for its failure to appreciate the talents of Mackintosh and Baillie Scott, Hermann Muthesius found reason to praise the country's generally high standard of commercial production: 'England is the one country in which one can nowadays find in furniture shops a selection of furniture that, while it cannot pretend to great art, yet meets with the requirements of good taste, and at extremely reasonable prices.'[1] Another critic, Haldene MacFall, singled out Hampton & Sons of Pall Mall East, Gill & Reigate, Mallett of Bath and Waring & Gillow as reason for there being 'nowadays no slightest excuse for a man, even with a scant purse, having an ugly home'.[2]

By 1900 the largest of these 'merchant houses' was Waring & Gillow, formed through the amalgamation of retailers S.J. Waring & Sons with the cabinetmakers Gillow & Co., the eighteenth-century firm 'Gillows of Lancaster', which had itself already absorbed Collinson & Lock and Jackson & Graham. As three-quarters of the illustrations in H.J. Jennings's *Our Homes and How to Beautify Them* (1902) were of Waring & Gillow interiors, the author could hardly 'omit to offer his admiration for their elevating influence':[3] 'Messrs Waring and Gillow', he went on, 'have been practically the leaders in the new English Renaissance and it is not their least merit that they have shown Art and Economy to be reconcilable terms.'[4] Loathing *L'Art Nouveau*, Jennings felt comfortably at home with the Edwardian taste for Chippendale and Sheraton revival furniture in which Waring & Gillow specialized. They did not only provide English styles: 'reproductions of any examples are undertaken, and their faithfulness would hardly be credited'.[5] As Muthesius acidly observed, in deference to their nineteenth-century record: 'Gillow deserves credit for upholding at least moderately good taste during the battle of styles'.[6] In Muthesius's judgement, most of the decent commercial furniture came from smaller firms such as Norman & Stacey of 118 Queen Victoria Street, who employed designers such as E.G. Punnett in order to 'supply every kind of Artistic Furniture ... payments for which may be extended over one or two years'.[7] Story & Co. was another of Muthesius's recommended manufacturers. Specialists in nursery decoration, their oak furniture and panelled walls were painted in boldly blocked colours to figurative designs by John Hassall and Cecil Aldin. Novelty prospered in the provinces too: Christopher Pratt & Sons of Bradford offered a complete house-furnishing service on which they turned in a profit of £44,000 in 1900. Pratts' honestly acknowledged in their catalogue of 1901 that 'modern furniture design consists very largely in the imitation of old styles';[8] nevertheless, the company offered their Bradford clients 'Voisey'[9] card tables, fine inlaid 'art nouveau' cabinets and made-to-measure chairs – the last in response, perhaps, to Lethaby's quip: 'Someone might even find a mission producing a human Christmas present.'[10]

The earliest furniture designed by Ambrose Heal (1872–1959) began to appear in the Tottenham Court Road

windows of Heal & Sons in 1896. His first catalogue (643) was not until 1898, too late to earn Heal more than brief mention by Muthesius in a list of designers who 'produced furniture of a notably high standard'.[11] A later commentator, the post-War furniture manufacturer Gordon Russell, was able to see Ambrose Heal in wider perspective, describing him as 'the only man in the retail trade of that time who had any real interest in and knowledge of design'.[12] Even a demanding modernist like Nikolaus Pevsner praised Heal's 'good progressive furniture ... living amongst such objects, we breathe a fresher air'.[13] Better remembered today for his scholarly *London Furniture Makers from 1660 to 1840*, published in 1953, Ambrose Heal has until now been unjustly neglected by collectors of Victorian and Edwardian designer-furniture.

When young Ambrose started at Heal's in 1893 – after three years' apprenticeship to the cabinetmakers Collier & Plucknett of Warwick – the family firm was known principally for the manufacture of beds and bedding, notably Le Sommier Elastique Portatif, a folding spring mattress patented in 1860 and still in production today. Inevitably Ambrose Heal turned his hand first to the design of *Plain Oak Furniture*, his catalogue title of 1898, and the following year to *Simple Bedroom Furniture* (649), a company catch phrase that lasted well into the twentieth century.

In fact, not all the early Ambrose Heal furniture was either 'plain' or 'simple' (648). An inlaid mahogany bedroom suite of 1898, for example, bears maddening inscriptions: 'Fine Feathers Make Fine Birds' on the wardrobe; 'If This Be Vanity Who'd Be Wise' on the dressing table mirror. Heal was clearly finding his way as a designer, taking basic eighteenth-century forms and throwing in a few contemporary details – pierced metal mounts and heart-shaped cutouts from Voysey, for example. The idea of inscriptions as

642 Ambrose Heal, photographed soon after joining the family firm in 1893.

643 Illustration by C. H. B. Quennell for the 1898 Heal's catalogue of 'plain oak furniture' designed by Ambrose Heal.

decoration was inherited from A.W.N. Pugin, who had covered Scarisbrick Hall with worthy quotations; in the 1850s and 1860s, Minton had produced numerous dinner services to leftover Pugin designs, the borders of the plates and dishes decorated with odd mottoes in Gothic script: 'Better is a dinner of herbs where love is than a stalled ox and hatred therewith'; and the un-Puginesque, 'Who deceives me once shame on him; if he deceives me twice shame on me.'

A distinctive Ambrose Heal style did not emerge till the Paris Exhibition of 1900 (650–651; most of the furniture was also shown at the Glasgow International Exhibition in the following year). At the centre of the stand, designed by the architect Charles Brewer, Heal's cousin, was a fully furnished 'Guest Bedroom' decorated with Godfrey Blount hangings. This bedroom furniture (653) was richer than Heal's previous work, and of greater individuality in design, the pewter and ebony inlay no longer a mere reflection of others' styles. The *Architectural Review* praised Heal's display: 'It almost goes without saying that the materials have been very carefully selected, and the work, which has been carried out under Mr Heal's supervision, is a triumph of craftsmanship.'[14] A critic in the *Studio* admired the furniture for being 'rich in effect, yet if compared with the average treatment of furniture of similar character, one cannot fail to be struck, not by the wealth of ornament, but by its extremely reticent use'.[15] In 1900 Heal also commissioned Brewer to build him a house in Pinner, Middlesex. Called The Fives Court – because it was designed around an open-air Rugby fives court, a favourite game of Heal's since his Marlborough schooldays – the house received the architectural draughtsman T. Raffle Davison's stamp of approval: 'The furniture and furnishings are very admirable, and illustrate what can be done by excellence in material and design in a very simple way.'[16]

What surprised Heal's contemporaries was not necessarily his furniture's simplicity *per se*, but the fact that manufactured products should remain so simple in style, in contrast to those of Waring & Gillow. Heal's cheap, stylish furniture was particularly suited to the new Garden City developments, and at the first Letchworth Exhibition of 1907 Ambrose Heal furnished a cottage built by Gimson's architect friend F.W. Troup. Heal designed quantities of 'Cottage Furniture' (657), silencing critics with: 'It may be objected that our designs err on the side of excessive plainness. Our answer is that economy has been studied everywhere except at the expense of sound construction.'[17] As a Heal's catalogue of 1904 pointed out, 'no-one has given more useful and intelligent study to the application of machinery in the manufacture of what is at once beautiful and useful',[18] an echo of the continuously quoted Morris adage: 'Have nothing in your houses that you do not know to be useful or believe to be beautiful.'[19] Ambrose Heal himself later wished to 'register a prophecy that in another fifty years amateurs and connoisseurs will be looking up Heal pieces … as fine examples of that revival of true craftsmanship of which that man of genius William Morris was the inspiration'.[20] As co-founder in 1915 – with Lethaby, Benson, Selwyn Image and Harry Peach – of the Design and Industries Association, Heal was instrumental in passing the Morris legacy on into twentieth-century manufactured design.

Arthur Lasenby Liberty (1843–1917) had a character very different from Ambrose Heal's. Heal, according to those who worked for him in later years, was intensely self-absorbed – like Pugin, he regularly incorporated his own initials as a decorative element in public designs. Liberty was a much more expansive individual, an energetic shopkeeper with his finger permanently held to the pulse of popular taste, a man of opinion who nevertheless relied

644 Mr and Mrs A. L. Liberty photographed in Granada in 1910, three years before Liberty was knighted.

almost entirely on the artistic judgement of others. Unlike Ambrose Heal, when success came to Arthur Liberty he acquired not a suburban villa, but a country mansion and three-thousand-acre estate in Buckinghamshire, and built a private road across his land to the local railway station at Great Missenden; he even installed his own marble bench at Marylebone Station on which to wait for the evening train. 'East Indian Merchants and Manufacturers of Art Fabrics to Queen Victoria; Manufacturers of Art Fabrics to King Edward VII; Gold and Silversmiths to Queen Alexandra; Silk Mercers to Queen Mary . . .':[21] honours never ceased being heaped on Liberty & Co.

The son of a country-town draper, Liberty began work at the age of eighteen as floorboy at Farmer & Rogers's Great Shawl and Cloak Emporium, where he was on hand to unpack purchases from Rutherford Alcock's Japanese display at the 1862 London International Exhibition. In 1864 young Liberty became manager of their Oriental Warehouse, and it was here that he learnt his trade before opening a small half-shop of his own at 218A Regent Street in May 1875. These were modest beginnings, with only three employees: a sixteen-year-old girl called Hannah Browning, a Japanese boy by the name of Hara Kitsui and a volunteer from Farmer & Rogers, William Judd, who later recalled: 'We just sold coloured silks from the East – nothing else. The sort of thing that William Morris, Alma Tadema and Burne-Jones and Rossetti used to come in and turn over and rave about.'[22] The timing was right, 'Japanese the style of the coming season,'[23] and Liberty's little shop instantly established itself on the aesthetes' round of morning calls. E.W. Godwin, who became manager of Liberty's costume department at its inception in 1884,

earlier described the crowds of fashionable visitors in these opening days: 'A distinguished traveller had buttonholed the obliging proprietor in one corner; a well-known baronet waiting to do the same, was trifling with some feather dusting brushes; two architects of well-known names were posing an attendant in another corner with awkward questions; three distinguished painters and their wives blocked the staircase; whilst a bevy of ladies filled up the rest of the floor space.'[24] By 1880 Liberty had widened his horizons to import shiploads of goods from Cairo, India and China, in addition to Japan. A writer in the *Cornhill Magazine* noted in July of that year: 'The Ganges and the Hoang-Ho overflowed the banks of the Thames. Benares metalwork and Lucknow jars, Indian dhurries and Chinese bronzes, jostled one another in half the windows of Regent Street.'

It soon became clear to Liberty that the demand for oriental furnishings far exceeded their supply, and in 1881 he placed his first order with Ursin Fortier, a Soho manufacturer, for made-up bamboo tables and chairs to flesh out the display of ivory inlaid Shishamwood occasional tables newly imported from the Punjab. On expanding into adjoining properties in 1883, Liberty set up the firm's own Furnishing and Decoration Studio which initially specialized in 'Moorish' furniture incorporating panels of imported 'musharabeyeh' latticework. Other manufacturers were already active in this field. H. & J. Cooper gave over a whole room of their Great Pulteney Street premises to prove 'how effectively we may orientalise our interiors ... using the Verandahad Meshrebiyeh of Old Cairo' (46).[25] With the popularity of their Arab Tea-Rooms in Regent Street,

however, Liberty's had no serious rivals and Leonard F. Wyburd, head of the design studio, soon cornered the market with his numerous Liberty variants of the celebrated Thebes Stool (663) – even Monsieur Samuel Bing felt obliged to stock them in his shop L'Art Nouveau when it opened in Paris in 1895. As with so much else at Liberty's, success with the Thebes Stool was the result of their marketing skills, not of any originality in design, for interest in this ancient Egyptian artefact was already recorded in 1853, in a drawing by J.G. Crace now at the Royal Institute of British Architects. It was probably Crace who made the inlaid ivory Thebes Stool Ford Madox Brown designed for Holman Hunt in about 1857, the father of numerous related designs of the 1870s by Godwin, Dresser, Tarver, Moyr Smith and Howard; evidence of the existing vogue for 'Eygptian' design is the particularly elaborate Egyptianesque interior published by H.W. Batley in the *Building News* of 28 January 1878, with togaed women added to his dining room design of 1872 (381).

Despite Wyburd's curious efforts at originality (667), the Liberty style always remained a hybrid of adapted styles and adopted designers. Even the most inventive of their manufactured goods, the silver and metalwork of Archibald Knox and the textiles of the Silver Studio (683), cannot strictly be described as in-house design. Certainly, all their best furniture was bought in from outside (676). Yet to blame Liberty's for plagiarization would be to misjudge the role they played as retailers of popular taste. Ashbee railed in vain against 'the great house of Novelty, Nobody & Co. who have done me the honour of stealing silverwork from me . . . [making] mechanical or underpaid imitations . . . in some filthy phthisical cubby hole in a black, back street in the model city of Birmingham'.[26] Other designers were only too pleased that their work should find its way to Liberty's: Voysey authorized the reproduction of his famous clock in plain oak (481) and Dresser of his 'Kordofan candlestick' in 'Liberty Art Colours';[27] Dresser was so impressed by Liberty's that he sent his son Louis to work in their furniture department in 1896 before leaving for Japan. G.P. Bankart, an influential member of the Bromsgrove Guild, regularly executed plasterwork in Liberty's commissioned interiors (674), work that the *Studio* admiringly described as: 'designed and carried out with skill and deftness . . . in this particular branch he is unrivalled at the present time'.[28]

No opportunites were missed. Liberty's textile printworks on the River Wandle at Merton were close enough to Epsom for them to produce a new scarf for Derby Day every year, with the winner's name already imprinted in time to sell in Merton High Street to the crowds of racegoers streaming back to London. Arthur Liberty's energetic salesmanship and his continuous search for the best in contemporary fashion led to the establishment of a worldwide reputation. By 1913, the year he received his knighthood, Liberty employed over a thousand people in London and two hundred in Birmingham and Paris. Incongruously, given Liberty's condemnation of Art Nouveau as 'erotic imaginings of morbid brains',[29] the Italians coined the phrase *Stile Liberty* to describe the style of the whole period. As George Bernard Shaw flatteringly concluded a letter to Sir Arthur: 'Go on and prosper: and the longer you go on, and the more you prosper the better for Art.'[30]

645 and **646** There were many provincial manufacturers considerably more adept than Liberty's at harnessing arts and crafts ideals to commercial practice: Marsh, Jones & Cribb of Leeds, for example, in their complete refurbishment (*left*) of the smoking room at The Knowle, Huddersfield, in 1904. It was as an importer of oriental textiles, old and new, that Arthur Lasenby Liberty both made and maintained his name, holding regularly impressive exhibitions in the Carpet Department at his shop (*right*) until 1914.

655

Pre-War Heal's

For over fifty years, until his retirement in 1953, Ambrose Heal was in autocratic control of Heal's, building on his commercial successes of the pre-1914 period. In order to cater for the needs of an expanding suburban middle-class he designed a range of expensively finished furniture, often in walnut, like a desk of 1908–9, now in the Victoria and Albert Museum (655), and a mother-of-pearl inlaid mirror (659). The sophisticated dining room table and chairs, made in the Heal workshops by William Jones for the Paris Exhibition of 1914, are known now only through period photographs (656).

Yet, according to Gordon Russell, Heal's 'outlook was not just a fashion of the moment. It was a deeply felt way of life with him and affected everything he did.' He continued to develop ideas for 'economical furniture', designing c. 1914 a kitchen dresser in elm (657) intended for use in

656

657

658

659

660

weekend cottages, with double doors that folded in to protect the crockery from dust. Although the price of such furniture had to be kept low, Heal still insisted on stylish details such as ebonized banding, chip-carving on the handles and light staining to bring out the grain. He also experimented with different woods: cherry and walnut for a bookcase (658) and chestnut and oak for this characteristic sideboard (661), which has recessed squashed-heart handles for the drawer and circular latches on the cupboard doors.

Just before the War Ambrose Heal introduced the first of an extensive range of painted furniture (660 and 662), painstakingly decorated by Miss Dix and Miss Dibbs. Other craftsmen and designers working at Heal's in 1915 included Hamilton Smith, Prudence Maufe and Mrs Cook, energetic head of the Emboidery and Decorating Studio.

661

662

Liberty's

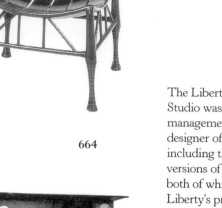

663

664

The Liberty Furnishing and Decoration Studio was founded in 1883 under the management of Leonard F. Wyburd, designer of most of their in-house furniture, including the three- and four-legged versions of the Thebes stool (**663** and **664**), both of which were patented in 1884; Liberty's produced many variations on this theme. The 'Valkyrie' piano (**665**), made for Liberty's in 1902 by J. J. Hopkinson, and a washstand (**667**), also designed by Wyburd shortly before his retirement in 1903, are marginally more original than this typical hall compendium (**666**), which incorporates a De Morgan tile panel, in the mock-Tudor style which was still favoured by Liberty's for their famous Great Marlborough Street facade built by Higgs & Hill in the 1920s.

Chairs in Liberty's turn-of-the-century catalogues (**668–673**) reflect established arts and crafts taste; the individuality of *Stile Liberty* was achieved largely through their fabric design, here illustrated in a Bedford Lemère photograph of 1897 (**675**); another Liberty interior (**674**), with plasterwork by G. P. Bankart, appeared in the *Studio Year-Book of Decorative Art* of 1910.

665

666

667

668

669

670

671

672

673

674

675

676

677

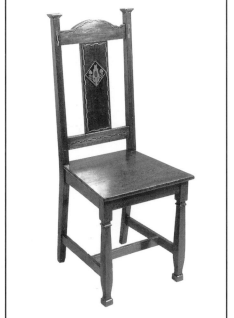

678

679

Outside designers at Liberty's

Despite the foundation in 1887 of its own cabinet workshops, Liberty's continued to stock quantities of furniture by outside manufacturers and designers. George Walton's easy chair (**676**), in walnut inlaid with mother-of-pearl, and E. G. Punnett's sturdy oak armchair (**677**) were both made by William Birch of High Wycombe on commission for Liberty's. Until opening his own showrooms at 134 New Bond Street in about 1905, J. P. White retailed through Liberty's much of the furniture made at his workshops in Bedford to the designs of M. H. Baillie Scott (**678**).

A number of Voysey's furnishing fabrics were woven by Alexander Morton & Co. for Liberty's (**679**). In 1898 Morton's began making hand-tufted 'Donegal' carpets and rugs (**680–682**): between 1900 and 1902 forty different Voysey designs were produced, many of them for sale through Liberty's. Outside designers were also largely responsible for the famous Liberty Art Fabrics, best known of which was the 'Peacock Feather' (**683**), a roller-printed cotton designed by Arthur Silver *c.*1887 and manufactured by the Rossendale Printing Company.

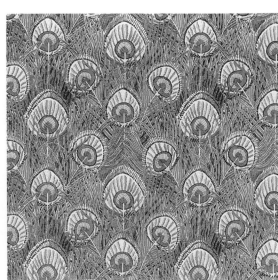

680

681

682

683

Gazetteer of public collections of Victorian and Edwardian furniture

ENGLAND

Barnsley *Cannon Hall Art Gallery and Museum*: small but instructive collection of nineteenth-century decorative arts.

Bedford *Cecil Higgins Art Gallery and Museum*: important collection, mostly displayed in period room settings, including over two hundred items from the Handley-Read collection; several pieces of Burges furniture; Waterhouse bookcase; Jeckyll fire-surround; etc.

Bibury, Gloucestershire *Arlington Mill Museum*: furniture by C.R. Ashbee, Ernest Gimson, the Barnsleys and other Cotswold craftsmen.

Birmingham *City Museum and Art Gallery*: important Morris & Co. tapestries designed by Burne-Jones; metalwork made by Hardman and other local manufacturers; furniture by A.W.N. Pugin, Burges, Chamberlain (the Everitt Cabinet), etc.

Bournemouth *Russell-Cotes Art Gallery and Museum*: Owen Jones piano and large collection of Victoriana displayed in a turn-of-the-century house.

Bradford *Cartwright Hall Art Gallery and Museum*: interesting collection of work by local cabinetmakers, in particular Pratts of Bradford.

Brighton *Art Gallery and Museum*: a collection unusually strong in Continental decorative arts of the Art Nouveau and Art Deco periods; includes examples by progressive British designers such as Mackintosh, Voysey and Baillie Scott.

Bristol *City of Bristol Museum and Art Gallery*: emphasis on the eighteenth rather than nineteenth century, but the collection includes pieces by Godwin and other designers with West Country connections.

Cambridge *Fitzwilliam Museum*: furniture by A.W.N. Pugin, Talbert, Owen Jones and Rossetti, as well as a substantial Morris & Co. collection (textiles, stained glass, ceramics, etc.).

Cheltenham *Art Gallery and Museum*: outstanding and ever-growing collection of arts and crafts furniture, including major pieces by Lethaby, Barnsley, Baillie Scott, Waals and Russell, as well as the largest public collection of Gimson furniture and designs.

East Grinstead, West Sussex *Standen*: fine Webb house, with the impressive Arthur and Helen Grogan collection of Morris movement furniture, textiles, ceramics, metalwork and pictures (National Trust).

Goole, Humberside *Carlton Towers*: gigantic country house by E.W. Pugin and Bentley; the most impressive furniture and interiors are Bentley's.

Lechlade, Oxfordshire *Kelmscott House*: Morris's country retreat from 1871, still with much of his own furniture. (Open by appointment only, through the Society of Antiquaries.)

Leeds *Temple Newsam House*: extensive collection of Bevan furniture made by Marsh & Jones for Titus Salt Jnr; other interesting pieces by A.W.N. Pugin, Voysey and Eastlake.

Leicester *Museum and Art Gallery*: fine collection of early Gimson furniture, mostly from the Gimson family.

Liverpool *Walker Art Gallery*: important pictures and sculpture of the nineteenth century; some decorative arts.

London *Bethnal Green Museum of Childhood*: the original building of the South Kensington Museum, re-erected in the East End; architectural dolls' houses, miniature furniture and all kinds of toys. *Geffrye Museum*: room settings through the ages, including three representing the Victorian and Edwardian periods. *Leighton House*: home of the painter Lord Leighton, built by George Aitchison; the extraordinary Arab Hall has tiles by William De Morgan. *Linley Sambourne House*: decorated and furnished by the *Punch* cartoonist Linley Sambourne in 1874 and virtually unaltered today (Victorian Society). *William Morris Gallery, Walthamstow*: substantial collection of furniture by Morris's circle as well as by Mackmurdo and the Century Guild; designs, reference library, etc. *Victoria and Albert Museum*: the largest and most important collection of nineteenth- and early twentieth-century British furniture in the world; reference library; significant holdings of furniture designs in the prints and drawings department; related ceramics, sculpture, textiles, metalwork.

Manchester *City Art Gallery*: the broadest-based provincial collection of Victorian furniture, including fine examples by A.W.N. Pugin, Burges, Talbert, Webb, Mackmurdo, Wood, Sellers, etc. *Whitworth Art Gallery*: extensive collection of Pre-Raphaelite art and designs.

Northampton *Central Museum and Art Gallery*: several Mackintosh pieces from local commissions for the Bassett-Lowke family.

Norwich *Castle Museum*: cast-iron furniture designed by Jeckyll for Barnard, Bishop & Barnard.

Oxford *Ashmolean Museum*: Webb's 1858-9 wardrobe; designs for the decorative arts by Morris, Ruskin, Rossetti and the Pre-Raphaelites.

Portsmouth *City Museum and Art Gallery*: important A.W.N. Pugin table, Godwin cabinet and interesting arts and crafts furniture.

Preston *Harris Museum and Art Gallery*: excellent nineteenth-century bronzes and sculpture and a smattering of decorative arts.

Rothbury, Northumberland *Cragside*: house designed by Richard Norman Shaw; the original furniture has been preserved.

Sheffield *Mappin Art Gallery*: strong nineteenth-century collection; notable metalwork.

Southampton *City Art Gallery*: specializes in twentieth-century arts and crafts.

Telford, Shropshire *Coalbrookdale Museum*: holds the records and designs of the Coalbrookdale Iron Foundry and of Maw & Co., the tile manufacturers; good collection of iron furniture and artefacts.

Tenterden, Kent *Smallhythe House*: home of the actress Ellen Terry, who for some years was Godwin's mistress; several pieces of Godwin furniture (National Trust).

Tiverton, Devon *Knightshayes House*: built and partly decorated to Burges's designs; his 1862 Exhibition bookcase and Worcester College chimneypiece are displayed here on long-term loan (National Trust).

Wolverhampton *Bantock House*: specialist collection of *papier-mâché* and other japanned ware. *Wightwick Manor*: decorated and furnished by Morris & Co.; good collection of Morris textiles and Pre-Raphaelite paintings (National Trust).

SCOTLAND

Glasgow *City Art Gallery and Museum*: strong general collection of Victorian and Edwardian fine and decorative arts. *Glasgow School of Art*: Mackintosh's masterpiece, with much of the original fittings and furniture intact. *Hunterian Art Gallery*: large collection of furniture and designs by both Whistler and Mackintosh; the interiors of Mackintosh's Glasgow home, 78 Southpark Avenue, have been reconstructed as part of the gallery. *The Willow Tea Rooms*: the Room-de-luxe has been reconstructed with reproductions of Mackintosh's furniture and fittings and now functions as a tea room again.

Helensburgh, Strathclyde *The Hill House*: designed and furnished by Mackintosh (National Trust for Scotland).

WALES

Cardiff *National Museum of Wales*: fine sculpture of the period; small collection of decorative arts, including Seddon's 1862 Exhibition roll-top desk. *Cardiff Castle*: sumptuous decoration and some original furnishings by Burges. *Castell Coch*: castle rebuilt and decorated by Burges; furniture by his assistant J.S. Chapple.

OTHER EUROPEAN COUNTRIES

Austria *Österreichisches Museum für angewandte Kunst, Vienna*: work by British designers exhibiting on the Continent at the turn of the century, notably Voysey, Mackintosh, Ashbee, Taylor, Armitage and Baillie Scott.

France *Musée d'Orsay, Paris*: museum of nineteenth-century art containing work by most major British furniture designers of the period, including A.W.N. and E.W. Pugin, Burges, Webb, Godwin, Dresser, Gimson, Voysey, Ashbee and Mackintosh.

Norway *Nordenfjeldske Kunstindistri Museum, Trondheim*: specialist arts and crafts and Art Nouveau collections, including items by Mackintosh, Walton, Ashbee, J.S. Henry & Co., Liberty's and Heal's.

UNITED STATES OF AMERICA

The USA contains no substantial collections of British furniture of the period 1837–1915, although some museums are currently making important purchases. Isolated pieces of interest may be seen in the following galleries: *Baltimore*: Walters Art Gallery; *Boston*: Museum of Fine Arts; *Chicago*: Art Institute; *Cleveland*: Museum of Art; *Dallas*: Museum of Fine Art; *Delaware*: Art Museum; *Detroit*: Institute of Arts; *Indianapolis*: Museum of Art; *Los Angeles*: County Museum of Art; *Louisville*: J.B. Speed Art Museum; *Minneapolis*: Institute of Arts; *New York*: Brooklyn Museum, Cooper-Hewitt Museum of Decorative Arts and Design, Frick Collection, Metropolitan Museum of Art; *Philadelphia*: Museum of Art; *Providence*: Museum of Art, Rhode Island School of Design; *Washington DC*: Freer Gallery.

Bibliography

Place of publication is London unless otherwise stated

Adams, M.B., *Artists' Homes*, 1883

Adburgham, A., *Liberty's: A Biography of a Shop*, 1975

The Aesthetic Movement (exhib. cat.), Fine Art Society, London, 1972

Agius, P., *British Furniture 1880–1915*, Woodbridge 1978

Alcock, R., *Capital of the Tycoon*, 1863

Anscombe, I., *Omega and After*, 1981

Anscombe, I., and Gere, C., *The Arts and Crafts Movement in Britain and America*, 1978

Architect-Designers: Pugin to Mackintosh (exhib. cat.), Fine Art Society, London, 1981

Armitage, G.F., *Decoration and Furnishing*, Manchester 1885

Ashbee, C.R., *Chapters in Workshop Reconstruction and Citizenship*, 1894

——*Craftsmanship and Competitive Industry*, 1908

——*The Guild of Handicraft*, 1909

C.R. Ashbee and the Guild of Handicraft (exhib. cat.), Cheltenham Museum, 1981

Aslin, E., *Nineteenth Century English Furniture*, 1962

——*The Aesthetic Movement*, 1969

——*E.W. Godwin: Furniture and Interior Decoration*, 1986

Aspects of the Aesthetic Movement (exhib. cat.), Dan Klein Ltd, London, 1978

Audsley, G.M., *The Practical Decorator and Ornamentist*, Glasgow 1892

Audsley, W. and G., *Outlines of Ornament*, 1878

——*Polychromatic Decoration as Applied to Buildings*, 1882

Baillie Scott, M.H., *The House of an Art Lover*, 1902

——*Houses and Gardens*, 1906

Batley, H.W., *A Series of Studies of Domestic Furniture*, 1883

Benson, W.A.S. *Elements of Handicraft and Design*, 1893

W.A.S. Benson—Metalworker (exhib. cat.), Haslam & Whiteway, London, 1981

Billicliffe. R., *Charles Rennie Mackintosh: The Complete Furniture, Furniture Drawings and Interior Designs*, 1979

——*Mackintosh Furniture*, Cambridge 1984

Blackburne, E.L., *Decorative Painting in the Middle Ages*, 1847

Blomfield, R., *Richard Norman Shaw*, 1940

Bridgens, R., *Furniture with Candelabra and Interior Decoration*, 1838

Brownlee, D., *The Law Courts: The Architecture of George Edmund Street*, Massachusetts 1984

Burges, W., *Art Applied to Industry*, 1865

——*Architectural Drawings*, 1870

William Burges (exhib. cat.), National Museum of Wales, Cardiff, 1981

William Butterfield (exhib. cat.), Fischer Fine Art, London, 1982

Carpenter, E., *My Days and Dreams*, 1916

Catleugh, J., *William De Morgan Tiles*, 1983

Charles, R., *The Cabinetmaker's Sketchbook*, 1866

——*Cabinet Maker: A Journal of Design*, 1868

Clark, K., *The Gothic Revival*, 1928 (new ed. 1962)

Cole, D., *The Work of George Gilbert Scott*, 1980

Colling, J.K., *Art Foliage for Sculpture and Decoration*, 1865

Collins, J., *The Omega Workshops*, 1984

Collinson & Lock, *Sketches of Artistic Furniture*, 1871

Comino, M., *Gimson and the Barnsleys*, 1980

Cooper, N., *The Opulent Eye*, 1976

Cottingham, L.N., *Working Drawings for Gothic Ornament*, 1824

Crane, W., *An Artist's Reminiscences*, 1907

Crawford, A., *C.R. Ashbee*, 1985

Crook, J. Mordaunt, *William Burges and the High Victorian Dream*, 1981

Darby, M., *John Pollard Seddon*, 1983

——*The Islamic Perspective*, 1983

Davis, O.W., *Instructions for the Adornment and Embellishment of Dwelling Houses*, c. 1880

Davison, T. Raffles, *Modern Homes*, 1906

——(ed.), *The Arts Connected with Building*, 1909

Day, L.F., *Every-Day Art*, 1882

——*William Morris and His Art*, 1899

Dixon, R., and Muthesius, S., *Victorian Architecture*, 1978 (2nd ed. 1985)

Dresser, C., *The Art of Decorative Design*, 1862

——*Principles of Decorative Design*, 1873 (repr. 1973)

——*Studies in Design*, 1874–6

——*Modern Ornamentation*, 1886

Christopher Dresser (exhib. cat.), Fine Art Society, London, 1972

Christopher Dresser (exhib. cat.), Camden Arts Centre, London, 1980

Eastlake, C.L., *Hints on Household Taste*, 1868 (rev.ed. 1878; repr. New York 1969)

——*A History of the Gothic Revival*, 1872 (repr. Leicester 1970)

——*The Present Condition of Industrial Art*, 1877

Edis, R.W., *Decoration and Furniture of the Town House*, 1881

——*Healthy Furniture and Decoration*, 1884

Franklin, J., *The Gentleman's Country House and its Plan*, 1981

Garrett, R. and A., *Suggestions for House Decoration*, 1876

Gebhard, G., *Charles F.A. Voysey, Architect*, Los Angeles 1975

Ernest Gimson (exhib. cat.), Leicester Museum, 1969

Girouard, M., *The Victorian Country House*, 1971 (rev.ed.1979)

——*Sweetness and Light*, 1977

The Glasgow Style (exhib. cat.), Glasgow City Art Gallery, 1984

Godden, S., *A History of Heal's*, 1984

Gradidge, R., *Edwin Lutyens*, 1981

Handley-Read, C., 'England 1830–1901', in *World Furniture* (ed. H. Hayward), 1965

Harbron, D., *The Conscious Stone. Life of E.W. Godwin*, 1949

Harrison M., *Victorian Stained Glass*, 1980

Haweis, M.E., *The Art of Beauty*, 1878

——*Beautiful Houses*, 1882

Heaton, J.A., *Catalogue of Furniture*, 1887

——*Beauty and Art*, 1897

Howarth, T., *Charles Rennie Mackintosh and the Modern Movement*, 1977

Jennings, H.J., *Our Homes and How to Beautify Them*, 1902

Jervis, S., *Victorian Furniture*, 1968

——*High Victorian Design*, 1983

——*The Penguin Dictionary of Design and Designers*, Harmondsworth 1984

Jones, O., *Plans, Elevations, Sections and Details of the Alhambra*, 1836–45

——*The Grammar of Ornament*, 1856 (repr. 1986)

Jonquet, A., *Original Sketches for Art Furniture*, 1877 and 1879

——*Present Day Furniture*, 1890

Joy, E.T., *Pictorial Dictionary of Nineteenth Century Furniture Designs*, Woodbridge, 1977

Kerr, R., *The Gentleman's House*, 1865

Kirkham, P., *Harry Peach*, 1987

Kornwulf, J.D., *M.H. Baillie Scott and the Arts and Crafts Movement*, 1972

Larner, G. and C., *The Glasgow Style*, 1979

Lasdun, S., *Victorians at Home*, 1981

Lethaby, W.R., *Architecture, Mysticism and Myth*, 1892

——*Ernest Gimson, His Life and Work*, Stratford-upon-Avon 1924

——*Philip Webb and His Work*, 1925 (new ed. 1979)

W.R. Lethaby (exhib. cat.), Central School of Art and Design, London, 1984

Lever, J., *Architects' Designs for Furniture*, 1982

Liberty's 1875-1975 (exhib.cat.) Victoria and Albert Museum, London, 1975

Light, C. & R., *Designs for Furniture*, c. 1880

Horatio Walter Lonsdale (exhib.cat.), Gallery Lingard, London, 1984

Loudon, J.C., *Encyclopaedia of Cottage, Farm and Villa Architecture and Furniture*, 1833

Lutyens (exhib. cat.), Arts Council, London 1981

MacCarthy, F., *The Simple Life. C.R. Ashbee and the Cotswolds*, 1981

Charles Rennie Mackintosh (exhib. cat.), Edinburgh Festival, 1968

Margaret Macdonald Mackintosh (exhib. cat.), Hunterian Art Gallery, Glasgow, 1983

Marble Halls (exhib.cat.), Victoria and Albert Museum, London, 1973

Massé, H.L.J., *The Art Workers' Guild*, Oxford 1935

Morris and Company (exhib.cat.), Fine Art Society, London, 1979

Morris and Company in Cambridge (exhib.cat.), Fitzwilliam Museum, Cambridge, 1980

William Morris and Kelmscott (exhib. cat.), Design Council, London, 1981

William Morris and the Middle Ages (exhib. cat.), Whitworth Art Gallery, Manchester, 1984

Morton, J., *Three Generations in a Family Textile Firm*, 1971

Muthesius, H., *Das Englische Haus*, Berlin, 1904–5 (English ed. 1979)

Muthesius, S., *The High Victorian Movement in Architecture 1850–1870*, 1972

Naylor, G., *The Arts and Crafts Movement*, 1971

Nesfield, W.E., *Specimens of Mediaeval Architecture*, 1862

Omega Workshops (exhib. cat.), Anthony D'Offay Gallery, London, 1984

Ottewill, D., 'Robert Weir Schultz', in *Architectural History*, 22, 1979

Panton, J.E., *Suburban Residences and How to Circumvent Them*, 1896

Parker, B., and Unwin, R., *The Art of Building a Home*, 1901

Parry, L., *William Morris Textiles*, 1983

Pevsner, N., *Pioneers of the Modern Movement*, 1936 (revised and reissued as *Pioneers of Modern Design*, 1960)

Port, M.H. (ed.), *The Houses of Parliament*, 1976

The Pre-Raphaelite Era (exhib. cat.), Delaware Art Museum, 1976

Pratts of Bedford (exhib. cat.), Bradford City Art Gallery, 1969

Pugin, A.W.N., *Gothic Furniture*, 1835

——*Contrasts*, 1836

——*Designs for Iron and Brass Work*, 1836

——*The True Principles of Pointed or Christian Architecture*, 1841

——*The Present State of Ecclesiastical Architecture in England*, 1843

——*Glossary of Ecclesiastical Ornament and Costume*, 1844

——*Floriated Ornament*, 1849

Pullan, R., *The House of William Burges*, 1885

——*The Designs of William Burges*, 1885

Quiney, A., *John Loughborough Pearson*, 1979

Richardson, M., *Architects of the Arts and Crafts Movement*, 1983

Rumens, G., *William Richard Lethaby*, 1986

Ruskin, J., *Seven Lamps of Architecture*, 1849

——*Stones of Venice*, 1851–3

Saint, A., *Richard Norman Shaw*, 1979

Savage, P., *Lorimer and the Edinburgh Craft Designers*, Glasgow 1980

Scott, G.G., *Personal and Professional Recollections*, 1879

Service, A. (ed.), *Edwardian Architecture and its Origins*, 1975

——*Edwardian Interiors*, 1982

Sewter, A.C., *The Stained Glass of William Morris and his Circle*, 1974

Shaw, H., *Specimens of Ancient Furniture*, 1836

Shaw, R.N., *Architectural Sketches from the Continent*, 1858

Simpson, D., *C.F.A. Voysey. An Architect of Individuality*, 1979

Smith, J. Moyr, *Ornamental Interiors, Ancient and Modern*, c. 1887

Sparrow, W.S. (ed.), *The British Home of Today*, 1904

——*Flats, Urban Houses and Cottage Homes*, 1906

——*Hints on House Furnishing*, 1909

——(ed.), *The Modern Home*, 1909

Spencer, C., *The Aesthetic Movement*, 1973

Spencer, I., *Walter Crane*, 1975

Stamm, M.D.E. Clayton, *William De Morgan*, 1971

Stamp, G., and Amery, C., *Victorian Buildings of London 1837–1887*, 1980

Stamp, G., *The English House, 1860 to 1914*, 1986

Street, A.E., *Memoir of G.E. Street*, 1881

Symonds, R.W., and Whinneray, B.B., *Victorian Furniture*, 1962 (repr. 1986)

Talbert, B.J., *Gothic Forms*, Birmingham, 1868

——*Examples of Ancient & Modern Furniture*, 1876 (repr. 1971)

——*Fashionable Furniture*, New York c. 1880

Thompson, E.P., *William Morris*, 1955 (rev. ed. 1977)

Thompson, P., *The Work of William Morris*, 1968

——*William Butterfield*, 1971

Truth, Beauty and Design (exhib. cat.), Fischer Fine Art and A.J. Tilbrook, London, 1986

Vallance, A., *William Morris*, 1897

Victorian and Edwardian Decorative Art: The Handley-Read Collection (exhib. cat.), Royal Academy of Arts, London, 1972

Victorian and Edwardian Decorative Arts (exhib. cat.), Victoria and Albert Museum, London, 1952

Victorian Church Art (exhib. cat.), Victoria and Albert Museum, London, 1971

Viollet-le-Duc, E., *Dictionnaire du Mobilier Français*, Paris 1858–75

——*Habitations Modernes*, Paris 1877

Voysey, C.F.A., *Individuality*, 1915 (repr. Shaftesbury 1986)

C.F.A. Voysey (exhib. cat.), Brighton Museum, 1978

Waring, J.B., *Masterpieces of Industrial Design*, 1868

Alfred Waterhouse (exhib. cat.), Heinz Gallery (RIBA), London, 1983

Watkinson, R., *William Morris as Designer*, 1967

Watt, W., *Art Furniture Designed by Edward W. Godwin FSA*, 1877

Wedgwood, A., *A.W.N. Pugin and the Pugin Family*, 1985

White, J.P., *Furniture Made at the Pyghtle Workshops . . . Designed by M.H. Baillie Scott*, Bedford 1901

Edgar Wood and J. Henry Sellers (exhib. cat.), Manchester City Art Gallery, 1975

Wyatt, M.D., *Industrial Arts of the Nineteenth Century*, 1851–3

Yapp, G.W., *Art Industry*, 1880

Periodicals and journals

The Architect, 1869–

The Architectural Review, 1896–

Art and Decoration, 1885–6

The Art Designer, 1884–

The Art Journal, 1839–1911

The Art Union, 1838–49

The Art Workman, 1873–83

The Artist, 1880–1902

The Artist and Journal of Home Culture, 1880–94

Arts and Crafts, 1904–6

The British Architect, 1874–

The Builder, 1843–

Building News, 1855–1926

The Cabinet Maker and Art Furnisher, 1880–

The Cabinet Maker's Assistant, 1853–

The Cabinetmaker's Monthly Journal of Design, 1856–

Cassells Household Guide, 1875–

The Craftsman, 1901–16

Decoration in Painting, Architecture, Furniture, etc., 1880–93

The Decorator, 1864

The Furnisher, 1899–1901

Furniture and Decoration, 1890–98

The Furniture Gazette, 1872–93

Hobby Horse, 1884–8

The House, 1897–1902

The House Furnisher and Decorator, 1872–3

The Journal of Decorative Art, 1881–1937

Journal of Design and Manufacturing, 1849–52

The Magazine of Art, 1878–1904

Sylvia's Home Journal, 1878–91

The Studio, 1893–

The Workshop, 1869–72

Notes on the text

Abbreviated references are to the editions listed in the bibliography.

Abbreviations: RIBA = Royal Institute of British Architects, London; V & A = Victoria and Albert Museum, London.

Preface
Pages 7–8
1   D. Lasdun (ed.), *Architecture in an age of Scepticism*, 1984
2   H.J. Jennings, *Our Homes and How to Beautify Them*
3   H. Muthesius, *Das Englische Haus*
4   Ibid.
5   W. Watt, *Art Furniture . . .*
6   W.R. Lethaby, *Philip Webb and His Work*

7   C.R. Ashbee, *Craftsmanship and Competitive Industry*
8   Charles Handley-Read (1916-71) began his pioneer research into nineteenth-century decorative arts in the early 1950s. With his wife, Lavinia, he assembled a vast private collection which was exhibited at the Royal Academy a few months after his death. Particularly strong in the Gothic revival, most of the furniture from the Handley-Read collection is now in public museums, notably the Cecil Higgins Art Gallery and Museum, Bedford.
9   *Magazine of Art*, 1883
10   *Gentleman's Magazine*, 1862
11   W.S. Gilbert, *Patience*, 1881
12   Ashbee Papers, King's College, Cambridge
13   Quoted by H. Binstead in *The Furniture Styles*, 1929
14   J. Gloag, *A Booklet to Commemorate the Life*

and Work of Sir Ambrose Heal, 1972
15   R.N. Shaw in W.S. Sparrow (ed.), *The British Home of Today*
16   Quoted by L. Parry in *William Morris Textiles*
17   Quoted by H. Hobhouse in *Prince Albert, His Life and Work*, 1983

Chapter One: A Matter of Style
Pages 9–25
1   Quoted by J. Mordaunt Crook in *William Burges*
2   *Building News*, 1875
3   M.E. Haweis, *Beautiful Houses*
4   Ibid.
5   Quoted by M. Harrison and B. Waters in *Burne-Jones*, 1973
6   J. Oldcastle in the *Magazine of Art*, 1881
7   W. Gaunt, *Victorian Olympus*, 1952

8   Quoted in the *Survey of London*, XXXVII, 1972
9   *Building News*, 1880
10   M.E. Haweis, *Beautiful Houses*
11   G. Stamp, *The English House 1860-1914* (exhib. cat.), Building Design Centre, London, 1980
12   M.E. Haweis, *Beautiful Houses*
13   Ibid.
14   *Building News*, 1866
15   R. Kerr, *The Gentleman's House*
16   W. Gaunt, *Victorian Olympus*, 1952
17   Song composed by Comyns Carr, founder of the Grosvenor Gallery
18   F.G. Stephens, *Artists at Home*, 1884
19   M. Wilson in *The Victoria and Albert Museum Year Book*, 1972
20   *Magazine of Art*, 1885
21   J.B. Waring, *Decorative Art in Furniture*, (?)1872
22   Quoted by V. Cecil in *Minton 'Majolica'*, 1982
23   Lord Overstone, *Correspondence*, 1971
24   M. Girouard, *The Victorian Country House*
25   R.W. Edis, *Decoration and Furniture of the Town House*
26   Handley-Read Archives, RIBA
27   O. Jones, *The Grammar of Ornament*
28   Ibid.
29   *Builder*, 1874
30   Ibid.
31   Ibid.
32   *Builder*, 1873
33   M.E. Haweis, *Beautiful Houses*
34   *Builder*, 1874
35   *Survey of London*, XXXIV, 1966
36   *Builder*, 1853
37   *Art Journal*, 1878
38   H. Stannus, *Alfred Stevens and His Work*, 1891
39   A. Hare, *The Story of My Life*, 1900
40   *Magazine of Art*, 1892
41   M. Girouard, *The Victorian Country House*
42   H. Shaw, *Specimens of Ancient Furniture*
43   C. Handley-Read, 'England 1830–1901'
44   *Building News*, 1872
45   J. Lever, *Architects' Designs for Furniture*
46   C.L. Eastlake, *Hints on Household Taste*
47   B. Ferrey, *Recollections of A.W. Pugin and His Father*, 1861
48   G. Burne-Jones, *Memorials of Edward Burne-Jones*, 1904
49   *Transactions of the RIBA*, 1865–6
50   C.L. Eastlake, *A History of the Gothic Revival*
51   *Ecclesiologist*, 1861
52   *Magazine of Art*, 1899
53   *Journal of the RIBA*, 1894
54   C.R. Ashbee, *Craftsmanship and Competitive Industry*
55   *Blackwoods Magazine*, 1862
56   Quoted by W.R. Lethaby in *Philip Webb and His Work*
57   Ibid.
58   *Gentleman's Magazine*, 1863
59   *Builder*, 1862
60   *Magazine of Art*, 1881

Chapter Two: A.W.N. Pugin
Pages 35–47
1   K. Clark, *The Gothic Revival*
2   *The Church and the World*, 1868
3   G.G. Scott, *Personal and Professional Recollections*, 1879
4   Ibid.
5   H. Muthesius, *Das Englische Haus*
6   N. Pevsner in the Preface to P. Stanton's *Pugin*, 1971
7   W.S. Sparrow (ed.), *The British Home of Today*
8   Quoted by A. Wedgwood, *A.W.N. Pugin and the Pugin Family*
9   Ibid.
10   K. Clark, *The Gothic Revival*
11   Letter to Pugin's second wife, Jane Knill, 26 June 1851 (V&A)
12   Undated letter inscribed by Crace: 'about December 185–' (RIBA)
13   Letter, 7 February 1852 (RIBA)
14   Undated letter (RIBA)
15   M. Trappes-Lomax, *Pugin, A Medieval Victorian*, 1932
16   Diaries (V&A)
17   Letter, 5 January 1841 (V&A)
18   Ibid.
19   Diary, 8 November 1835 (V&A)
20   Letter of 1851 (RIBA)
21   Quoted by P. Stanton in *Pugin*, 1971
22   W. Cobbett, *A History of the Protestant Reformation in England and Ireland*, 1829
23   Letter of 1840 (V&A)
24   Letter to Lord Shrewsbury (V&A)
25   Letter, 13 July 1847 (V&A)
26   C.L. Eastlake, *A History of the Gothic Revival*
27   A.W.N. Pugin, *Glossary of Ecclesiastical Ornament*
28   A.W.N. Pugin, *Floriated Ornament*
29   C. Handley-Read, 'England 1830–1901'
30   Letter, 15 May 1851 (RIBA)
31   A.W.N. Pugin, *True Principles*
32   Autobiographical notes, 23 November 1829 (V&A)
33   C. Handley-Read, 'England 1830–1901'
34   Ibid.
35   Letter, 1850 (RIBA)
36   Letter to Crace, 1850 (RIBA)
37   Ibid.
38   Letter, 11 November 1850 (RIBA)
39   Quoted by E.W. Pugin in *Who was the Art Architect of the House of Parliament?* 1867
40   Quoted by M.H. Port in *The Houses of Parliament*
41   Letter to the Earl of Shrewsbury, 1841 (V&A)
42   Letter, 14 July 1848 (V&A)
43   Ralph Sneyd, Sneyd Papers, University of Keele
44   J.D. Crace Papers (V&A)
45   Letter to Crace (RIBA)
46   Ibid.
47   S. Jervis, *High Victorian Design*
48   *Illustrated London News*, 25 October 1879
49   C.R. Ashbee, *Craftsmanship and Competitive Industry*

Chapter Three: William Burges
Pages 55–69
1   See J. Mordaunt Crook's definitive biography *William Burges and the High Victorian Dream*, from which much of the information in this chapter has been culled
2   Quoted by J. Mordaunt Crook, ibid.
3   *Transactions of the RIBA*, 1883–4
4   *Builder*, 1861
5   *Architect*, 1881
6   Reprinted in W. Burges, *Art Applied to Industry*
7   W.M. Rossetti, *Reminiscences*, 1910
8   W.M. Rossetti, *Rossetti Papers*, 1903
9   Letter to the future Lady Bute, 7 February 1872 (Mount Stuart papers)
10   Letter to her sister, September 1873 (Mount Stuart papers)
11   Quoted by J. Mordaunt Crook in *William Burges*
12   *Architect*, 1881
13   G. Murray, *Sidelights on English Society*, 1883
14   Worcester College Archives
15   *Building News*, 1858
16   *Art Journal*, 1886
17   RIBA Drawings Collection
18   W.R. Lethaby, *Architecture, Mysticism and Myth*
19   W.R. Lethaby, *Philip Webb and His Work*
20   M.E. Haweis, *Beautiful Houses*
21   RIBA Drawings Collection
22   R. Pullan, *The House of William Burges*
23   M.E. Haweis, *Beautiful Houses*
24   H. Holiday, *Reminiscences of My Life*, 1914
25   *Western Mail*, 15 October 1900
26   Lady Bute (Mount Stuart papers)
27   Quoted by J. Mordaunt Crook in *William Burges*
28   H.S. Goodhart Rendel, *English Architecture Since the Regency*, 1953
29   Quoted by J. Mordaunt Crook, *William Burges*

Chapter Four: Geometric Gothic
Pages 77–101
1   *Art Journal*, 1867
2   J. Ruskin, *Seven Lamps of Architecture*
3   O. Jones, *The Grammar of Ornament*
4   C.L. Eastlake, *A History of the Gothic Revival*
5   Ibid.
6   Ibid.
7   P. Thompson, *William Butterfield*
8   Quoted by P. Thompson, ibid.
9   *Building News*, 1886
10   P. Thompson, *William Butterfield*
11   M. Girouard, *The Victorian Country House*
12   Ibid.
13   C.L. Eastlake, *A History of the Gothic Revival*
14   *Victorian and Edwardian Decorative Art*
15   Quoted by J. Mordaunt Crook in *William Burges*
16   C.L. Eastlake, *A History of the Gothic Revival*
17   S. Jervis, *Penguin Dictionary of Design and Designers*
18   J.C. Fergusson, *History of the Modern Styles of Architecture*, (?) 1882
19   M. Girouard, *The Victorian Country House*
20   C.L. Eastlake, *A History of the Gothic Revival*
21   *Builder*, May 1873
22   *Civil Engineer*, 1862
23   *Bentley's Miscellany*, August 1862
24   *Illustrated London News*, 18 October 1862
25   *Building News*, 28 April 1865
26   *Journal of the RIBA*, 1905–06
27   K. Clark, *The Gothic Revival*
28   Ibid.
29   J. Lever, *Architects' Designs for Furniture*
30   G. Stamp and C. Amery, *Victorian*

Buildings of London 1837–1887
31   Quoted in *Alfred Waterhouse* (exhib.cat.)
32   A. Hare, *The Story of My Life*, 1900
33   *Building News*, 1905
34   *Alfred Waterhouse*, where Sally MacDonald acknowledges Simon Jervis's comparisons
35   M. Girouard, *The Victorian Country House*
36   Sneyd Papers, University of Keele
37   C.R. Ashbee, *Craftsmanship and Competitive Industry*
38   Quoted by J. Mordaunt Crook in *William Burges*
39   Handley-Read Archives, RIBA
40   Quoted by B. Morris in *The Harborne Room*, V&A Bulletin, 1968
41   M.E. Haweis, *The Art of Beauty*
42   This is a mistake; Eastlake never received a knighthood. The author is confusing him with his uncle, the painter Sir Charles Lock Eastlake
43   *Cornhill Magazine*, July 1880
44   C.L. Eastlake, *Hints on Household Taste*, 1878 edition
45   C. Dresser, *Principles of Decorative Design*
46   C.L. Eastlake, *Hints on Household Taste*
47   *Building News*, 1881
48   *Cabinet Maker and Art Furnisher*, 1 July 1881
49   H. Muthesius, *Das Englische Haus*
50   Ibid.
51   The engraved titlepage is dated 1867, but the preface is dated January 1868
52   B.J. Talbert *Gothic Forms*
53   Ibid.
54   Ibid.
55   B.J. Talbert, *Examples of Ancient & Modern Furniture*
56   B.J. Talbert, *Fashionable Furniture*
57   C. Dresser, *Principles of Decorative Design*
58   *Cabinet Maker and Art Furnisher*, 1 July 1881
59   Ibid.
60   Handley-Read Archives, RIBA
61   M. Girouard, *The Victorian Country House*
62   *Building News*, July 1865
63   Quoted by S. Jervis in the *Penguin Dictionary of Design and Designers*
64   *House Furnisher*, May 1871
65   Handley-Read Archives, RIBA
66   W. Smith, *Household Hints*, 1876
67   *Builder*, 22 January 1881
68   *Art Journal Supplement*, 1878
69   Handley-Read Archives, RIBA
70   *Art Journal Supplement*, 1867

Chapter Five: From 'Nankin' to Bedford Park
Pages 115-137

1   *Furniture Gazette*, 4 July 1874
2   Quoted by E. Aslin in *The Aesthetic Movement*
3   *Studio*, 1894
4   *Furniture Gazette*, 1874
5   *Decorative Art from a Workshop Point of View* (paper read by Ashbee at the Edinburgh Art Conference 1889)
6   Quoted by M. Girouard in *The Victorian Country House*
7   *Studio*, October 1897
8   *Art Journal*, 1893
9   Letter, 31 October 1877 (University of Glasgow)
10   Letter, 17 July 1877 (University of Glasgow)
11   *Studio*, 1904

12   C.L. Eastlake, *A History of the Gothic Revival*
13   *Architect*, 1876
14   Reproduced in the *Builder*, 20 August 1870
15   Godwin MSS (RIBA)
16   Ibid.
17   J. Forbes-Robertson, *A Player Under Three Reigns*, 1925
18   *Architect*, 1876
19   M. Girouard, *Country Life*, 23 November 1972
20   Letter quoted by H. Montgomery Hyde in A. Service (ed.), *Edwardian Architecture and Its Origins*
21   Ibid.
22   E. Terry, *Memoirs*, 1933
23   Quoted by E. Aslin in *E.W. Godwin*
24   *Building News*, 16 January 1874
25   W. Watt, *Art Furniture . . .*
26   *Magazine of Art*, 1878
27   *Artist*, 1882
28   'Studies and Mouldings', *Building News*, 1879
29   *All the Year Round*, August 1862
30   *Studio*, 1899
31   Reprinted as *Principles of Decorative Design*, 1873
32   *Builder*, 13 December 1873
33   Quoted by W. Halen in *Christopher Dresser and Japan Observed*, The Society for the Study of Japonisme, 1984
34   W. Halen, doctoral thesis, University of Oxford
35   *Studio*, 1899
36   *Magazine of Art*, 1881
37   Ibid.
38   C. Dresser in a paper read to the Society of Arts, 8 February 1871, reported in *The House Furnisher*, 1 March 1871
39   C. Dresser, *The Art of Decorative Design*
40   *Builder*, 3 May 1873
41   H. Muthesius, *Das Englische Haus*
42   J. Cash in W.S. Sparrow (ed.), *The British Home of Today*
43   'Jack Easel' in *London Society*, August 1862
44   Letter of 1869 published in *The Swinburne Letters*, ed. C.J. Young, 1959–62
45   *Magazine of Art*, March 1883
46   'The Ballad of Bedford Park', *St James Gazette*, 17 December 1881
47   R.N. Shaw in W.S. Sparrow (ed.), *The British Home of Today*
48   R. Blomfield, *Richard Norman Shaw*
49   *Cornhill Magazine*, July 1880

Chapter Six: Morris and Company
Pages 153–165

1   W. Morris, *The Decorative Arts – Their Relation to Modern Life* (undated pamphlet published by Ellis & White)
2   C.R. Ashbee, *Craftsmanship and Competitive Industry*
3   Quoted by W.R. Lethaby in his 1901 Birmingham lecture, *Morris as Work-Master*
4   Quoted by E.P. Thompson in *William Morris*
5   *Studio*, 1899
6   G.B. Shaw, *Morris as I Knew Him*, William Morris Society Reprint, 1966
7   E.P. Thompson in the Postscript to the 1977 edition of his 1955 Morris biography
8   W. Morris, *The Decorative Arts . . .* (see note 1)

9   P. Henderson (ed.), *The Letters of William Morris to his Family and Friends*, 1950
10   Quoted by E. Carpenter in *My Days and Dreams*
11   Quoted by W.R. Lethaby in *Philip Webb and His Work*
12   W.B. Scott, *Autobiographical Notes*, 1892
13   R.W. Edis, *Decoration and Furniture of the Town House*
14   *London Society*, August 1862
15   *Building News*, August 1862
16   W.R. Lethaby, *Philip Webb and His Work*
17   H. Muthesius, *Das Englische Haus*
18   *Country Life*, 1915
19   *Studio*, 1899
20   Quoted in the *Survey of London*, XXXVII, 1972
21   Quoted by W.R. Lethaby in *Philip Webb and His Work*
22   Ibid.
23   L.F. Day in the *Art Journal*, 1893
24   *Studio*, 1897
25   H. Muthesius, *Das Englische Haus*
26   M.E. Haweis, *The Art of Beauty*
27   Quoted by W.R. Lethaby in *Philip Webb and His Work*
28   Quoted by M. Girouard in *The Victorian Country House*
29   J. Broadwood, *Album of Artistic Pianos*, 1898
30   W.S. Sparrow (ed.), *The British Home of Today*
31   W.R. Lethaby, *Morris as Work-Master*, 1901
32   *Clarion*, 19 November 1892
33   Original catalogue at the William Morris Gallery, Walthamstow
34   W.S. Sparrow (ed.), *The British Home of Today*
35   *Studio*, 1902
36   *Building News*, 24 January 1890
37   Quoted by L. Parry in the *Journal of the William Morris Society*, VI, 1985–6.
38   *Franco-British Exhibition–Illustrated Review*, 1908
39   Original catalogue at the William Morris Gallery, Walthamstow
40   W. Morris, *The Decorative Arts . . .* (see note 1)
41   Letter of 1890 in P. Henderson (ed.), *The Letters of William Morris to his Family and Friends*, 1950
42   W. Morris, *The Decorative Arts . . .* (see note 1)

Chapter Seven: The Arts and Crafts Movement
Pages 179–197

1   C.R. Ashbee, *Memoirs*, 1938
2   A. Romney Green, 'The Influence of Tools on Design' in T. Raffles Davison (ed.), *The Arts Connected with Building*
3   C.R. Ashbee, *Craftsmanship in Competitive Industry*
4   *Journal of the RIBA*, 1894
5   H. Muthesius, *Das Englische Haus*
6   *Magazine of Art*, 1896
7   Quoted in *W.R. Lethaby*
8   J. Cash in W.S. Sparrow (ed.), *The British Home of Today*
9   H. Ricardo in *The Modern Home*, 1909
10   A. Crane, 'My Grandfather' in *Yale University Library Gazette*, 1957

11   *Hobby Horse*, 1884
12   *Magazine of Art*, 1885
13   *Builder*, 1885
14   *Studio*, 1899
15   Watts & Co. is still in business
16   C.R. Ashbee, *Craftsmanship in Competitive Industry*
17   Ibid.
18   C.R. Ashbee, *Chapters in Workshop Reconstruction and Citizenship*
19   Ibid.
20   Ashbee Journals, King's College, Cambridge
21   *Studio*, 1897
22   Ibid.
23   Quoted in *C.R. Ashbee and The Guild of Handicraft*
24   A. Crawford, *C.R. Ashbee*, 1985
25   Published by the Essex House Press, 1898
26   C.R. Ashbee, *Craftsmanship in Competitive Industry*
27   Ibid.
28   L. Weaver, *The House and its Equipment*, 1912
29   Quoted by M. Comino in *Gimson and the Barnsleys*
30   Quoted by G. Rumens in *W.R. Lethaby*
31   W.R. Lethaby, *Ernest Gimson, His Life and Work*
32   *Journal of the RIBA*, 1931
33   Letter,16 February 1924 to S.C. Cockerell, British Library
34   *Architectural Review*, 1897–8
35   Letter from Sidney Barnsley to Philip Webb, 30 June 1901
36   W.R. Lethaby, *Ernest Gimson, His Life and Work*
37   Ibid.
38   Ibid.
39   Quoted by M. Comino in *Gimson and the Barnsleys*
40   Ibid.
41   Ibid.
42   *Architectural Review*, 1931
43   *Journal of the RIBA*, 1934
44   *Studio*, 1896
45   *British Architect*, 1910
46   Quoted in *C.F.A. Voysey*
47   *Magazine of Art*, 1896
48   *Studio*, 1896
49   Handley-Read Archives, RIBA
50   Instructions written on a drawing, RIBA

51   T. Raffles Davison, *Modern Homes*
52   Quoted in *C.F.A. Voysey*
53   *Studio*, 1896
54   C.R. Ashbee, *Craftsmanship in Competitive Industry*
55   H. Muthesius, *Das Englische Haus*
56   C.H. Spooner in W.S. Sparrow (ed.), *The British Home Today*
57   R. Blomfield, *Richard Norman Shaw*
58   *Architectural Review*, 1898
59   E.W. Godwin in the *British Architect*, 1882
60   H. Muthesius, *Das Englische Haus*
61   Letter from Daphne Phelps, 23 November 1965. Handley-Read Archives, RIBA.
62   C. Handley Read, letter of 27 October 1965 to Daphne Phelps. Ibid.
63   H. Muthesius, *Das Englische Haus*

Chapter Eight: The 'New Art'
Pages 211-225
1   H.J. Jennings, *Our Homes and How to Beautify Them*
2   *Magazine of Art*, 1904
3   W.R. Lethaby, *The Study and Practice of Artistic Arts* (lecture to the Birmingham School of Municipal Art), 1901
4   Quoted by H. Binstead in *The Furniture Styles*, 1929
5   H. Muthesius, *Das Englische Haus*
6   Ibid.
7   *Studio*, 1906
8   M.H. Baillie Scott, in T. Raffles Davison (ed.), *The Arts Connected with Building*
9   Quoted by T. Howarth in *Charles Rennie Mackintosh and the Modern Movement*
10   H.J. Jennings, *Our Homes and How to Beautify Them*
11   H. Muthesius, *Das Englische Haus*
12   N. Pevsner, *Pioneers of the Modern Movement*
13   *Studio*, 1905
14   *Studio*, 1903
15   Quoted in *The Glasgow Style*
16   H. Muthesius, *Das Englische Haus*
17   RIBA Sketchbook
18   H. Muthesius, *Das Englische Haus*
19   J.S. Henry & Co., *Catalogue*, c. 1910
20   *Franco-British Exhibition, An Illustrated Review* (ed. F.G. Dumas), 1908
21   N. Pevsner, *The Buildings of England: South Lancashire*, 1969
22   Letter of 1933–4, transcribed by Dylis

Sheldon-Williams in her letter to C. Handley-Read of 14 November 1970. Handley-Read Archives, RIBA
23   B. Parker and R. Unwin, *The Art of Building a Home*
24   Ibid.
25   R. Fry, *Omega Catalogue*, c. 1915
26   *Dryad Catalogue*, 1908–10
27   W.S. Sparrow (ed.), *The British Home of Today*, 1904

Chapter Nine: Heal's and Liberty's
Pages 235-239
1   H. Muthesius, *Das Englische Haus*
2   *Franco-British Exhibition, An Illustrated Review* (ed. F.G. Dumas), 1908
3   Ibid.
4   H.J. Jennings, *Our Homes and How to Beautify Them*
5   H.J. Jennings in W.S. Sparrow (ed.), *The British Home of Today*
6   H. Muthesius, *Das Englische Haus*
7   *Artist*, May 1898
8   Quoted by C. Gilbert in *Pratts of Bradford*
9   Ibid.
10   W.R. Lethaby, *The Study and Practice of Artistic Crafts*, 1901
11   H. Muthesius, *Das Englische Haus*
12   *Mobilia*, September 1964
13   N. Pevsner, *Pioneers of the Modern Movement*
14   *Architectural Review*, 1900
15   *Studio*, 1901
16   T. Raffles Davison, *Modern Houses*, 1909
17   Heal's catalogue, *Cottage Furniture*, 1918
18   Heal's catalogue of 1904, quoted by S. Godden in *A History of Heal's*
19   Quoted by H. Ricardo in W.S. Sparrow (ed.), *The Modern Home*
20   J. Thorp, *An Aesthetic Conversation*, 1912
21   A. Adburgham, *Liberty's*
22   Ibid.
23   *Furniture Gazette*, 1878
24   *Architect*, December 1876
25   *Magazine of Art*, 1884
26   C.R. Ashbee, *Craftsmanship in Competitive Industry*
27   *Liberty's 1875–1975*
28   *Studio Year-Book of Decorative Art*, 1910
29   Quoted by A. Adburgham in *Liberty's*
30   Ibid.

Location of illustrated furniture and drawings

Illustrations taken from period printed or photographic sources are included in this list only when the present location of the furniture is known.
Abbreviations: Cec. Hig. = Cecil Higgins Art Gallery and Museum, Bedford; Chelt. = Cheltenham Art Gallery and Museum; Man. City. = Manchester City Art Gallery; P of W = Palace of Westminster, London; Priv. Coll. = Private Collection; RIBA = Royal Institute of British Architects, London; V&A = Victoria and Albert Museum, London.

5,6 RIBA; 7 Cardiff Castle; 8 David Robinson; 11, 12 RIBA; 13, 14, 16 Priv. Coll.; 23 Richmond Fellowship, London; 24 RIBA; 26, 34 Priv. Coll.; 35, 36; V&A; 44 Rhinefield Lodge Hotel, Hants.; 49 Walter D'Arcy Hart; 51 V&A; 54 Windsor Castle, Berks.; 55 RIBA; 56 Priv. Coll.; 57 The Fine Art Society Ltd; 60 V&A; 61, 62 Priv. Coll.; 63 V&A; 64, 65 Priv. Coll.; 66 V&A; 70, 71, 72 Priv. Coll.; 74 Public Record Office; 75 P of W; 76, 77 Priv. Coll.; 78 P of W; 79, 81, 82 Priv. Coll.; 85, 86 RIBA; 87, 88 Carlton Towers, Yorks.; 89 V&A; 90 Art Institute, Chicago; 91 Priv. Coll.; 92 V&A; 94 Priv. Coll.; 95 V&A; 96, 97 Priv. Coll.; 98 Temple Newsam House, Leeds; 99 V&A; 100, 101 Priv. Coll.; 103 RIBA; 104 P of W; 105 Temple Newsam House, Leeds; 106 (desk) Priv. Coll.; 111 Lord Wraxall; 112 (chairs) Priv. Coll.;

113 (chair) Gilbert and George; 117, 119, 120 Priv. Coll.; 121 P of W; 123 V&A; 124 Cardiff Castle; 125 Castell Coch; 126 RIBA; 127 Castell Coch; 128 Cardiff Castle; 129 Man. City.; 130 Auberon Waugh; 131 Andrew Lloyd Webber; 132 Cardiff Castle; 134 Andrew Lloyd Webber; 139 Castell Coch; 140 Cardiff Castle; 144 Worcester College, Oxford; 145 RIBA; 147, 148 Cardiff Castle; 149 Knightshayes Court, Devon; 150 (Yatman Cabinet), 151 V&A; 152 The Fine Art Society Ltd; 153 V&A; 154 Auberon Waugh; 155 Priv. Coll.; 156 Auberon Waugh; 157 Cec. Hig.; 158 V&A; 162, 163 Tower House, London; 165 (bed, dressing table) V&A; 166 Priv. Coll.; 167 Cec. Hig.; 170 Man. City.; 171 V&A; 176 Elvetham Hall, Hants.; 178, 186, 187 Priv. Coll.; 188 Ivor Braka Ltd; 189 Priv. Coll.; 190 Gilbert and George; 191, 201, 206

Priv. Coll.; 207 V&A; 209, 210 Priv. Coll.; 212 Keble College, Oxford; 213, 214, 215 V&A; 217, 218, 219 Priv. Coll.; 220 V&A; 221 (desk) National Museum of Wales, Cardiff; 222, 223 V&A; 224 Priv. Coll.; 225, 226 V&A; 227 Priv. Coll.; 230 RIBA; 231, 232, 233, 236 Priv. Coll.; 237 RIBA; 239 Temple Newsam House, Leeds; 240, 241, 245, 246, 252, 253, 256, 257, 258, 259, 260 Priv. Coll.; 264 V&A; 265, 266 Temple Newsam House, Leeds; 267, 268, 269, 280 Priv. Coll.; 286 V&A; 288 Priv. Coll.; 289 RIBA; 290 Priv. Coll.; 291 Gilbert and George; 292 Freer Gallery, Washington DC; 293, 294, 295 Priv. Coll.; 296 Cragside, Northumberland; 298, 299 Smallthwe, Kent; 300, 303 Priv. Coll.; 306 Cragside, Northumberland; 307 RIBA; 312, 313 Sir Stephen Lycett Green; 316 V&A; 317 Priv. Coll.; 318 Hunterian Museum, Glasgow; 319 California Palace of the Legion of Honour; 321 V&A; 322, 323 RIBA; 325, 326 Smallthwe, Kent; 327 Priv. Coll.;328, 329 RIBA; 330 Institute of Arts, Detroit; 331 V&A; 332 Ivor Braka Ltd; 335 Hunterian Art Gallery, Glasgow; 337 Ivor Braka Ltd; 341, 342 V&A; 343, 344 Priv. Coll.; 345 V&A; 350, 351, 352, 357 Priv. Coll.; 360, 361 V&A; 363 Royal Academy; 366 RIBA; 372 V&A; 377, 379 Priv. Coll.; 383 V&A; 388 Priv. Coll.; 389 V&A; 390, 391, 393 Priv.

Coll.; 397 National Portrait Gallery; 401 RIBA; 402 V&A; 403 Musée d'Orsay, Paris; 404 RIBA; 407 V&A; 408 Priv. Coll.; 409 Wightwick Manor, Staffs.; 411 Chelt.; 414 Musée d'Orsay, Paris; 415 Kelmscott Manor, Lechlade; 416, 417 Red House, Bexley Heath; 419, 424 Kelmscott Manor, Lechlade; 425 Fitzwilliam Museum, Cambridge; 426 Birmingham City Art Gallery; 427, 428, 429, 430 Priv. Coll.; 431 Fitzwilliam Museum, Cambridge; 432 Priv. Coll.; 435 Kelmscott Manor, Lechlade; 436 V&A; 437 Ruskin Gallery, Isle of Wight; 440 V&A; 441 St James's Palace; 442 V&A; 443 Priv. Coll.; 444 V&A; 450 Standen, Sussex; 452 Wightwick Manor, Staffs.; 453 Priv. Coll.; 454 Fitzwilliam Museum, Cambridge; 455 Priv. Coll.; 456 Birmingham City Art Gallery; 458, 459, 460, 461 Priv. Coll.; 463 V&A; 464, 465, 466, 467, 468, 469, 470, 471, 472 Priv. Coll.; 477 Bedales School, Hants.; 478 Priv. Coll.; 479 RIBA; 481 Priv. Coll.; 482, 483 Fischer Fine Art and A.J. Tilbrook; 484 Priv. Coll.; 486, 487 V&A; 495 Chelsea Public Library; 496, 497 RIBA; 499 Priv. Coll.; 503 (desk) A. Davies; 504 V&A; 505 National Portrait Gallery; 506 Geffrye Museum, London; 514 William Morris Gallery, Walthamstow; 515 (cabinet on left) Man. City.; 515 (chair) V&A; 519 Priv. Coll.; 520

Österreichisches Museum für angewandte Kunst, Vienna; 521 (cabinet) Chelt.; 523 Toynbee Hall, Whitechapel; 525, 526 Chelsea Public Library; 533 (throne) St John the Baptist Church, Aldenham, Herts.; 534: Musée d'Orsay, Paris; 535 Priv. Coll.; 537 Cragside, Northumberland; 538 Priv. Coll.; 539 RIBA; 552 Chelt.; 554 Fine Art Society Ltd; 555 Priv. Coll.; 556 R. St John Hornby; 557 A. Davies; 559 (sideboard) Edward Barnsley; 562, 563, 564 Priv. Coll.; 565 (candlesticks) Chelt.; 566 (clock) V&A; 568 Priv. Coll.; 569, 571 V&A; 572 Priv. Coll.; 573 Temple Newsam House, Leeds; 575 (chair on right), 576 Priv. Coll.; 577, 578 V&A; 579 Priv. Coll.; 584 Glasgow School of Art; 585 National Museum of Antiquities of Scotland, Edinburgh; 588 Musée d'Orsay, Paris; 589 Chelt.; 590 Priv. Coll.; 591 Art Institute, Chicago; 592 Hill House, Helensburgh; 595, 597 Priv. Coll.; 598 Man. City.; 607, 608 The Hill House, Helensburgh; 611 Royal Ontario Museum, Toronto; 612, 613, 614, 615, 616, 617, 622, 624, 627 Priv. Coll.; 629 Chelt.; 631 Priv. Coll.; 632 Man. City.; 633 V&A; 634, 635 Priv. Coll.; 636 Fischer Fine Art and A.J. Tilbrook; 637 (screen at back) Charleston, Sussex; 655 V&A; 663, 664, 666, 667 Priv. Coll.; 676 V&A; 677, 678, 679 Priv. Coll.; 683 Liberty's.

Acknowledgments for photographs

My principal debt of gratitude is to those collectors, by choice anonymous, who allowed their furniture to be photographed, and to Ken Jackson, Philip de Bay and Mike Jones who took the majority of the specially commissioned photographs. In addition to the individuals and institutions credited below, I would like to thank the following for their help with photographs: Elisabeth Aslin, Keith Baker, John Bonython, Ivor Braka, the Marquess of Bute, Dermot Chichester, Jacqueline Childs, Donald Cooper, Robert Copley, Stephen Croad, Michael Darby, Martin Drury, Robert Ellwell, Celina Fox, Jim Garrett, Christopher Gilbert, Gilbert and George, Halina Grubert, Robin Hartley, Hermione Hobhouse, Peter Humphries, Ralph Hyde, James Joll, Neil Jones, Dan Klein, Susan Lasdun, Ian Leith, Jill Lever, Martin Levy, Sally MacDonald, Peter Miall, Chris Payne, Simon Peers, Nicola Redway, Hugh Roberts, Jean Robinson, Pauline Sargent, Maria Schleger, John Scott, Cindy Shaw-Stewart, Peyton Skipwith, Louise Spence, Jane Taylor, Simon Taylor, Françoise Terrin, Clive Wainwright, Lynne Walker, Jan van der Wateren, Charles Wood III, and Elizabeth de Wouters.

Photographs are reproduced by kind permission of: Her Majesty the Queen 54; T.&R. Annan and Sons Ltd 582–4, 602–3, 605–6, 610, 612; Isabelle Anscombe 639; Birmingham City Art Gallery 426; H. Blairman and Sons 56, 94, 97, 129, 232, 269, 327, 427, 581; British Rail 195; CADWR (Welsh Historical Monuments) 125, 127, 139; Cardiff City Council 7, 124, 128, 132, 140, 147–8; Central School of Art and Design 538; Chelsea Public Library 495, 525–6; Christie's (Photo: A.C. Cooper) 16, 63, 91, 96, 109, 131, 134, 158, 246, 267, 335, 337, 391,

443, 466, 616; Christie's and Edmiston's 617; *Country Life* 75, 81, 198, 229, 312–13, 445, 449; Alan Crawford 521–3, 532; Anthony D'Offay Ltd 598, 637; Edgar Jones Photography 3-4, 14, 17-20, 32, 37, 40, 45, 102, 138, 141, 159, 169, 175, 177, 179-82, 204-6, 208, 228, 238, 240-4, 248, 250-1, 254, 257, 260-3, 270, 281, 284, 287, 297, 311, 314, 346-9, 353-6, 368-71, 373-6, 384-7, 394, 399-400, 406, 410, 412, 480, 485, 489-90, 494, 498, 509, 511-13, 517-18, 527-31, 556, 558, 561, 566-7, 570, 580, 586, 593-4, 596, 599, 601, 604, 621, 623, 625-6, 630, 638, 640, 665, 668-74, 680-2; Edward Barnsley Educational Trust 501, 503, 559; Fine Arts Museums of San Francisco 319: The Fine Art Society Ltd 57, 82, 152, 288, 303, 316-17, 332, 388, 398, 414, 454, 458-9, 468, 471, 534, 554, 557, 591, 595, 611, 676; Fischer Fine Art and A.J. Tilbrook 64, 215, 217, 224, 245, 351, 482-4, 579, 636; Fitzwilliam Museum, Cambridge 425, 431; Freer Gallery, Washington DC 292; Greater London Council Photograph Library 28; Bob Hall 77, 189, 209, 325, 352, 612; Jonathan Harris 62, 377, 379, 564; Haslam and Whiteway Ltd 78, 157, 160-1, 164-6, 207, 213, 330, 334, 408, 411, 433, 467, 574, 588, 629; Hawkley Studio Ass. Ltd. 258-9, 679; Heal's 600, 641-3, 647-62; Hunterian Art Gallery, Glasgow 318; Ken Jackson and Philip de Bay 70, 76, 101, 117, 155, 178, 186-8, 190-1, 227, 231, 233, 252-5, 291, 293-5, 300, 343-4, 350, 393, 519; Jeremy Cooper Ltd 26, 55, 93, 100, 118, 121, 143, 168, 202, 247, 249, 268, 280, 285, 304, 333, 336, 338-40, 364, 378, 381-2, 395, 403, 428-30, 462, 477, 486, 499, 520, 535, 540-9, 562-3, 569, 571-2, 628; A.F. Kersting 27, 130, 135, 144, 154, 156, 162-3; King's College, Cambridge (Courtesy F. Ashbee) 491; Leicestershire Museums, Art Galleries and Records Service 500; Liberty's 683; Lingard Gallery 219; Manchester City Art Gallery 632; National Museum of Antiquities of Scotland 585; National Museum of Wales, Cardiff 122,

167; National Portrait Gallery, London 397, 505; National Trust 146, 149, 296, 298-9, 306, 326, 409; Phillip's 290, 590, 631, 677; Public Records Office 74; David Robinson 8; Royal Commission on Historical Monuments (England) 1-2, 9-10, 21-3, 29-30, 38-9, 42-4, 46-7, 50, 52-3, 67, 69, 87-8, 104, 106-8, 110-16, 142, 172-4, 176, 196, 199-201, 234-5, 320, 358, 380, 405, 415-17, 424, 441, 446, 450-2, 473-6, 488, 492, 516, 536-7, 645, 675; Royal Commission on Historical Monuments (Scotland) 607-9, 619-20; Royal Institute of British Architects, London 5-6, 11-12, 24, 41, 85-6, 103, 126, 145, 197, 216, 230, 237, 289, 307, 315, 322-3, 328-9, 362, 366-7, 392, 401, 404, 447-9, 493, 496-7, 508, 539; Ruskin Gallery, Isle of Wight 437; Andrew Saint 359, 363, 365; Saint Bride's Printing Library (Photo: Godfrey New) 438-9; Fritz von der Schulenburg 592; Jason Shenai 79; Sims, Reed and Fogg Ltd (Photo: Mike Jones) 15, 25, 58-9, 80, 133, 136-7, 183-5, 193, 203, 273-9, 283, 302, 493; Sotheby's Belgravia 61, 71-2, 90, 256, 361, 390, 453, 456, 460-1, 465, 555, 576, 667; Sotheby's 13, 35-6, 65, 119-20, 170, 210, 357, 360, 396, 413, 455, 464, 469-70, 472, 478, 481, 568, 578, 597, 613-15, 622, 624, 627, 634-5, 663-4, 666, 678; Spinks 34; Gordon Taylor 218; Temple Newsam House, Leeds (Photo: Chris Hutchinson) 98, 105, 239, 265-6, 573; Templer Papers 305; Thomas-Photos 212; Paul Thompson 211; A.J. Tilbrook 31, 83, 301, 418, 420-3, 434, 502, 507, 510, 524, 533, 550-3, 565; Eileen Tweedy 646; Victoria and Albert Museum, London 33, 51, 61, 66, 68, 89, 92, 95, 99, 123, 150-1, 153, 171, 192, 194, 214, 220, 222-3, 225-6, 264, 286, 308, 321, 324, 331, 341-2, 345, 372, 383, 389, 402, 436, 440, 442, 444, 457, 463, 487, 504, 514-15, 577, 633; John Webb 49, 407; Westminster City Libraries 644; West Surrey College of Art and Design 419, 435; Stephen Wildman 221; Christopher Wood 432.

Index

Page numbers in **bold** indicate the principal biographical references; numerals in *italic* refer to illustration numbers. Exhibitions are indexed by name under their location.